Marketing Planning Guide

Third Edition

Marketing Planning Guide

Third Edition

Robert E. Stevens
David L. Loudon
Bruce Wrenn
Phylis Mansfield

Routledge
Taylor & Francis Group

LONDON AND NEW YORK

First published 2006 by Best Business Books

Published 2013 by Routledge
2 Park Square, Milton Park, Abingdon, Oxon OX14 4RN
711 Third Avenue, New York, NY 10017, USA

Routledge is an imprint of the Taylor & Francis Group, an informa business

First edition published 1991.
Second edition published 1997.

Cover design by Marylouise E. Doyle.

Library of Congress Cataloging-in-Publication Data

Marketing planning guide / Robert E. Stevens . . . [et al]. — 3rd ed.
    p. cm.
    Includes bibliographical references and index.
    ISBN-13: 978-0-7890-2337-7 (hard : alk. paper)
    ISBN-13: 978-0-7890-2338-4 (soft : alk. paper)

    1. Marketing—Management. I. Stevens, Robert E., 1942- II. Title.
HF5415.13.S874 2005
658.8'02—dc22

                                                         2005008559

ISBN 13: 978-0-7890-2338-4 (pbk)

CONTENTS

ABOUT THE AUTHORS

Robert E. Stevens, PhD, is Professor of Marketing in the Department of Management and Marketing at the University of Louisiana at Monroe. During his distinguished career, Dr. Stevens has taught at the University of Arkansas, the University of Southern Mississippi, and Hong Kong Shue Yan College. His repertoire of courses has included marketing management, business research, statistics, marketing research, and strategic management. The author or co-author of twenty books and well over 150 articles, he has published his research findings in a number of business journals and in the proceedings of numerous professional conferences. He also serves on the editorial boards of four professional journals. Dr. Stevens has acted as a marketing consultant to local, regional, and national organizations and is the owner of two small businesses.

David Loudon, PhD, is Professor of Marketing in the School of Business at Sanford University. He has also taught at the University of Louisiana at Monroe, Louisiana State University, the University of Rhode Island, Hong Kong Shue Yan College, and the North American Executive program in Monterrey, Mexico. He has taught a variety of courses but focuses on marketing management and consumer behavior. Dr. Loudon is co-author of twelve books and has conducted research in the United States, Europe, Asia, and Latin America on topics such as services marketing, marketing management, consumer behavior, and international marketing. He has also written over 100 articles, papers, and business cases, and his research findings have been published in a number of journals and in the proceedings of numerous professional conferences. Dr. Loudon is co-editor of Best Business Books, an imprint of The Haworth Press, Inc.

Bruce Wrenn, PhD, is Associate Professor of Marketing in the Division of Business and Economics at Indiana University South Bend. The author of several books on marketing management, planning, research, and marketing for religious organizations, Dr. Wrenn has also written numerous articles on marketing strategy, research, and marketing techniques for nonprofit and health care organizations. He spent several years with a major pharmaceutical company performing market analysis and planning and has served as a consultant to a number of industries, religious denominations, and organizations in the food, high tech, and health care industries.

Phylis Mansfield, PhD, is Assistant Professor of Marketing at Penn State University, Erie. Her research and teaching interests include consumer complaint resolution, service quality, and social issues and ethics in marketing. She teaches in the areas of marketing principles, business-to-business marketing, and services marketing. Dr. Mansfield has previous industry experience as a product manager, a business systems analyst, and a corporate training manager. Her industry experience has been with SunTrust Bank, National City Bank, and in administration at Vanderbilt University. She has published several cases and articles that have appeared in such publications as the *Journal of Business Ethics*.

Preface

Many changes have occurred in the business environment since the second edition of the *Marketing Planning Guide* was published in 1997. The third edition includes new orienting examples and text material, including a section on e-marketing and a section on ethics.

The book was written for two groups: (1) practitioners who are preparing marketing plans and need background material to guide them through the process, and (2) as a college text for upper-division marketing courses where instructors want to use a practical "hands-on" approach for teaching the planning process to students. The ancillary material includes an instructor's manual with a test bank and PowerPoint slides for adopters.

PART I:
INTRODUCTION TO MARKETING PLANNING

Chapter 1

The Importance of Marketing Planning

MARKETING PLANNING IN ACTION:
STARBUCKS

Most Americans have heard of the company Starbucks. The proliferation of Starbucks stores has been the subject of late-night television jokes and watercooler discussions, yet the company continues to open an average of three stores every day. When hearing about the company's debut on the Fortune 500 earlier this year, its founder, Howard Schultz, admitted that it would be arrogant to say that ten years ago he thought Starbucks would be where it is today, but from the very beginning of the company's inception, his goal was to dream big. And dream big it does. In fact, the seemingly oversaturation of many retail markets is the very goal of his business strategy.

Starbucks' strategy is surprisingly straightforward: "Blanket an area completely, even if the stores cannibalize one another's business." Today the company has 6,000 stores in more than thirty countries despite the fact that it does not franchise. Its goal is to have a minimum of 10,000 stores worldwide. Yet Schultz's goal for the company has as much to do with its philosophy of business as it does in becoming a multinational icon. Starbucks strives to be the kind of company everyone wants to work for, where even the part-time employees receive benefits such as health insurance and stock options. This nurturing environment transfers over to the employee's belief in the company, its product, and sense of community, which in turn provides an atmosphere that is the key to success in service companies.

The omnipresence of Starbucks adds to its success in spite of the fact that stores may literally be across the street from each other. When a new store opens it will often cannibalize a sister store, sometimes up to 30 percent of the existing store's business. Although this may seem to be an inappropriate strategy to some, it does provide the company several operational benefits. With stores so close together it cuts down on delivery and management costs, it can help to shorten customer lines in each store (particularly during the morning rush), and helps to increase total customer traffic. In a given week, 20 million people will buy a cup of coffee from a Starbucks store. The typical customer visits Starbucks four to five times each week—an unheard of frequency for customer visits to a retailer.

The proliferation of stores also helps to bring a sense of "presence" to the customer, similar to the impact of multiple shelf facings of a product in a grocery store. The fact that Starbucks is everywhere and readily available contributes to its brand awareness despite the fact that it spends only 1 percent of its annual revenues on advertising. Typically, retailers spend close to 10 percent on ads each year.

The company has also managed to have a significant impact on the way America views coffee and community. Starbucks' $3 cup of coffee was viewed as a West Coast fad that would soon die out. It is far from a fad, and this premium pricing strategy certainly appeals to a specific segment of the total coffee market. Starbucks has successfully created a niche for a premium-priced product by offering consistent quality and a neighborhood conclave. It appears to serve that niche well, even though it captures just 7 percent of the total coffee-drinking market in the United States and less than 1 percent abroad.

When Schultz took Starbucks public in 1992, the company had only 165 stores around Seattle and in neighboring states. Eleven years later it made its first appearance on the Fortune 500. What is Schultz's goal for the next ten years? "We want to become one of the most respected and recognized brands in the world. Like Coke," he adds.[1]

INTRODUCTION

Planning is one of the keys to success of any undertaking, and nowhere is it more important than in business. Every study dealing with business failures uncovers the same basic problem, whether it is called undercapitalization, poor location, or simply a lack of managerial skills. All these problems have their roots in planning. Marketing is one of the most important types of business activity that must be planned. The marketing plan defines the nature of the business and what that organization will do to satisfy its customers' needs in the marketplace. As such, the marketing plan is not just an "academic" concept of use to educators, but is a ruthlessly practical exercise that can spell the difference between success and failure to all types of organizations—big or small, producing for businesses or consumers, goods or services, for-profit or not-for-profit, offering domestic or international.

For planning to be successful, it must be founded in a root philosophy or conceptual framework that provides a basis for analysis, execution, and evaluation. A thorough understanding of both marketing and planning must precede any manager's attempt to develop and execute a marketing plan. This chapter focuses on marketing and planning and their relationship in the planning process.

WHAT IS MARKETING?

Various definitions of marketing have evolved over the years, but one that appears to be fairly complete is as follows: *Marketing directs those activities that involve the creation and distribution of products to identified market segments.* Several key words in this definition need further explanation. First, marketing directs. This is a managerial perspective rather than a residual perspective, which is concerned only with what has to be done to get goods and services to customers. Thus, marketing is not just a group of activities but more specifically is activities that are controlled in their execution to attain identifiable objectives. Second, marketing involves the performance of specific activities or functions. These functions constitute the work or substance of what marketing is all about. To be involved in marketing means to be involved in the planning, execution, and/or control of these activities.

Third, marketing involves both creation and distribution of goods and services. Although the product or service is actually created by the production function, marketing personnel are very much concerned not only about the creation of goods and services from a physical perspective but also from the perspective of customer need. Marketing needs to have a vital role in creation as well as distribution of goods and services. In fact, a well-conceived product or service makes the rest of the marketing tasks easier to perform.

Finally, marketing's concern is with customers and meeting a need in the marketplace. However, its concern is not just with any or all customers but particularly with those preselected by management as the market segment(s) on which the company will concentrate. Thus, specific customers with their specific needs become the focal point of marketing activities.

Marketing Orientation

True marketing thought focuses on addressing the needs and wants of a targeted segment of the market. Other business philosophies or orientations may be put into practice by managers with marketing titles, but they do not reflect authentic marketing thought. Exhibit 1.1 shows five different business orientations that have been used as the operating philosophies behind management decision making. The term *dominant* identifies the core objective that gives the orientation its name. *Present* means that the orientation includes that objective, but does not use it as the centrally controlling goal in orienting the manager's thoughts about his or her company, its products, and its customers. *Notpertinent* means that a particular objective has no relevance, pertinence, or connection with the orientation described. This exhibit makes it clear that the production, product, and selling orientations are internally driven. Managers using such orientations are determining what they want to dictate to the market. Only the last two orientations—marketing and societal marketing—contain the elements of an "outside-in" or market-driven philosophy, which stresses discovery of market opportunities, marketplace input regarding the organization's claim of a competitive advantage, and the integration of effort across all areas of the organization to deliver customer satisfaction. These two orientations reflect the competitive realities facing organizations of all types.

The societal orientation is particularly well-suited to internal and external environmental forces currently facing managers. It includes all of the positive contributions of the other four orientations, but adds concerns for the long-term effects of the organization's actions and products on its customers, as well as the desire to consider the effects of the organization's actions on society at large. In other words, it recognizes the sovereignty of the marketplace and uses both deontological (rights of the individual) and teleological (impact on society) ethical frameworks as part of the decision-making process. Putting this philosophy in practice requires a planning procedure that transforms this consumer orientation into marketing activities.

EXHIBIT 1.1. Business orientations.

	Production	Product	Selling	Marketing	Societal marketing
Desire to capitalize on synergies and efficiencies in production process	Dominant	Present	Present	Present	Present
Attention to design and production of a quality product	Not pertinent	Dominant	Present	Present	Present
Dedicated resources to stimulating interest and desire for product purchase	Not pertinent	Not pertinent	Dominant	Present	Present
Focus on identifying and satisfying needs and wants of customers	Not pertinent	Not pertinent	Not pertinent	Dominant	Present
Consideration of the short- and long-term effect of actions on customers and on society	Not pertinent	Not pertinent	Not pertinent	Not pertinent	Dominant

WHAT IS PLANNING?

Anyone studying managerial functions soon learns that although the list of specific functions may vary from author to author, one function common to all lists is planning. Planning may be defined as a managerial activity that involves analyzing the environment, setting objectives, deciding on specific actions needed to reach the objectives, and providing feedback on results. This process should be distinguished from the plan itself, which is a written document containing the results of the planning process. The plan is a written statement of what is to be done and how it is to be done. Planning is a continuous process that both precedes and follows other functions. Plans are made and executed, and then results are used to make new plans as the process continues.

Reasons for Planning

With today's fierce business competition and economic uncertainty, traditional management approaches are becoming less effective. In the past, the attention was on boosting profit by cutting expenses, conducting operational efficiency, and doing things right. Downsizing the firm's workforce to cut costs became a popular reaction to profit squeezes for many organizations during the late 1980s and 1990s. However, it became obvious only later that such efforts to reduce costs may be sacrificing long-term competitive strengths for short-term financial gain. Gains in efficiency cannot deliver long-term benefits unless they are coupled with gains in effectiveness. A survey of 250 senior executives revealed that profit management in the future will require attention to effective marketing planning and strategy (doing the right things as well as doing things right). The survey found that regardless of the type of business, remaining competitive will require companies to:

- reorient planning techniques and processes with competitive marketing strategy as the driving force;
- develop sound forecasts; and
- realize "marketing strategy' is a productive adaptation of all corporate resources to new opportunities in the marketplace.[2]

Planners cannot control the future, but they should attempt to identify and isolate present actions and forecast how results can be expected to influence the future. The primary purpose of planning, then, is to see that what we do now will be used to increase the chances of achieving future objectives and goals; that is, to increase the chances for making better decisions today that affect tomorrow's performance.

Unless planning leads to improved performance, it is not worthwhile. To have an organization that looks forward to the future and tries to stay alive and prosper in a changing environment, there must be active, vigorous, continuous, and creative planning. Otherwise, management will only react to its environment.

Some managers and organizations with poor planning skills constantly devote their energies to solving problems that would not have existed, or at least would be less serious, with adequate planning. Thus, they spend their time fighting fires rather than practicing fire protection.

Reasons Given for Not Planning

In many small firms, managers may object to planning, thinking that it makes no sense for them because each knows what happened in the past year and what is likely to happen in the coming year. Another objection often voiced is that there is no time for planning. A third objection is lack of enough resources to allow for planning. All of these objections actually point out the necessity for planning—even in the small firm. Such a firm may actually be a million-dollar business, making it imperative to have a plan of where the business is heading. The objection to the lack of time for planning may seem accurate, but simply reflects the fact that the lack of planning in the past has left insufficient time for attention to such necessities. Finally, the argument of insufficient resources should justify the role of planning to obtain the maximum benefit from the firm's resources. Planning is a critical element in any organization's success.

Advantages of Planning

Planning has many advantages. For example, it helps management adapt to changing environments, take advantage of opportunities created by change, reach agreements on major issues, and place responsibility more precisely. It also gives a sense of direction to members of an organization as well as provides a basis for gaining commitment from employees. The sense of vision that can be provided in a well-written plan also instills a sense of loyalty in organization members.

A firm can benefit from the planning process because it is a systematic, continuous process that allows the firm to do several activities:

1. *Assess the firm's market position*—This involves what is termed a SWOT analysis, which is an examination of the firm's internal strengths and weaknesses, external opportunities, and threats. Without explicit planning, these elements may go unrecognized.
2. *Establish goals, objectives, priorities, and strategies to be completed within specified time periods*—Planning will enable the firm to assess accomplishment of the goals that are set and take corrective action to achieve the desired goals.
3. *Achieve greater employee commitment and teamwork aimed at meeting challenges and solving problems presented by changing conditions*—Success is not achieved by everyone doing their best. Success is the result of everyone doing their best to support an overall objective that everyone understands and performs as team members to achieve.
4. *Muster its resources to meet change through anticipation and preparation*—"Adapt or die" is a very accurate admonition.

Disadvantages of Planning

Planning also may have several disadvantages. One disadvantage is that the work involved in planning may exceed its actual contributions. Planning tends to delay actions and may cause some administrators not to exercise initiative and innovation. Sometimes the best results are obtained by an individual appraising the situation and tackling each problem as it arises. Yet, in spite of these disadvantages, the advantages of planning far outweigh them. Planning not only should be done, it must be done.

PLANNING'S PLACE IN THE ORGANIZATION

All managers engage in planning to some degree. As a general rule, the larger an organization becomes, the more primary planning is associated with groups of managers rather than individual managers. Many larger organizations develop a professional planning staff for one or more of the following reasons:

1. *Planning takes time.* A planning staff can reduce the workload of individual managers.
2. *Planning takes coordination.* A planning staff can help integrate and coordinate the planning activities of individual managers.
3. *Planning takes expertise.* A planning staff can bring to a particular problem more tools and techniques than any single individual.
4. *Planning takes objectivity.* A planning staff can take a broader view than one individual and go beyond projects and particular departments.

A planning staff generally has three basic areas of responsibility. First, it assists top administration in developing goals, policies, and strategies for the organization. The planning staff facilitates this process by scanning and monitoring the organization's environment. A second major responsibility of the planning staff is to coordinate the planning of different levels and units within the organization. Finally, the planning staff acts as an organizational resource for managers who lack expertise in planning. Managers who are new to their positions and administrators of relatively new units in the organization may fall into this category.

In smaller firms, planning and execution must be carried out by the same people. The greatest challenge is setting aside time for planning in the midst of all the other activities needed on a day-to-day basis.

Types of Plans

Programs and projects usually require different types of plans. A program is a large set of activities involving a whole area of a firm's marketing capabilities, such as introducing a new product. Planning for programs involves the following:

1. Dividing the total set of activities into meaningful parts
2. Assigning planning responsibility for each part to appropriate personnel
3. Assigning target dates for completion of plans
4. Determining and allocating the resources needed for each part

A project is generally of less scope and complexity, and is not likely to be repeated on regular basis. A project may be part of a broader program or may be a self-contained event. Even though it is a one-time event, planning is an essential element to accomplishing the objectives of the project and coordinating the activities that make up the event. For example, a plan to respond to the promotional moves of a competitor in a particular region would be an example of a project plan.

Planning Levels

In large, multiproduct line companies, planning typically occurs at three levels: (1) *corporate level* planning, which generates what is usually referred to as a strategic plan; (2) *strategic business unit (SBU)* planning, which generates what is referred to as a strategic marketing plan; and (3) *product/market level* planning, which is referred to as an operating marketing plan. Exhibit 1.2 illustrates the typical questions and outcomes addressed at each of these levels. In moderate-size businesses with a single SBU, the strategic marketing and operating marketing planning may be conducted as a single process, with longer-term strategic planning being conducted at the corporate level. In smaller organizations, the planning process incorporates all three levels simultaneously.

Our primary focus is on strategic and operating marketing planning, which consist of planning issues at the SBU and product/market level. In Chapter 2, we will address those aspects of corporate-level strategic planning that heavily influence the development of plans at the other two levels. Our focus on marketing planning means that we will be concerned with the identification and exploitation of a competitive advantage for products targeted at specific customer groups. As indicated in Exhibit 1.2, we are finding answers to the following questions: "Where should we be going (given our corporate purpose and mission)?" and "How do we get there?" Answers to these questions will be governed by the philosophy embodied in the societal

EXHIBIT 1.2. Levels of planning.

Level	Name	Question	Output
Corporate	Strategic plan	What is our business? What should it be?	Mission Objectives SBU portfolio
SBU	Strategic marketing	Where should we be going?	Marketing strategy indicating where we gain a sustainable competitive advantage
Product/ market	Operating marketing	How do we get there?	Marketing plan

marketing concept—a customer-needs-driven orientation with long-range concerns for the welfare of our current and potential customer and one that is cognizant of the impact of our actions on society as a whole.

THE MARKETING PLANNING PROCESS

Nowhere in the organization is planning more needed than in marketing. The complexity of today's environment in terms of social, legal, environmental, economic, competitive, technological, and resource constraints requires a high degree of skill to provide structure to a course of action an organization can follow to achieve desired results.

For marketing managers, the marketing planning process becomes paramount. The societal marketing orientation has no impact on an organization's operating procedures unless it is reflected in the performance of the administrative function of planning. The customers' needs are the focus of an organization's operations under the marketing philosophy, and this is made evident in the planning process. Which customer segments will the organization try to serve? Where will we gain a competitive advantage in serving those targeted segments? How will the marketing functions be performed? Who will perform them? What sales volume will be generated? What are the short- and long-term consequences to our customers and society from performing these marketing actions? These questions can all be answered by a well-thought-out and carefully written marketing plan. In essence, the plan becomes a tool through which the societal marketing orientation is implemented into decision-making procedures.

An understanding of the marketing planning process is also a valuable aid in helping managers organize their thinking about the marketing process and the various methods and procedures used. When they talk about sales volume, managers relate such figures to objectives accomplished. A study reporting customer attitudes toward the firm's activities becomes another aspect of situation analysis. Managers begin to think systematically and analytically about the marketing process in their organization. This may be one of the most crucial contributions of a manager's involvement in marketing planning.

Before discussing the details of a marketing plan, specify the relationship between the strategic marketing plan and the operating marketing plan. The strategic marketing plan is the long-term marketing plan for the marketing area. It deals with the overall marketing objectives of the organization and how the organization plans to accomplish these objectives. The operating marketing plan, by contrast, is a detailed plan indicating the results of a situation analysis and offering a set of objectives to be attained by the end of the year. It is a detailed tactical statement explaining what must be done, when, and how. In other words, the strategic marketing plan deals with what is to be accomplished in the long run, while the operating marketing plan deals with what is to be done in a given period, usually a year.

The strategic marketing plan does not necessarily differ in format from the operating marketing plan. In fact, it must cover some of the same basic topics, objectives, strategies, and so forth. The difference is in scope and may lay out a strategy that indicates in which product/markets the company wishes to compete. The operating marketing plan focuses on the tactical marketing decisions needed to carry out the strategic marketing plan. The time frame for the operating marketing plan is usually a year and normally coincides with the organization's fiscal year. The situation analysis deals only with the current operating environment and details only important events that influence changes in marketing activities. The strategy portion contains the detailed tactical decisions that spell out changes in such items as advertising themes, new products, etc.

The interrelationships between the corporate strategic plan, the strategic marketing plan, and the operating marketing plan will be discussed more fully in Chapter 2. Since formats of the strategic marketing plan and the operating marketing plan usually differ more in scope and time frame than in what is covered, the term marketing plan will be used throughout the book. If you are working on an operating plan, remember the need for specific details in your plan. The worksheets provided in Appendix A will permit you to begin work on the details of what is to be done in the marketing area during that time frame.

The marketing plan is a written document containing four basic elements:

1. A summary of the situation analysis, including general developments, consumer analysis, and opportunity analysis.
2. A set of objectives.
3. A detailed strategy statement of where the competitive advantage lies and how the marketing variables will be combined to achieve the objectives as well as the financial impact.
4. A set of procedures of monitoring and controlling the plan through feedback about results.

The logic of this approach to planning is clear. We must (1) determine where we are now (situation analysis); (2) decide where we want to go (objectives); (3) decide how we are going to get there (strategy); and (4) decide what feedback we need to let us know if we are staying on course (monitor and control). A complete marketing plan provides the answers to these questions. The marketing planning process should not be confused with departmental or personnel plans developed under a system such as management by objectives (MBO). Even though the processes used to develop both types of plans are compatible, the MBO plans usually deal with personnel activities rather than marketing activities.

The feasibility of combining products for planning purposes depends on the similarities of customer needs and the importance of each product to the firm's market position. For example, a firm may develop a plan for a whole line of products aimed at the same customers. Yamaha uses this approach with its musical instrument line. The basic advertisement theme is used for different instruments: "Welcome to the world of Yamaha."

One of the most important contributions of this type of planning process is the perspective managers must take to use it properly. Managers must study the entire marketing process from the customer's vantage point, which creates new patterns for administrative development and organization. An understanding of the planning process provides a framework for organized thought patterns for the variety of marketing activities that take place in an organization.

THE MARKETING PLAN FORMAT

An outline of the format for marketing plans is provided in Exhibit 1.3. Subsequent chapters discuss in detail the rationale and procedures used to develop the plan. This book focuses on marketing planning as a process and suggests tools and techniques that can be used in developing a marketing plan. A sample marketing plan for a firm adding a new product is provided in Appendix B.

Budgeting for Marketing

Marketing efforts require that expenditures of funds be budgeted. A manager should budget expenditures to ensure that the financial

---

EXHIBIT 1.3. Outline of a marketing plan.

I.   Situation analysis
    A. Market analysis
    B. Customer analysis
    C. Competitive analysis
    D. Opportunity analysis
II. Objectives
    A. Sales objectives
    B. Profitability objectives
    C. Customer objectives
III. Strategy
    A. Overall strategy
    B. Marketing mix variables
    C. Financial impact statement
IV. Monitoring and control
    A. Performance analysis
    B. Customer data feedback

support needed to undertake marketing activities is available. The three most commonly used budgeting methods are the percentage of sales approach, the "all-you-can-afford" approach, and the task or objective approach.

Percentage of Sales Approach

This common marketing budgeting approach is determined by applying a fixed percentage of either past or forecasted sales. The proportion of sales allocated to marketing may be based upon past results or on management judgments about the future.

This method is widely used for many reasons. Besides being simple to calculate, it is exact and easy to define by administrators who are accustomed to thinking of costs in percentage terms. Also, it is financially safe, since it links expenditures directly to revenues.

The major problem with the percentage approach is its inherent fallacy of implying that sales determine marketing expenditures rather than vice versa. However, this method can legitimately be used as a starting point for budgeting and can offer good direction in this process.

"All-You-Can-Afford" Approach

Some organizations set marketing budgets on the basis of availability funds. Here the organization spends as much as it can afford without impairing financial stability. Thus, the budget adopted and the monies needed to accomplish the required marketing tasks may be unrelated. On the one hand, the organization could miss opportunities because of underspending. Conversely, it could easily spend too much.

Task or Objective Approach

Because the methods discussed so far have major faults, none closely approximates a good standard. Consequently, the task or objective approach—or the build-up approach, as it is often called—is an alternative that has the most merit. This method requires that marketing objectives be stated clearly, and then expenditures necessary to reach these objectives be determined. The implementation of this method is more complex, but the end result is that only what is needed in a give period is spent to accomplish the stated objectives. This approach requires a great deal of experience to know what can be accomplished with a specific level of expenditures.

SUMMARY

The marketing planning process should be intimately tied to the societal marketing orientation. The marketing process described in this text ensures that the societal marketing orientation will be put into the organization's operations through the planning process. The process begins with a detailed analysis of clients and their operating environment before any attention is devoted to what objectives should be sought or what strategies are needed.

Chapter 2 addresses the organizational aspects of marketing planning in terms of the firm's purpose, objectives, and responsibility for planning. Chapter 3 discusses the need and procedures for building a database for planning. Part II, which includes Chapters 4 through 7, presents the concepts used in the situation analysis portion of the marketing plan. Part III, Chapter 8, reviews the details of the objective-setting step in the marketing planning process. Part IV, Chapters 9 through 14, addresses the strategy-related elements of the plan; Part V, Chapters 15 and 16, covers controlling the plan; and Part VI, Chapter 17, discusses a planning audit and the implementation of the marketing plan.

Chapter 2

Organizational Considerations in Marketing Planning

MARKETING PLANNING IN ACTION: SIMPLE IS BEST

The fact that organization is the key to a company's marketing success is a myth that will not die. Marketing departments are reorganized more often than other functional units. The most frequent reason given is to gain a greater sense of marketing orientation. Many times, however, a company has discarded a perfectly sound plan for one that is complicated and costly.

Management has apparently forgotten two important facts. First, marketing concentrates on fulfilling customer needs rather than being a functional part of a business. Second, the marketing strategy of a business depends not on its organizational structure, but on the philosophy of its top management. Marketing activities can be organized four ways: by function, by orientation, by product orientation, and by a combination of market and product orientation.

Organizing around functions is the simplest approach. Separate divisions for each major activity, including sales, research, etc., can be set up, which are then reported to the president or general manager. Despite this simplicity, many companies have added so many new products that they have consequently adopted more complex forms of organizing marketing activities.

Companies selling many different products favor a product-oriented system, with the responsibility for each line given to the product manager. Companies with homogeneous or related product lines, however, favor a market-oriented system to appeal to different markets. Marketing responsibility is divided among managers responsible for certain market segments or channels. When product and market structures are complex, a combination of market and product orientation is often used.

These systems can have problems. First, responsibility is difficult to define, being shared by product and market managers and functional marketing specialists. Second, development and coordination of strategy is difficult because the manager responsible is usually a junior member of the management team. It may be difficult for that person to set priorities and negotiate trade-offs with nonmarketing functions.

The simple method should be tried first and for as long as possible. A more complex approach can be tried if it does not work. If a more complex, nonfunctional organizational structure is chosen, however, it will command nontraditional management functions to work. Many times, simple is best.[1]

INTRODUCTION

The organization in which marketing plans are made directly influences the nature and scope of the plans and also who participates in the planning process. This chapter focuses on the impact of organizational characteristics on the marketing planning process. One of the aims of this chapter is to emphasize the need to assign specific responsibility for marketing plan development. The planning processes, which take place in every area of an organization, must be coordinated and must be compatible with the overall mission and with corporate objectives and strategy. This chapter moves from a discussion of organizational concepts to tools used to control and coordinate marketing planning.

ORGANIZATIONAL PURPOSE

Drucker has referred to an organization's purpose as its mission or reason for being.[2] To define a business' purpose is to ask, "What is our business and more importantly, what should it be?" Drucker further states the following:

> Only a clear definition of the mission and purpose of the business makes possible clear and realistic business objectives. It is the foundation for priorities, strategies, plans, and work assignments. It is the starting point for the design of managerial jobs and above all for the design of managerial structure.[3]

One aspect of every firm's purpose should be to meet a need in the marketplace. However, a statement of purpose needs to be a written statement that spells out in some detail the uniqueness that has led to the creation of the business enterprise. Such a statement becomes a reference point for subsequent managerial action. In effect, it becomes the reference point upon which all operating areas in a firm must reflect as a part of their decision-making processes. Typical types of questions faced by most firms include the following: "Should we enter this market?" and "Should we introduce this particular product?" The starting point in answering should be how the decision relates to accomplishing the stated purpose of the organization. If it does not help the organization accomplish its stated purpose, it should not be undertaken, no matter how profitable or otherwise successful it appears to be; it is not aligned with the basic purpose of the enterprise. One problem that makes this dictum difficult to follow for some organizations is too much prosperity. This might not appear to be a "problem," but it becomes one if it means that the organization cannot turn away "found" business. If an organization is constantly modifying or even designing products or bidding for jobs for every potential customer who walks through the door, it is failing to make the hard decisions involved in determining where it wants to be at some point in the future. Its future is going to be determined by default—it will consist of a dilution of resources and a diffuse market focus, which will result in a failure to establish a strong competitive position in any market. A firm's purpose can be altered over time to reflect changing environmental conditions or changing managerial philosophies, but at any given point there must be a standard of relevance for managerial thought and action.

The marketing manager must have a clear understanding of company purpose to ensure alignment of marketing activities with the way the firm has defined its mission. Otherwise, attempted activities will be across purposes with the organizational mission, or on the other hand, there will be a failure to attempt activities beneficial to fulfillment of its purpose. Common vision and unity can be achieved only by common purpose.

The following information is adapted from the statement of purpose and mission prepared by Ben & Jerry's management. This type of statement can be developed to provide unit and guidance in decision making. Ben & Jerry's mission statement is presented in three interrelated parts, its mission with regard to the product(s) it sells, its mission with regard to the economic health of the company, and its mission with regard to its impact on the social environment within which it operates.

> *Product mission:* Ben & Jerry's strives to make ice cream and other novelties with the highest quality ingredients available.
>
> *Economic mission:* The company's goal is to maintain sustainable growth, increasing the value for all of its stakeholders, including its employees.
>
> *Social mission:* Ben & Jerry's strives to be an integral part in the communities it touches, from local to international, and to improve their quality of life.[4]

A few of the implications of this statement for marketing management within the organization will help show how to relate corporate purpose to the development of marketing plans.

The paragraph on product mission, for example, states that the company will produce the finest quality product with a commitment to wholesome ingredients, and at the same time promote business practices that respect the environment. This means that the marketing plans must not be based on profit expansion by using more economical food ingredients that were developed through methods requiring toxic chemicals or that created excessive or harmful waste by-product that would devalue farms and rural communities.

Another marketing constraint can be derived from the social mission. This stipulation restricts marketing any products or using any marketing techniques that would negatively impact the quality of life of the worldwide community. For example, the company would not support the use of promotion techniques that may be misleading to children or other vulnerable consumer groups.

These examples illustrate the impact of statements of purpose on marketing planning. Marketing activities must be consistent with overall purpose of an effective organization.

ORGANIZATIONAL OBJECTIVES AND STRATEGIES

Most managers are aware of the need for objectives, and their importance has been well stated, as follows:

The importance of objectives is widely accepted; most managers agree that they are vital. Inappropriate and inadequate objectives can retard the management and suffocate the operations of any organization. Too frequently, objectives are not stated, are overlooked, forgotten, or ignored. Objectives can be called the neglected area of management. It is common for a manager to find that the details of an immediate operation have occupied so much of his time that he has lost sight of the basic overall objective.[5]

With most companies, a single set of overall objectives does not provide sufficient detail for operating management. Rather, a hierarchy of objectives reflects the specificity of the contribution of the part to the whole. In other words, overall company objectives would be expected to be more general in nature than divisional ones. Divisional objectives, in turn, would be more general than departmental objectives. The closer the planning activity gets to the tactical implementation stage, the more specific are the objectives (e.g., "Each salesperson should make a call on every distributor in their territory during the next thirty days and detail the advantages of using X product for Y purpose, leaving Z promotional brochure outlining the advantages over the market leader.").

Although objectives may originate anywhere in the organization, the most logical sequence is to start at the top and flow down to lower levels in the structure. Later in this book, an entire chapter is devoted to the actual process of setting objectives, which directly affects the objectives set for any single marketing plan. Knowledge of and alignment with this hierarchy is mandatory to integrate the total organization by fostering commonality of purpose and unity in decision making.

In most planning scenarios, strategy follows objectives. Thus, the development of the corporate strategy follows the identification of corporate objectives. Just as there is a hierarchy of objectives, which flows from corporate to functional to operational, there is also a hierarchy of strategies. Strategies in the functional areas (marketing, production, and finance) must support the overall corporate strategy.

In their book *The Discipline of Market Leaders,* Treacy and Wiersema refer to the overriding strategic direction of an organization as its "value discipline," which defines the value it can deliver to a chosen market.[6] Organizations are most successful when they pursue one of the three value disciplines and then develop strategic marketing plans and operating plans that are consistent in their support of the overall corporate strategy or value discipline. The characteristics of these three value disciplines are shown in Exhibit 2.1.

Strategic marketing and operating plans need to be consistent with the overall value discipline used by the firm in order to maximize the effectiveness of the organization's strategic thrust. Exhibit 2.2 shows an example for the Eli Lilly Pharmaceutical Co. of how objectives and strategy should be consistent as you move through the planning levels.

In this example, they have chosen the product leadership value discipline to provide strategic direction at the corporate level. The corporate level objective is general in nature and consistent with the value discipline. At the strategic marketing level, this corporate strategic direction is focused in one instance on objectives and strategies for their nonnarcotic analgesic line. The leading product in the line, Darvon, will be going off patent during the year. The objective of

EXHIBIT 2.1. Value disciplines.

| Company traits | Discipline | | |
	Operational excellence	Product leadership	Customer intimacy
Core business processes that . . .	Sharpen distribution systems and provide no-hassle service	Nurture ideas, translate them into products, and market them skillfully	Provide solutions and help customers run their businesses
Structure that . . .	Has strong, central authority and a finite level of empowerment	Acts in an ad hoc, organic, loosely knit, and ever-changing way	Pushes empowerment close to customer contact
Management systems that . . .	Maintain standard operating procedures	Reward individuals' innovative capacity and new product success	Measure the cost of providing service and of maintaining customer loyalty
Culture that . . .	Acts predictably and believes "one size fits all"	Experiments and thinks "out of the boxes"	Is flexible and thinks "have it your way"

Source: Treacy, M. and Wiersema, F. How Market Leaders Keep Their Edge. *Fortune,* February 6, 1995, pp. 88-98.

EXHIBIT 2.2. Eli Lilly Pharmaceutical Co.

<table>
<tr><td colspan="2">Corporate level</td></tr>
<tr><td>Objective:</td><td>Maintain product leadership in each market we enter.</td></tr>
<tr><td>Strategy:</td><td>Adopt a product leadership value discipline.</td></tr>
</table>

<table>
<tr><td colspan="2">Strategic business unit level</td></tr>
<tr><td>Objective:</td><td>Maintain a market share of the nonnarcotic analgesic market of 80 percent + for the next five years.</td></tr>
<tr><td>Strategy:</td><td>Introduce new products to take place of high-revenue-producing products when they lose patent protection.</td></tr>
</table>

<table>
<tr><td colspan="2">Product market level</td></tr>
<tr><td>Objective:</td><td>Call on physicians to detail Darvocet as a more advanced analgesic than Darvon with more efficacy and fewer side effects; call on pharmacists to leave order blanks for Darvon at sale prices.</td></tr>
<tr><td>Strategy:</td><td>Product line extension and aggressive pricing.</td></tr>
</table>

maintaining a high market share in this market would be impossible, given the influx on new generic competitors for Darvon, unless new patent-protected products can be introduced and physician prescribing habits are changed so that an increasing number of prescriptions will be written for the new drug. This new product entry strategy is an embodiment of the product leadership corporate value discipline. At the operating level, one of several objectives deals with tactical implementation of the product line extension and aggressive pricing strategy. The objective is to get the word to the physicians that a new and improved product, Darvocet, is now available with advantages over Darvon, so they should change their prescribing to write for the new drug. Simultaneously, detail calls should be made to pharmacists to let them know that Darvon is now on sale for 30 percent off the usual price. If successful, this sale should cause the pharmacists to stock up on Darvon, so that prescriptions written for it will be filled with the Lilly product and not some generic equivalent. Although the pharmacists work off their Darvon inventory, the objective will be to have affected a change in physician-prescribing to Darvocet. Hence, a consistency emerges between objectives and strategies among the three levels, and within any particular level. It should also be noted that these objectives and strategies are only a sample of what would be set for sales volume, growth, share, percentage of prescriptions written for new versus old products, etc. Finally, objectives set in functional areas other than marketing (finance, R&D, production, etc.) must support the overall corporate strategy to pursue product leadership.

ORGANIZING FOR PLANNING

The terms *organizing* and *organization* refer to two different concepts. *Organizing* is a process that involves a series of steps that lead to an end product—the organization. The *organization,* then, is the result of the organizing process.[7] The organizing process is not a one-time effort to develop an organization but a continuous process that changes as the operating environment of the firm changes. The organization can be thought of as a snapshot of the company's managerial structure at a given time, whereas the organizing process can be thought of as a film of the changes taking place over time.

Organizing for marketing planning refers to the process of developing a structure to accommodate and assign responsibility for the marketing planning activity. Organizing may be defined simply as the process of:

1. determining what must be done if a given set of objectives is to be achieved;
2. dividing the necessary activities into segments small enough so that each can be performed by one person; and
3. providing means of coordination to ensure that there is no wasted effort and that the members of the organization do not get in each other's way.[8]

This process should produce a structure of task and authority relationships that enhance the firm's ability to accomplish stated objectives. The end result of the process is usually represented by an organizational chart that shows individuals' positions and their formal relationships of authority. When detailed job descriptions, which specify duties and responsibilities, are prepared for each position, the foundations for the managerial system have been laid. If current job descriptions do not state that the development of strategic and annual marketing plans is a responsibility of marketing managers, the job description should be rewritten to state their responsibility to that task. This, of course, does not mean that each manager would individually carry out all the activities necessary to develop a plan, but only that he or she is responsible for seeing that one is prepared or providing input for it.[9]

ORGANIZATIONAL STRUCTURE

The organizational structure reveals the relationships between activities, authority, and responsibility at a given time within the organization. The nature of a firm's organization greatly influences not only who will be responsible for marketing planning but also how much assistance the planner can expect from others in the organization.

Two basic types of organizational structures are (1) the line organization, and (2) the line and staff organization. The distinction between the two is the separation of planning from operating tasks in the line and staff approach. The line organization is the simplest form and will be described first.

In a line organization, authority flows directly from the chief executive to the first subordinate, then to the second, and so forth. Few, if any, specialists are present in the line organization, and planning and operating activities are usually performed by the same individual. The chief executive might do all the planning for all areas and maintain primary authority and responsibility for all areas. This type of organizational structure is depicted in Exhibits 2.3 and 2.4.

In the marketing line organization, the marketing manager is responsible for planning and for the operations in marketing. The sales supervisor and distribution supervisor carry out the manager's plans through supervision of other employees. Although this type of orga-

EXHIBIT 2.3. Company line organizational structure.

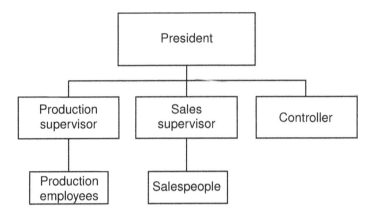

EXHIBIT 2.4. Marketing line organizational structure.

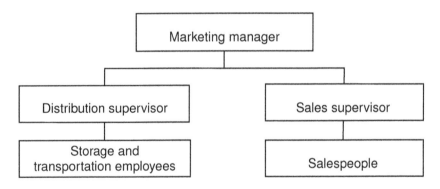

nization may be successful for small organizations, its usefulness in larger, more complex situations is limited. To be effective, there must be a division of effort, and this is exactly what staff positions provide. Staff personnel are added to help the line personnel perform the various functions carried out in an organization, especially the planning function.[10] A marketing manager in a line organization must not only develop plans but also carry them out. Less time is available for planning because the manager is involved in operative tasks of the organization. Good planning procedures can still be used under these conditions, especially if there are only a few products and/or customers.

However, the analysis section of the plan usually will not be as thorough simply because of less time and fewer resources available to the manager.

The line and staff organization, depicted in Exhibit 2.4, illustrates the addition of staff specialists to the organization. This approach permits separation of planning and operating activities, which in turn means more time and resources available for marketing planning. The results should be more thorough plans.

The structure in Exhibit 2.5 has added staff positions at both the headquarters and regional level. This makes staff specialists available to coordinate overall company efforts in their areas of specialization at the headquarters level, and also takes into consideration regional differences that warrant additional specialization by geographical area. Of course, there are many other ways to specialize staff personnel—products, customer type, channel of distribution, etc. A wide variety of potential organizational structures can be adapted to a specific organization's needs.

One other organizational structure will be illustrated because of the way it facilitates the marketing planning process. The geographic structures shown in Exhibit 2.5 has one staff position with primary responsibility for marketing planning but without authority for marketing execution. That is, a staff person has the responsibility for planning, but must count on others to actually make the decisions related to the marketing area unless given functional authority—which seems unlikely. If a firm is organized by products, the marketing planning process is greatly facilitated because it becomes easier to assign responsibility for planning to those individuals who have the authority to carry out the plans. This structure is shown in Exhibit 2.6.

In this partial organizational structure, each product manager reports directly to the chief marketing officer. Each product manager would be assigned the responsibility for developing a short-term marketing plan for each product, and the chief executive officer would be responsible for overall coordination and plan approval. For the strategic plan, the chief executive in marketing would take responsibility for development of the plan and use other key executives as resources for plan development and approval. In firms that have few products or where one product is key to the firm's success, the president of the company may assume responsibility for developing the strategic plan.

EXHIBIT 2.5. Marketing line and staff organizational structure.

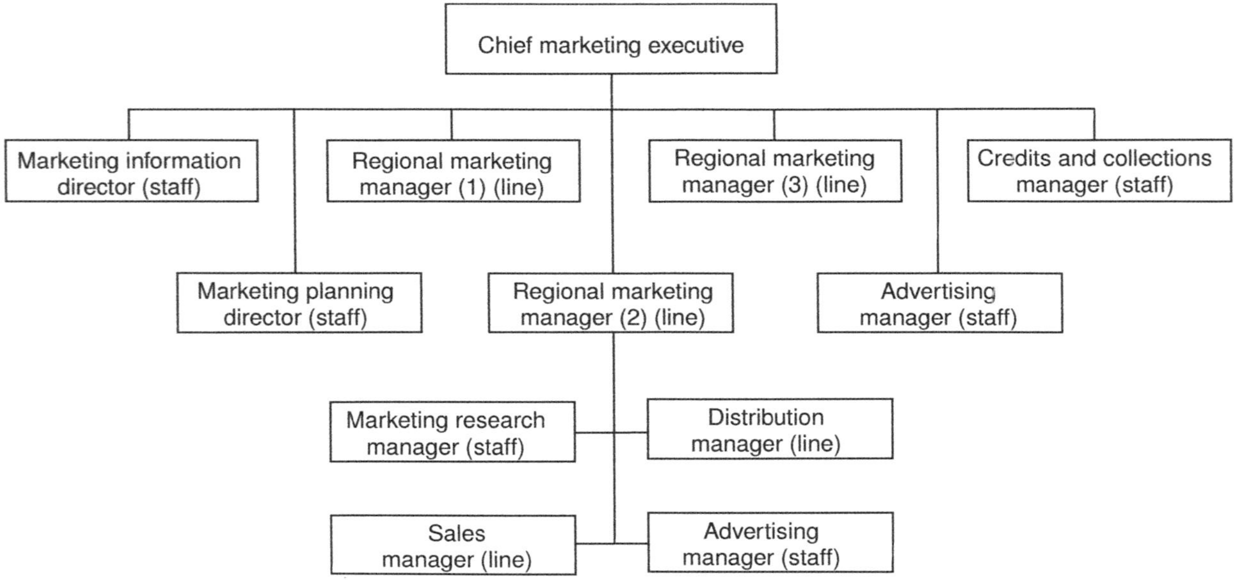

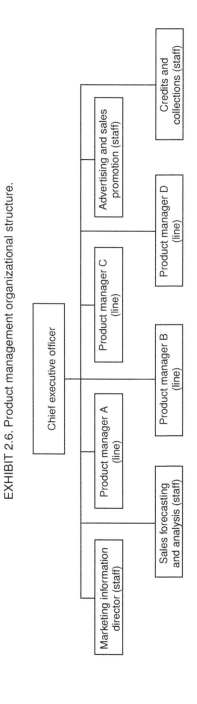

EXHIBIT 2.6. Product management organizational structure.

Two trends in organizational design could influence structures of the future.[11] The first is *managing business processes* rather than functional areas. For example, new product development as a business process might include people with expertise in marketing, R&D, finance, manufacturing, service, and distribution. A material flow process area would have individuals from purchasing, production, logistics, billing, and warehousing. For businesses organized around processes, planning would require a coordination of objectives and strategies with other process structured units so that an externally oriented objective (e.g., customer satisfaction rather than, say, sales volume) could be simultaneously pursued by the different process units.

Another trend affecting future structures is the use of *self-managing teams*. The term *empowerment* has been frequently used to describe the belief that those people doing the work should have the means to achieve the desired outcome of their work—satisfying the customer. Such an approach requires that evaluation of worker performance and rewards be linked to the desired customer satisfaction measures. The team is responsible for planning its activities in coordination with other teams to achieve the successful implementation of corporate strategies.

COORDINATION AND THE PLANNING PROCESS

One other organizational factor influencing the planning process is the degree and nature of the coordinating methods used in an organization. In multiproduct and multimarket companies, this factor is a necessity because there are many plans that constitute the corporate marketing program, which is the composite of all marketing plans, properly balanced and coordinated, for an organization. Many aspects of a company's operations may already serve as an aid to coordination. For example, the budgeting process can force allocation of resources to products in such a way that marketing effort is somewhat balanced and coordinated. However, this balance is only in monetary terms. Many decisions about information, advertising approaches, package design changes, sales training efforts, and so on, must be balanced and coordinated to ensure organizational effectiveness. For greatest effectiveness, the maximum contribution should be achieved from each area involved, but in relation to the entire process and to other corresponding areas.

Coordination can be defined as the synchronization of efforts. It permeates all managerial activities and must be both horizontal and vertical within the organization. That is, coordination must be achieved within the plan for a given product or group of products and also between products or groups of products.

The relationship between marketing and marketing communications is similar to the relationship between a pitcher and a catcher. Without clear signals from the marketing plan, advertising, public relations, and other marketing tools can curve high and wide of the company's strategy.

Solid links between marketing and marketing communications have been established by some business-industrial companies. For example, some firms have a central corporate marketing communications group. Formal reporting methods might be established to ensure that marketing communicators receive planning information, or they may depend on a strong corporate culture that emphasizes teamwork between the two groups.

Dow and Kodak have decentralized market communications by placing the function's staff members inside divisions or product groups, where they work directly with marketing executives. Communication between the groups is enhanced by their close proximity to one another. The communications executives can build a stronger understanding of marketing strategy since they are involved in it on a daily basis. This leads to more effective promotions and advertising being produced.

Marketing consultants and business marketers agree, however, that a gap usually exists between marketing and marketing communications. The problem is especially severe in firms where marketing communications is a separate corporate group. Sometimes marketing people are so involved in sales support that communications people are left to their own devices. Without complete information, the marketing communications group has a difficult time producing messages that match a company's strategy, which results in costly and inefficient selling.[12]

Techniques for Coordination

Several techniques are available to ensure coordination of effort. The most obvious is to assign the specific responsibility to the line executive at the next highest level in the organization. For example, if a multiproduct firm is using a product management system, several product managers will usually report to a group product manager. The product managers are responsible for coordination of efforts within their own plans, and the group product managers have responsibility for coordinating individual product plans. If the chief marketing executive is the next highest level above the group product manager, then he or she will be assigned responsibility for coordinating the plans for each product group and ensuring their congruence with the strategic plan. This responsibility may seem obvious, but the point is to assign specific responsibility for coordination to the positions in order to provide for the performance of this task. It should be a part of the job description.

Another approach to coordination is the linear organizational chart. With this approach, a diagram is prepared showing at a glance the functions to be performed and who has responsibility for each, who must supervise and coordinate them, who must be consulted about a decision, and who must be notified about a decision. This chart provides for coordination and also identifies working relationships with others in the coordinating effort. This type of chart (see Exhibit 2.7) is used to clarify who does what, and it can serve as a good device to show various relationships in the planning process. The product managers, for example, must take responsibility for the development of the short-term marketing plans for their products, but they must coordinate approval or notification with various other areas. Specifically, the product manager must seek help from other departments, the group product manager must supervise and coordinate the various individual product marketing plans, and the chief executive officer must supervise overall planning.

In some organizations, management introduces staff meetings and committees for the express purpose of coordinating efforts. A marketing planning committee, for example, would be made up of line and staff personnel directly involved in the planning process plus someone from production and finance. This arrangement should fos-

EXHIBIT 2.7. Linear organizational chart.

Code of Responsibilities

WD = Work is done by this person | D = Decision on specific points
GS = General supervision | C = Must be consulted
DS = Direct supervision | N = Must be notified
SC = Supervision with coordination | EV = May be called for exchange of views

Functions	Board of Directors	President	VP marketing	Manager	Group product manager	Other departments
Interpret and apply company policy	—	D	WD	EV	N	N
Develop strategic marketing plan	GS	GS	WD	C	N	N
Prepare and submit territorial sales forecast	—	—	N	C	WD	WD
Prepare economic and industry forecast	—	C	GS	EV	EV	WD
Prepare company forecast by product	—	N	GS	EV	WD	WD
Approve company sales forecast	GS	WD	N	N	N	N
Develop and administer short-term marketing plans	—	—	GS	SC	WD	EV
Administer expenses under budget	—	GS	DS	SC	WD	EV
Issue sales performance reports monthly	—	N	GS	N	N	WD
Analyze sales performance reports and summary reports	N	GS	N	N	WD	—

Source: Adapted from Tinsley Jr., George M. A Simplified Approach to Charting Sales Functions. *Sales Management,* November 18, 1960, p. 79.

ter coordination vertically within the marketing activity and horizontally across the various business functions.

The key to effective coordination is communication. Communication of what *should* be done and what *can* be done serves as the basis for deciding what *is* to be done in any given plan.

ORGANIZATIONAL STRUCTURE AND MARKET RESPONSIVENESS

If management is truly committed to making its plans responsive to the marketplace, as is characteristic of the societal marketing orientation, then it will make decisions with regard to organizational structure and coordination processes with the objective of increasing the organization's market responsiveness. Organizational structure may be required to evolve just as the markets the organization serves evolve. Since the form to which the market will evolve cannot be known with certainty in advance, the attribute most valuable to management is the flexibility of line and staff employees to change to fit new realities. Experience suggests that people can and will adapt to change as long as they understand what is expected of them, know the reasons necessitating a change, and have latitude in designing the new organizational structure.[13] Formulation of a marketing plan that identifies a competitive advantage, which must be exploited before it vanishes, requires that the organization have a structure and a management and employee culture that can quickly adapt to changed conditions in order to capitalize on temporal market opportunities.

SUMMARY

The organization in which plans are made influences the planning process. Because each organization is different—in personnel, structure, procedures, purpose, and objectives—the marketing planner must work within the established framework or attempt to alter it as plans are developed. Who does what and when must be decided on in an established organizational environment. Understanding how those factors can influence planning is a first step in approaching an organizational perspective in the marketing planning process. Definition of acceptable objectives, strategies, and procedures must be viewed from this perspective to ensure unity and consistency within the organization.

Chapter 3 discusses the procedures used to collect information for use in marketing planning. The resulting information becomes the basis for a well-thought-out plan.

Chapter 3

Database Marketing Planning: Getting Needed Information

MARKETING PLANNING IN ACTION: HYUNDAI MOTOR COMPANY

Hyundai Motor Company, a unit of Seoul, Korea-based Hyundai Corporation, is a distant tenth in United States automobile sales. In an increasingly competitive market, Hyundai had to develop a unique plan for marketing its vehicles against the other U.S. and Japanese giants. Recently, Hyundai began to display its Santa Fe sport utility vehicle inside the Las Vegas airport. In previous months, it had mailed thousands of invitations to homeowners on specific city blocks in Baltimore, Maryland, and Minneapolis, Minnesota, offering them a chance to test-drive its sleek Sonata sedan.

Hyundai recognized the benefit of combining marketing research and information databases to reach its target customers. The company began to get involved with census-based marketing when it sought to determine households that fit into its target market and then identify their specific neighborhood by using the U.S. Census data. Hyundai also uses the census information to help it plan locations for its dealerships. Hyundai combined this data with information from the Claritas PRIZM Lifestyle Segmentation software program, which divides Americans into sixty-two "clusters" or consumer types.

With both census data and buyer profiles, the company can determine which side of town is best to locate the dealership, and which type of vehicles to stock, from the entry-level Accent to the sport-utility Santa Fe, and the more upscale Sonata.

Hyundai pays about $200,000 each year for the information, which it uses not only to identify targets but do direct mailings to them as well. The company recently identified the cluster "urban achiever" as one of interest. This cluster was composed of white-collar, middle-class couples who tended to live in cities, go to rock concerts, and read *Gourmet* magazine. Hyundai thought they fit perfectly with the upscale sedan, Sonata. However, when sent the invitation for a test-drive, they failed to show up, and instead, older couples, possibly interested in the warranty program that offers increased security, were the ones to come in. David Axline, Hyundai's manager of database marketing says, "Sometimes things pop up and make you think, where did that come from? Then you look a little deeper, and it starts to make sense."[1]

INTRODUCTION

Managers seeking to use a societal marketing orientation approach to their planning have, by definition, committed themselves to listening to the voice of the marketplace before developing marketing plans that can deliver customer satisfaction at a competitive advantage. Hence, those managers need to develop the means by which the market can register needs, desires, levels of satisfaction, buying motives, evaluations of competitors, etc. with the firm. Typically, the means by which the firm acquires and uses such information in its marketing planning are the development of market databases and the use of marketing research.

DATABASE MARKETING

True database marketing creates customer intelligence that contributes to the development of profitable customer relationships. Database marketing is an organizational process that is customer research-driven. The information base is dynamic and evolving, preferably with two-way dialogue with the customer.[2] This measure of the importance of creating and maintaining a good database of market information is why *Business Week* devoted the cover story of its September 5, 1994, issue to the subject of database marketing, calling it "one of the biggest changes in marketing since 'new and improved.'"[3] Since that time the concept of database marketing, coupled with new technologies, has grown to the point that a new generation of marketing professionals has been created. These new database marketing professionals offer skills in four primary areas:

1. Secondary data acquisition, including analysis of the value of lists
2. Database building, including the understanding of computer hardware and software

3. Target marketing, including maximizing database record use
4. One-to-one marketing, managing and refining the targeting process to customize contacts for every customer[4]

The popularity of database marketing is grounded in the belief that marketing planning begins by understanding the customer—his or her buying and consumption patterns, location, interest, and other aspects of buying behavior discernable from databases—and then formulating plans that attempt to weave the firm's product or service into the consumer's pattern of behavior. The basic idea behind use of databases is, "If that is what consumers are doing, how can we make them want to do that more often and with our product?" This approach to satisfying customers adheres to the belief that the best indicator of future behavior is past behavior. Thus, if American Express sees its card frequently used by a cardholder to purchase works of art, it assumes an advertisement for artworks in its monthly bill will generate a better response than it would with a cardholder who uses the card for travel in the Caribbean, who gets advertisements for travel specials to that region. In fact, by monitoring cardmembers' shopping, travel, and eating patterns, plus the economic and weather patterns in which they live, the database may trigger an ad to be sent to someone who has traveled in the past to warmer climates during a particularly inclement winter month, in a calculated effort to "strike while the iron is hot." The process of data collection and manipulation, which allows such powerful tactical marketing actions to occur, consists of the following steps:

1. *Consumer action.* The process begins with consumers taking some form of action—they use a coupon, fill out a warranty card, make a purchase, enter a sweepstakes, place a toll-free call to request information, fill out a business reply card, order from a catalog, etc. This behavior is combined with other information in public records to identify a broad profile of each consumer in the database.
2. *Digesting the data.* Sophisticated statistical techniques are used to merge data on the consumer into a coherent, consolidated database. Other software allows the marketer to "drill down" into the data to reveal patterns of behavior for classes of customers.

3. *Profiling the ideal customer.* Neural networks that "learn" from the data are used to identify a model consumer, i.e., the common characteristics held by the high-volume customer. This allows the marketer to find customers or potential customers who share those characteristics in common with the high user.

4. *Using the knowledge.* This data can be used in many ways: determine who gets which sales promotions, to develop attributes for new products or services with a targeted list of customers for new product introduction announcements, to tailor ad messages and target them by customer groups, etc.

5. *Sharing data with channel members.* For consumer package goods marketers, it is possible to merge the manufacturers' database previously described with individual store's scanner data to help plan local promotional mailings, fine-tune shelf displays, and design store layouts.

Using modern technology, marketers can do extensive searches through a large database, essentially mining the data. Data mining is the process of sorting through the data to find hidden patterns, potential trends, and correlations between customers, or within a single customer's data. Data mining is predominantly accomplished through mathematical and statistical processes and is typically done utilizing software developed for this purpose.[5]

Although modern technology, including neural network software and parallel processor hardware, makes the use of such database marketing possible, old-fashioned objectives drive the interest in databases—marketers are seeking to know their customers so well that they can anticipate their needs and provide those products and services to customers before they even know they want them. This is relationship marketing at its most efficient evolutionary stage. Computer technology allows the marketer to acquire knowledge of the purchasing habits of millions of individual customers and to "weave relationships" with them by anticipating their needs and informing them of need-satisfying products specifically suited to their situation. By successfully weaving those relationships, the marketer makes it inconvenient or costly for the customer to switch to a competitor. The information required for this relationship management sometimes comes from loyalty programs, where marketers have some type of method for obtaining customer information at every purchase, usually through plastic membership cards or online accounts. Bookstores, hotels, grocery-store chains, and even casinos have established loyalty accounts. The idea of cultivating relationships with customers and identifying those that are most profitable is called customer relationship management. Customer relationship management may very well be the key marketing trend for the new millennium.[6] Marketers can acquire and manage the information necessary for customer relationship management in several ways. For example, Philip Morris has built a 26 million-name database of smokers, which it uses to target a complete line of Marlboro Man merchandise as well as other direct marketing and lobbying appeals. Blockbuster Entertainment recommends new movies based on a customer's past rentals. Frequent customers of Fairfield Inn are offered discounted stays at a Marriott resort, its parent company.

To some degree, the marketing plans of companies actively engaged in database marketing are driven by the desire to maximize the use of their databases and the technology that allows manipulation of those databases. In other words, the ability to use the database in certain ways means those uses will become the implementation of the marketing plan (i.e., the plan conforms to fit the technology available). This is not necessarily an inappropriate or "backward" approach to marketing as long as marketers do not lose sight of the fact that the ultimate goal of any use of technology or objective of a marketing plan is to identify how a company can gain a competitive advantage in satisfying customer needs and wants.

Jackson and Wang identified fifteen ways to use a marketing database.[7] These are described in depth in their book and the following list illustrates the spectrum of possibilities for the use of databases in data-based marketing planning.

1. Identify your best customers.
2. Develop new customers.
3. Deliver a message consistent with product usage.
4. Reinforce consumer purchase decisions.
5. Cross-sell and complementary-sell products.
6. Apply three-tiered communications.
7. Improve delivery of sales promotion.
8. Refine the marketing process.
9. Increase the effectiveness of distribution channel marketing.

10. Maintain equity.
11. Establish a management resource.
12. Take advantage of stealth communications.
13. Conduct customer, product, and marketing research.
14. Personalize customer service.
15. Provide program synergy and integration.

MARKETING RESEARCH

Although database marketing has increasingly been adopted by organizations and accounts for a significant amount of the funds used to acquire information from the marketplace, it is not the only means by which an organization can hear the voice of the market. Another important method of determining what target market customers are doing, thinking, and saying, which is relevant to your company's marketing planning, is to conduct marketing research to study the market.[8]

Research is defined as an organized, formal inquiry into an area to obtain information. When the adjective "marketing" is added to "research," the context of the area of inquiry is defined. Marketing research, then, refers to procedures and techniques involved in the design, data collection, analysis, and presentation of information used in making marketing decisions. More succinctly, marketing research produces the information needed to make marketing decisions.

The benefits of research are endless, however the following are a few mentioned by Sablosky with regard to bank marketing:

1. Research can confirm your hunches about the customer's perceptions,
2. It can reveal additional customer information that can have a major impact on your business plan,
3. It can identify unseen opportunities, and
4. It can clarify advertising campaign targets and the media needed to reach them.[9]

Although many of the procedures used to conduct marketing research can also be used on other types of research, marketing decisions require approaches that fit the decision-making environment to which they are being applied. Marketing research can make its greatest contribution to management when the researcher understands the environment, organization, management goals and styles, and decision processes that give rise to the need for information.

DECISION MAKING

Although the performance of the activities that constitute marketing research requires a variety of research techniques, the focus should be on the decisions to be made and not the techniques used to collect the information. This focus is central to an understanding of the marketing research function and to the effective and efficient use of research in decision making. Any user or provider of marketing research who loses sight of this central focus is likely to end up in one of two awkward and costly positions: (1) failing to collect the information actually needed to make a decision, or (2) collecting information that is not needed in a given decision-making context. The result of the first situation is ineffectiveness—not reaching a desired objective. The result of the second is inefficiency—failing to reach an objective in the least costly manner. The chances of either of these problems occurring are greatly reduced when the decision itself is the focus of the research effort.

To maintain this focal point, one must understand the purpose and role of marketing research in decision making. The purpose of marketing research is to reduce uncertainty or error in decision making. The uncertainty of the outcomes surrounding a decision is what makes decision making difficult. If you knew for sure the outcome of choosing one alternative over another, then choosing the right alternative would be simple, given the decision-making criteria. If you knew for sure that alternative A would result in a $100,000 increase in income and alternative B would result in a $50,000 income increase, and if the decision criterion was to maximize income, then the choice of alternative A would be obvious. However, most decisions must be made under conditions of uncertainty, in which you do not know for sure if alternative A will produce $50,000 more than B. In fact, neither of the alternatives may be effective. The degree of uncertainty surrounding a decision, the importance of the decision, and the amount of uncertainty that the information will reduce, cause information to have value.

Decision making involves choosing among alternative courses of action. Decision making can be viewed in Exhibit 3.1 as a four-step process that involves (1) identifying the problem or opportunity, (2) defining the problem or opportunity, (3) identifying alternative courses of action, and (4) selecting a specific course of action.

Problem/Opportunity Recognition

A problem or opportunity is the focus of management efforts to maintain or restore performance. A *problem* is anything that stands in the way of achieving an objective. An *opportunity* is a chance to improve on overall performance.

Managers need information to help them recognize problems and opportunities. A problem must be recognized before it can be defined and alternatives developed. An example of this type of information is customer activity data. If new customer generation activity were expected to total twenty new accounts per salesperson during a six-month period, but only ten new accounts per salesperson were to be brought in, this information would make the manager aware of the existence of a potential problem.

Defining the Problem or Opportunity

Once a problem or opportunity has been recognized, it must be defined. Until a clear definition of the problem is established, no alternative courses of action can be considered. The symptoms of the problem are recognized first, and there may be several problems that produce the same set of symptoms. This is analogous to someone with a headache (symptom), who may be suffering from a sinus infection, stress, the flu, or a host of other illnesses (potential problems). Treating the headache may provide temporary relief, but not dealing with the root problem will ensure its return, perhaps with worsening physical conditions.

EXHIBIT 3.1. Steps in decision making.

Step 1	Step 2	Step 3	Step 4
Recognize existence of problems and opportunities	Define the exact nature of problems and opportunities	Identify alternative courses of action	Select a specific course of action

The same type of phenomenon may occur in a business firm. A decline in sales (symptom) may be the result of a decline in the overall economy, losses to another firm, or a myriad of other potential problems. No alternative courses of action should be considered until the actual problem is defined. Information aids the manager at this stage in the decision-making process by defining the problem.

One way problems can be uncovered is through the use of a focus group. This is an exploratory research technique typically involving from eight to ten persons who discuss their attitudes about various products and services or companies. The individuals chosen for the focus group should be representative of the firm's customer base in order to generalize from their comments to other customers not included. This is the inherent danger in focus groups—or any research sample for that matter—that they are not actually representative of others. Ideally, the focus group should be guided by a trained moderator who knows when and how to elicit productive comments from the group. By starting the discussion with a broad general question such as, "How do you feel about current financial services offered to you?" the marketer may be able to obtain useful insight into the feelings of customers about financial services generally and specific services offered by the company. Focus groups are very useful and a relatively economical means for obtaining helpful insights about customers' opinions on a broad variety of subjects related to the firm's marketing strategy.

Identifying Alternatives

The third stage in the decision-making process involves identifying viable alternatives. For some problems, developing alternatives is a natural outcome of defining the problem, especially if that particular problem or opportunity has occurred before. A manager's past knowledge and experiences are used to develop the alternatives in these situations. However, in other situations, a real contribution of research is to inform the decision maker of the options available. A firm considering introduction of new services may use customer information to evaluate different ways in which the new service might be offered. Information from potential customers about various needs not being met could open up many new types of programs that could be offered, thus identifying new alternatives.

Selecting an Alternative

The final stage in the decision-making process is the choice among the alternative courses of action available to the decision maker. Information provided by research can aid a manager at this stage by estimating the effects of the various alternatives. For example, a firm evaluating two alternate prices may use information from a group of customers to decide which one to use.

Information collected through research must be directly related to the decision in order to accomplish the purpose of risk reduction. Thus, the focus of research should be on the decision-making process in general and, specifically, the decision to be made in a given situation rather than the data or the techniques used to collect the data.

TYPES OF DATA

Two basic types of data can be used in decision making: secondary and primary. Secondary data have already been collected and published. The major task of the researcher is to locate the data and then evaluate its appropriateness for the decision at hand.

Secondary data offer two major advantages: (1) low cost and (2) quick access. The major cost of most secondary data is the labor involved in locating and extracting it. Even if the data have to be purchased, the cost is usually low compared to the cost of collecting the data yourself.

Primary data are collected by or for the firm. Although primary data cost more to obtain and also will take longer to access, it may be the most appropriate choice. No secondary data may exist on a particular subject of interest; or if it does exist, it may not be in the necessary units or for the time period of interest. Securing primary data is like obtaining a tailor-made suit rather than one off the rack. It may cost more, but has a much better fit if tailored properly.

The most logical approach to getting the information you need is a two-step process. First, determine if the data have already been collected and, if so, evaluate its appropriateness in terms of your specific information needs. Use secondary data if it is adequate. However, if the secondary data cannot be located or are not of sufficient quality or detail to meet your needs, then collect primary data. This approach would be the most cost-effective and would prevent you from "reinventing the wheel." The steps involved in collecting primary data are the focus of the remainder of this chapter.

STEPS IN A MARKETING RESEARCH PROJECT

Ensuring that data collected in a research project are not only related to the decision maker's information needs but also fit the time frame requires a research approach that is centered on the management problem—the decision to be made. This approach is divided into two phases: (1) the planning phase and (2) the execution phase. The steps in a research project include the following:

1. Define the marketing problem.
2. State research objectives.
3. Develop research methodology.
   a. Define information problem—specific information needs.
   b. Define population to be studied.
   c. Develop sampling technique and determine sample size.
   d. Determine how to measure variables or attributes to be studied.
   e. Determine how to collect data.
   f. Determine how to analyze data.
4. Collect data.
5. Analyze and interpret data.
6. Present findings.

An old work adage states, "Plan your work; work your plan," and this approach should be used in carrying out a research project. A research project does not begin with a questionnaire, a focus group interview, or any other research technique, but with a carefully conceived plan for the research, including (1) a statement of the marketing problem or opportunity, (2) a set of research objectives, and (3) a statement of the research methodology to be used in the project.

The Marketing Problem

The starting point in a research project should be an attempt by both the user and the provider of information to clearly define the problem. Nowhere in the research process is their mutual understanding and agreement more necessary than at this point. Failure by either party to understand or clearly define the major issue will surely lead to disappointment and wasted effort. Many information users, especially the uninitiated, have been "burned," never to be "burned" again, by someone who has collected some data, collected their money, and left them with a lot of "useful" information. One manager recently related such a story. He had heard a lot about marketing and the need to have information about his customers, although he was really unclear about both. He was approached by someone who offered to supply much "useful marketing information" for a reasonable fee. Several months after he had received the final report and paid the fee, he realized that he had no idea how to use the information or if it was what he really needed.

This type of problem can be avoided, or at least minimized, through user-provider interaction, analysis, and discussion of the key administrative issues involved in the situation. The information provider's task is to convert the manager's statement of symptoms into a list of likely problems, decision issues, and, finally, information issues. Two key questions must always be asked at this stage:

> What information does the decision maker feel is needed to make a specific decision?
> How will the information be used to make the decision?

Asking these questions will cause the information user to begin thinking about the information needed rather than the decision itself. Also, the user can start thinking specifically about how the information will be used.

Two types of investigative inquiry should be used by the researcher to generate answers to the two key questions. Managers should be asked "why" and "what-if" questions. The "why" questions help to determine what is known from what is merely assumed to be true, the "what-if" question helps to determine the value of the information in arriving at the decision. For example, consider the following dialogue between a researcher and a decision maker:

DECISION MAKER: We need to get a new advertising agency. Our market share is slipping.

RESEARCHER: Why do you think the decline in market share is due to the poor performance of our ad agency?

In this scenario, the "why" question and a series of related "why" questions that follow it will be used to distinguish between what is known (i.e., where evidence exists to support a contention), from what is assumed (i.e., where no evidence exists but strongly held opinions are voiced). The researcher can then begin to determine what information is needed to make a decision.

A "what-if" question can be used in the decision maker/researcher dialogue as follows:

RESEARCHER: What if the research indicated the problem were to be centered on our price disadvantage rather than poor advertising? How would that information affect your decision making?

DECISION MAKER: Well, I do not think that is true, but if it really were we would have to reevaluate our pricing policies.

In this instance, the researcher has discovered how different pieces of information will affect the decision-making process, helping the researcher to determine the scope and focus of the research. If the decision maker cannot identify how the information described in the "what-if" questions will make a difference in his or her decisions, the researcher knows not to waste time and money collecting that information.

Clearly defining the real issues must be foremost in the researcher's thinking. Information, regardless of quality or quantity, collected for the wrong problem or unrelated to the right decision represents wasted resources and may even be misleading.

If the problem cannot be defined based on current information, an entire study may be necessary just to clearly identify the problem. This type of research may involve identifying the variables in a given decision-making situation and developing a clear definition of the problem or opportunity facing the organization.

Research Objectives

A logical flow develops from the statement of the problem to the identification of specific objectives to be accomplished in the research project. The objectives represent a decomposition of the problem into a series of statements that constitute the end results sought through the research project. The objectives should be stated so that their accomplishment will provide the information necessary to solve the problem. The objectives serve to guide the research results by providing the direction and scope of a given project, and they are the basis for developing the project's methodology.

Objectives are another area in which the user and provider should interact so that the research will produce results that both the user and provider are anticipating. The information provider's role is usually to interpret needs and develop a list of objectives that serve as a basis of negotiation for final research objectives. Objectives should be stated in the form of questions so that the researcher can think in terms of providing answers to those questions. The following is an example:

> *Management problem:* A person who has a small company that installs in-wall wiring for home stereo systems wants to know if a market opportunity exists to work with builders of expensive "spec" homes to provide prewired installations for audio/video (A/V) systems.

> *Research objectives:*
> 1. What building contractors are building "spec" homes costing $250,000+?
> 2. What product and service features would have to be present to interest them in subcontracting for prewired A/V installations?
> 3. Would they want a variety of product/service packages at different price points?
> 4. What role does a home buyer play in making A/V installation decisions?
> 5. Should A/V equipment, satellite dishes, etc., be offered with the prewiring installation?
> 6. Who are my competitors and what do they offer?

Research Methodology

After the management problem has been defined and research objectives agreed upon by both user and provider, the next step in the research process is to develop a research methodology that will accomplish the objectives and provide the information needed to solve the management problem. The specific decisions about methodology are discussed in the following.

Defining Information Needs

The first step in developing the research methodology is to identify the specific types of information needed to accomplish the research objectives. Although this might appear to be an inherent part of the process for developing the objectives, it is usually wise to approach the activity in a more formal way by identifying specific information types. For, example, a research objective could be stated as follows: What are the characteristics of heavy, light, and nonusers of our product? The word *characteristics* can take on a wide variety of definitions—socioeconomic, psychological, behavioral, and physical. What specific types of information are needed? Answering this question forces the researcher to consider research objectives, the management problem, and the decisions to be made based on the research.

This step could be completed under the measurement area—deciding what is to be measured—and this is acceptable. However, since every aspect of research methodology is directly influenced by the type of information to be collected and analyzed, there are advantages to using this as the initial step in methodology.

Population or Universe

The next step in developing the research methodology is to define the population or universe of the study. The research universe includes all of the people or places that possess some characteristic that management is interested in measuring. The universe must be defined for each research project, and this defined universe becomes the group from which a sample is drawn. The list of all universe elements is sometimes referred to as the sampling frame.

The sampling frame must include all members of the population. Failure to meet this requirement can result in bias. If, for example, a researcher were trying to determine the number of families in an area who had purchased a product or service and used the telephone book as the list of respondents to call, three problems would be encountered. First, new residents would not be listed. Second, a significant percentage of phone owners have unlisted numbers. Third, some people are moving away from having a land line in their home to only a cell phone, which would not be listed in the phone book. The difference between the list (telephone book) and area residents could be substantial and could bias the results.

Sampling Technique and Sample Size

Two separate decisions are called for in this step. The first is to determine how specific sample elements will be drawn from the population. The approach selected depends on the nature of the problem and the nature of the population under study. For probability sample designs, the objective is to draw a sample that is both representative and useful. For nonprobability designs, the objective is to select a useful sample even though it may not be representative of the population. The sample design influences the applicability of various types of analysis; some types of analysis are directly dependent upon how sample elements are drawn.

Sampling issues are pertinent even when we are dealing with decision makers who say, "I can't afford the time or money to do a big survey. I just want to get a feel for the market opportunity and then I'll take my chances." For example, if the installer of prewired A/V systems previously mentioned held such an attitude, the researcher is still faced with the need to define the population of interest (building contractors of expensive homes), develop a sampling frame (list) of these people, and determine how many and who to talk with in order to get answers to the research questions.

Sample size represents the second part of the decision. Determining how many sample elements are needed to accomplish the research objectives requires both analysis and judgment. Cost, response rate, and homogeneity of sample elements must be considered when deciding on sample size. For small organizations, cost may dictate the sample size.

Measurement Decisions

Another tough question is, "How will we measure what we need to measure?" The answer is one of the most difficult ones facing the researcher. Researchers must often rely on what has been used in past studies and on their own judgment to decide upon the appropriate technique.

Researchers must develop operational definitions of the concepts to be measured, and these definitions must be stated explicitly. Even seemingly simple concepts, such as product "awareness," can be defined in several ways, with each definition having a different meaning and relative importance. For 60 percent of the respondents to say they have heard of your product is not the same as 60 percent saying that your firm is what comes to mind when they think of the product. Yet both of these approaches measure awareness.

Once the planning stages are complete, the written results of the plan should be embodied in a document called a research proposal. A proposal should be prepared whether the project is done in-house or by an outside organization because it is the basis for allocating funds internally and for an agreement when an outside research group is involved. If an outside firm is used, their staff normally prepares the proposal based on interaction with the information users and those with authority to expend funds for outside research.

Data Collection

The next decision area involves how to collect the data. The first choice is between observation and interrogation, and the second choice is which specific observation or interrogation technique to use. These decisions, in turn, depend on what information is needed, from which sample elements, over what time frame, and at what level of cost.

Data collection can be the single most costly element in a project or it can be of low relative cost, depending on the nature of the project. However, data collection is always an important determinant of research value because of the influence of the conditions surrounding data collection on the validity of the results obtained. Some companies have developed unique solutions to ongoing data-collection projects. Blockbuster Video collects point-of-purchase data from the customer each time a video, DVD, or video game is rented. Bacardi-Martini, in an attempt to target its young adult and student market, collects data through games and other "taste" tests at spring break events. This type of simultaneous marketing and data collection is called experiential marketing.[10] (More about this topic can be found in Chapter 12.) A Canadian cigarette company uses its sales staff as market researchers. Using a portable computer, sales representatives of Rothmans Pall Mall brand record marketing and sales information when they visit retailers. At the conclusion of each day, the sales representatives connect to a central computer via modem and upload the information they have collected, while also receiving electronic messages from the home office. By utilizing the online computer system, information on company marketing programs and competitors' shelf space can be collected, analyzed, and be made immediately available to sales and marketing managers. The program is designed to give Rothmans a competitive edge in the Canadian cigarette market by using the company's sales force to collect market data in the course of doing business, and allowing marketing management to obtain an analysis of the data immediately.[11]

Using untrained interviewers to collect data, for example, can produce not only invalid data, but also data that can lead administrators to make the wrong decision. Careful control of data collection is essential to effective research. Some companies have utilized new forms of technology in their collection of data, such as Web surveys and cellular phones. Online surveys represent about 10 percent of all market research conducted in the United States, and both academics and practitioners recognize the benefit in using this type of technology.[12] In addition, the wireless survey is a data-collection technique that uses standard wireless phones to conduct marketing surveys in the field. Information is input by the customer and is up-linked from multiple sites to a single processing unit, where it can be analyzed immediately and stored.[13]

Data Analysis

One final research methodology decision area concerns the methods used to analyze the data. The major criterion here is the nature of the data to be analyzed. The purpose of the analysis is to obtain meaning from the raw data that have been collected.

For many researchers, the area of data analysis can be the most troublesome. The ability to choose the appropriate technique and carry out the calculations or interpret them from a computer printout marks the difference between a seasoned researcher and a novice. Failure to use the appropriate techniques can result in not getting enough out of the available data or trying to go beyond the data limits in the analysis.

Project Implementation

Once the previous steps have been completed and the planning stage of the research project has been carried out, you are now ready for the execution stages. The execution stages involve carrying out the research plan, collecting the data from the population sampled in the ways specified, and analyzing the data using the techniques already identified in the research plan. If the research plan or proposal has been well-thought-out and "debugged" through revisions of objectives and research designs, then the implementation steps will flow much better and may be completed in a few weeks.

Once the data are collected and analyzed, the researcher must interpret the results of the findings in terms of the problem studied. This means determining what the results imply about the solution to the problems and recommending a course of action to solve the problem. If the purpose of the research project were the determination of the feasibility of introducing a new product and the results of the research project were to show that the product would produce an acceptable level of profits, then the researcher would be smart to recommend introduction of the product unless there are known internal or external barriers that cannot be overcome. This means that the researcher must move beyond the role of the scientist in objectively collecting and analyzing data. Now the role is as a consultant in a framework that states, "Given these facts and this interpretation, I recommend this action." This does not, of course, mean that the action recommended will be pursued by the organization. The researcher usually only makes recommendations. Other administrators have the prerogative of accepting or rejecting the recommendations. However, the researcher must still recommend the action.

The researcher should be involved in the problem definition and objective-setting stages in order to be able to recommend courses of action based on interpretation of research results. To some, this approach may seem to be overstepping the researcher's responsibility to make recommendations, yet most administrators appreciate this approach since it at least represents a starting point in deciding what action should be taken, given certain findings. Information has not really served its basic purpose until it is used in decision making.

SUMMARY

Adopting a market-driven approach to planning means that managers must determine where the market is driving their organization. Understanding consumer needs, behavior, interests, etc., is the first step in developing products and services that are capable of delivering customer satisfaction. Currently, organizations obtain such an understanding from the use of extensive databases and from marketing research projects directed at addressing specific management problems. Chapter 4 begins the sequence of chapters focused on the first stage of the marketing planning process—situation analysis—by discussing how to conduct a product/market analysis.

PART II:
SITUATION ANALYSIS

Chapter 4

Product/Market Analysis

MARKETING PLANNING IN ACTION: NAPSTER AND THE ADVENT OF MUSIC FILE SHARING

In 1999, a nineteen-year-old college student launched what was to become a revolution of sorts in the recorded music industry. Napster, the first music file-sharing service, had become a way to download music from the Internet without payment. What must have at first seemed to be a benign event, the recording industry in the United States soon took notice as its revenues began to fall. Since Napster's inception, unit sales of recorded music have dropped more than 26 percent and the recording industry's revenues have fallen 14 percent—a $2 billion decline. The industry responded by suing the Internet pirates for theft of intellectual property.

Indeed, music is a universal form of communication throughout the world, an industry worth $40 billion annually. In the United States alone, revenues are close to $13 billion, representing the livelihood of thousands of people, from songwriters to record promoters. Only a few short years ago there were several barriers for entering the recording industry market, however, technological advances, consumer attitudes, and the way in which the public uses music has begun to change and affect the way in which music is produced. So much in fact, that it is now possible for someone with minimal sound equipment and a computer, to begin a record label and promote the CD around the world through the Internet in a matter of minutes. At the other end of the recording industry spectrum, the powerhouse recording companies continue to grow through merger and acquisition. Five recording companies share the control of about 70 percent of the global recorded-music market. European regulators have historically blocked any merger among these five, however recently, these sanctions were lifted and two of the world's largest companies, Sony Music and Bertelsmann's BMG, merged. Consolidation is one of several strategies the industry hopes will help it to survive. In addition to reducing costs, the newly created company, Sony BMG, plans to transform more narrowly defined record firms into broader music companies, adding revenues from global concerts and sponsorships. Re-cording companies have also begun to embrace their former adversary, the Internet. Even though Napster was eliminated through the courts, other online music-swapping services quickly sprung up in its place, cre-ating a problem that would not go away. Record labels are now making deals with online providers to offer for-pay subscription services. Just two weeks after the debut of iTunes, more than 2 million downloads at ninety-nine cents each were sold. Record companies are also recogniz-ing the power of online marketing, offering real-time broadcasts of popu-lar bands' concerts, and showcasing new artists' videos to broadband users in an attempt to stimulate sales.[1]

INTRODUCTION

Effective marketing plans must be rooted in a factually based situa-tion analysis. The first step in the situation analysis is a product and market analysis, which involves developing a general understanding of the factors that influence a given market and how a company and/or a product fit into that market. Trends and factors must be iden-tified in the market and in a firm's sales and cost patterns to under-stand what has happened in a market over time.

This chapter focuses on external and internal analyses and their re-lationship to marketing planning. Internal data sources are described and their uses in understanding the dynamics of a market are ex-plained. Thus, the external and internal factors influencing a product or service are analyzed to provide a basis for the marketing plan.

ENVIRONMENTAL SCANNING

Evidence suggests that the first firm to exploit an environmental opportunity for a new product/market will enjoy market share and profitability advantages over later entrants. A study of 371 mature consumer goods businesses discovered a mean market share of 29 per-cent for those first to market, 17 percent for those firms that followed the pioneer quickly, and an average market share of 12 percent for late entrants when the market reached maturity.[2] The first market may not gain long-term profitability and market share advantages. An-other study discovered that because some firms have talents at lead-ing and others at following, entry timing depends upon the company's success in assessing internal skills and resources relative to the market's requirements.[3] Therefore, advantages can be gained by a firm conducting an analysis of the environment surrounding a particular market as well as assessing internal skills and resources before planning a market entry strategy.

Environmental scanning involves identifying those realities in a firm's operating sphere that directly or indirectly influence a firm's plans and operations. They include economic, technological, cultural, social, legal, political, competitive, and organizational environments. The most important point a manager can learn from an analysis of environmental factors is the answer to the following question: "How do these factors influence marketing plans being developed or precipitate changes in an existing plan?" The answer involves keeping in tune with the operating environment and relating environmental changes to the planning process. Managers continually need to ask themselves two basic questions: "Are we doing the right things?" and "Are we doing things right?" The first question is concerned with direction and adaptation, or keeping in the mainstream of what is going on in the world in which we operate. The second question is concerned with effectiveness and efficiency.

Since the environment is so large and complex, a manager must establish a standard of relevance in the analysis, which means developing an approach to determine whether or not an environmental factor is important to the company and/or product. This can be accomplished by developing a list of words that can be used as a focus when sifting through the various sources of information. For example, in developing a marketing plan for a water-related recreational park, the following key word list was used:

- Water
- Recreation
- Leisure activities
- Theme parks
- Leisure expenditures
- Recreational expenditures

In the information search process, the environmental factors were identified as shown in Exhibit 4.1 at the time of the study. In developing a list of key words or phrases, and in the information search stage,

EXHIBIT 4.1. Environmental factors for a water-related recreational park.

1. Americans have a growing preoccupation with outdoor recreation.
2. Based on past trends, a doubling of recreational expenditures can be expected in the next eight to ten years.
3. Expenditures for leisure activities are increasing faster than consumer spending as a whole.
4. More and more people are moving to the Sunbelt; the South and Southwest are expected to be major growth areas, and people tend to be more recreationally active in these geographical areas.
5. Leisure spending does not appear to be as heavily influenced by adverse economic conditions as other expenditures.
6. Total leisure spending is expected to grow by 76 percent to $300 billion over six years.
7. Tops on the list of popular sports in the United States is swimming—some 103 million people regularly swim.
8. Admission revenues for sporting events grew by 150 percent to $9 billion over twelve years.
9. Water-related activities account for five of the top twenty-five outdoor recreational activities.
10. Experts predict that participation in summertime outdoor recreational activities will be four times greater in the year 2000 than in 1960.
11. Many theme parks are currently in trouble financially because of saturation, competition, and inflation.
12. Experienced theme park operators have learned how to keep guests for several hours and offer many alternative ways to spend money.
13. A major cost problem for theme parks is the attempt to add newer, more thrilling rides every two years—at continually inflated costs.
14. A comparable outdoor water recreation project is successful—but appeals mainly to a young market (ages 8 to 23); very few families participate.

a basic question continually asked was, "Could this factor directly or indirectly influence the market, objectives, or strategy of the marketing plan?" If the answer is yes, the factor is examined. If the answer is no, the factor is omitted. This question is the standard of relevance used to judge the importance of the various environmental factors.

For companies having access to computer search facilities, the same process is involved. The user must develop a list of key words and a potential title of the types of information that may be pertinent, and then the computer searches information sources using those criteria.

An examination of the list in Exhibit 4.1 demonstrates how this process works. Each of those statements was derived from an article or group of articles and reflects important aspects of the environment, both positive and negative, that should influence the planner's thinking about the product or service for which the plan was being developed. Statements 6 and 8, for example, support the idea that the market, of which the water-related recreation park would be a part, is indeed a growth market. Statements 7 and 9 provide a basis for viewing the park as having a high-traffic potential, which, in turn, is useful in forecasting market demand.

This type of analysis provides initial insight into the nature of the environment in which the firm operates or plans to operate and serves as a part of the factual base for planning. It helps the planner understand in a clearer way the market of a specific company and/or product.[4]

THE STRATEGIC IMPLICATIONS OF PRODUCT/MARKET ANALYSIS

Industry analysis describes the study of the economics, structure, forces, etc., that dominate particular groups of companies producing similar products, such as the bicycle industry or cosmetics industry. However, the use of such a term to describe the level of analysis we are discussing in this chapter suggests more of a company-centered approach than the customer-centered approach we are stressing in this book. Customers do not think in terms of doing business with an industry, they think in terms of satisfying their needs. Thus, on Saturday night, a young married couple wants to "have some fun," not buy one of the offerings from the movie industry. Firms should think in terms of "product/markets" rather than industries. By product/market we mean the set of products that serve a certain need of a certain market segment with a certain technology.[5] (See Exhibit 4.2 example for home computers.)

One obvious implication of viewing a product/market in this way is that changes in the product/market may occur along each of these three dimensions, perhaps simultaneously. Therefore, environmental scanning should identify forces at work on any of these three dimensions, which could change the nature of the product/market. A related

EXHIBIT 4.2. Home computer product/market.

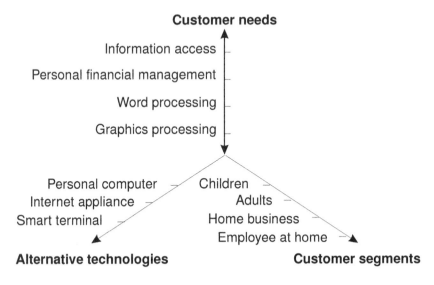

implication is that product/markets evolve over time as movement occurs along the three dimensions. This evolution is reflected in the group of competitors competing for market share and the sales growth and share of market for different technologies over time. Consider, for example, what competitors and products have defined the home computer product/market over time (see Exhibit 4.3).

Clearly the definition of what constitutes a "home computer" has dramatically changed over time, as have the group of competitors competing in this market, the needs that home computers are intended to fulfill, and the customer segments existing in the market. Marketing plans must address in the product/market analysis section the evolving nature of their markets so that the company does not fail to take advantage of emerging opportunities or deal with emerging threats along the three dimensions of a product/market.

Analysis of Markets and Company Market Positions

Although the dimensions of a market analysis will vary to include relevant aspects of each unique market, some variables will typically be found in most analyses:

- Market growth
- Key success factors
- Sales analysis
- Cost analysis

EXHIBIT 4.3. Evolution of competition and technologies in the home computer product/market, 1981-2003.

1981-1982	1983	1984
Commodore 64-64K $600 Atari 400-64K $500 Timex 1000-2K $100	Atari 800XL-64K $300 Coleco Adam-80K $700 Commodore 64-64K $500	Apple IIC-128K $1,200 IBM PC Jr-128K $1,000
1985	**1986**	**1991**
Leading Edge D-256K $1,500 Tandy 1000-256K $1,750 Apple II E-128K $1,500	Zenith Z–148-256K with 2 drives $1,800	IBM Compact Turbo XT—640K RAM, keyboard, 20MB hard floppy, 14" monitor $600
1992	**1994**	**1996**
386SX-16 HZ 1MB RAM 40MB hard drive, 3.5" floppy disk drive, 14" VGA monitor, keyboard, DOS, $688	Gateway 2000 $1,500, 33 MHZ 486SX, 4 MB RAM, 340 MB hard drive, CD-ROM, 2400/9600 data fax/modem, 3.5" disk drive, 14" color SVGA monitor, keyboard, mouse, MS-DOS 6.2	Intel 100MHZ Pentium $1,649, video graphics card, 8 MB EDD RAM, 1.2 gigabyte hard drive, 3.5" 1.44 MB disk drive, 4X CD ROM drive, 28.8 bps fax/voice modem, keyboard, mouse, 15" color monitor, Windows 95, one year in-home service
1998	**2000**	**2005**
Gateway $1,299, Intel Celeron 400 MHz, 64 MB SDRAM, 17" monitor, 6.4GB ultra hard drive, CDROM, 56K modem, Windows 98	Compaq Presario 8000T, $1,299, Intel Pentium 1.80GHz, 128 MB SDRAM, 40 GM ultra hard drive, 48X CDROM 56K V90 modem, digital audio, 17" monitor, Windows XP	Gateway 7310S $799, Intel 915G, 512MB, 400MHz DDR SDRAM, 160GB hard drive, 15" flat panel color monitor, 16X DVD Writer, Windows XP. Dell Insipiron 6000 Note-book, $649, 1.3GH, 1MB, 400MH, 256MB, 40GB hard drive, 8X DVD, ninety-day warranty and service plan.

Each of these areas can have a significant impact on the ability and willingness of a firm to compete in a market. They will be briefly described here.[6] The checklist in Exhibit 4.4 includes other considerations for analyzing a market's direction.

Market Growth

The rate of growth of a market can affect the way in which a firm competes. If a market is showing a significant rate of annual growth, a firm may be able to have increased sales without having to fund market programs intended to increase market share. In mature or declining markets, however, "experience curve" pricing and a more aggressive posture of firms trying to maintain their growth in a declining market may force firms into a different strategic position.

Market growth factors are those realities in the market that allot the demand for the product. For example, a market growth factor for baby cribs is the number of babies born each year. Since a market consists of people with money and a motivation to buy, population

EXHIBIT 4.4. Product/market evaluation checklist.

1. Growth	☐ Slow	☐ Medium	☐ Fast
2. Customers	☐ Growing	☐ Declining	☐ No change
3. Technology	☐ Low	☐ Medium	☐ High
4. Product change	☐ Slow	☐ Medium	☐ Fast
5. Danger of obsolescence	☐ Low	☐ Medium	☐ High
6. Ease of entry	☐ Low	☐ Medium	☐ High
7. Quality of suppliers	☐ Low	☐ Medium	☐ High
8. Possibility of regulation	☐ Low	☐ Medium	☐ High
9. Availability of raw materials/resources	☐ Low	☐ Medium	☐ High
10. Amount of capital required	☐ Low	☐ Medium	☐ High

and income figures are commonly used as market growth factors. However, you can be much more specific in identifying market growth factors for a given company, product, or service. The interest in market growth factors is threefold: (1) to identify the factors that influence a product or service's demand, (2) to determine the relationship between the factor and the product or service, and (3) to forecast that market growth factor into the future. Since many of the factors are used by different forecasters, much of the forecasting work may have already been completed and simply needs to be located. Population projections, for example, are available through many sources, so there is usually no need to develop your own forecast of population.

Two basic techniques available for selecting and determining the impact of market growth factors on a given product or service are arbitrary judgment and correlation analysis. Arbitrary judgment makes use of the decision maker's own experience and judgment in selecting factors and weighing them. For new products or services, this is a common technique since no sales history is available, unless, of course, a test market is used. It can also be used for established products. For example, a drug manufacturer might determine from historical data that two dollars worth of prescription drugs per month are purchased for each person residing in a given market area. The number of consumers in a market area is the market growth factor for that product, and projection of population for that market area would be used to obtain information on its future size. It might also be discovered from past data that the company's market share has been 12 percent for the past three years. This figure could be used to estimate expected growth in company sales for the next time period, all other things being equal.

A more complex, yet usually more reliable, approach is to use correlation analysis to help identify and weigh growth factors. Although it is not appropriate to discuss the details of this technique here, there is a specific technique in correlation analysis called step-wise regression analysis, which not only weighs the various factors but also provides a measure of what the addition of each factor adds to an explanation of changes in sales. Because this method requires a sales history, it is limited mainly to existing products even though it could be used on test-market data for new products.

Regardless of the techniques used in analyzing market growth factors, the basic information sought involves understanding the factors that influence demand for a product or service and their historical and future trends. This information helps develop the basis from which objectives and strategies are developed. This concept will be more evident in the discussion in Chapter 5, which discusses the use of factors to estimate market potential.

Key Success Factors

An important component of a thorough market analysis is the identification of key success factors (KSF)—the resources and skills the market dictates companies must have to successfully compete (i.e., the factors thay are key for success). The most basic of these factors are similar to an "ante" in a game of poker—if you cannot come up with them, you cannot be a "player." Establishment of an intensive distribution system would be a basic key success factor for a manufacturer of chewing gum, as would time slots and gates at airports for an airline. Obviously, these key success factors will vary by industry and product/market within an industry. The failure of Philip Morris and Procter & Gamble (P&G) to gain entry into the soft-drink market was due to a lack of access to soft-drink bottlers, a KSF for that industry. Other examples of key success factors follow:

Book (or Movie) Market

- Relationships with authors (or producers), with a balance between established and emerging talents
- The capacity to market the resulting product effectively, coupled with a quick response system to exploit a hit when it occurs
- The ability to control fixed and marginal costs and to obtain scale economies
- Relationships with the distribution channel
- A strategy for the Internet, including an e-book route to market[7]

Firms must understand the KSF's for each product/market in which they operate or are considering future entry. Studies have shown that firms having strengths that match the market's KSF's outperform other firms in those markets by a substantial margin.[8] KSF's can change as product/markets evolve over time. Therefore, market analysis, including marketing research, should be ongoing to identify in a timely fashion changes that can impact an organization's ability to gain and maintain a competitive advantage. The objective is to discover the KSF's at the "crest of the wave" as a market evolves to a new stage; that is, when the KSF is changing from one which constitutes the "ante" to one which is emerging and when capitalizing on it will grant a firm a competitive advantage in the market's next evolutionary stage. For example, car companies that foresaw the shift in financing from purchase to leasing were able to develop attractive leasing programs and gain a competitive advantage over companies who continued to think their business was in "selling" autos. Such an advantage must be aggressively pursued, however, before the wave crests and the KSF becomes the basic condition that everyone must meet in order to be a viable firm in the market.

SALES ANALYSIS

For firms already in a market, other types of analysis are possible. One extremely beneficial form is sales analysis, two types of which are: (1) analysis of net sales volume, and (2) analysis of sales by segments—products, customers, areas, etc.

Analysis of Net Sales Volume

Analysis of net sales of a company or a specific product or service is extremely useful in developing trends or patterns of sales activity. Exhibit 4.5 illustrates this approach by presenting sales for an actual restaurant, total food sales of eating places in the city, and a calculation of market share for a four-year period.

Two important points can be derived from this illustration. First, you must put sales figures for any given year in some type of perspective. One way to do so is to compare sales over a period of time. In the example, sales were increasing but at a slow rate.

Although this figure may provide some insight into the company's role in the market, it can be misleading. When the total sales of eating places for the city was used to calculate the firm's market share, a distinct pattern emerges—the firm's market share had declined. The question that must be answered is "why." If the increase in total city

EXHIBIT 4.5. Restaurant market share data.

Year	Total city sales of eating places	Restaurant sales	Market share (percent)
1	$9,410,931	$219,184	2.3
2	8,932,350	222,723	2.4
3	9,446,857	222,793	2.3
4	11,008,016	238,439	2.1

sales is due to several new restaurants in the city, the small decline may be explained by increased competition. However, if the same number of firms were still in the market, they were growing faster relative to this restaurant, and we must suspect something is wrong with the restaurant's marketing strategy.

The second point is that although this type of analysis does not reveal why a condition exists or what action to take, it does indicate potential problems. Projecting these data trends into the following year would suggest a worsened condition for this firm in relation to the total market. Certainly, the marketing plan would need to incorporate objectives and strategies aimed at uncovering the cause for the decline and then at stopping or reversing the trend.

Sales Analysis by Segment

Analysis of net sales can provide some insight into a firm's sales pattern and historical market share, but more specific information is needed. This information can be obtained through analysis of sales by segments—products, product groups, customers, divisions, geographical areas, and so on. The purpose is to find the contribution to total net sales from each segment that is analyzed. An example of this type of analysis is shown in Exhibit 4.6 for a manufacturer of industrial parts. In this illustration, a two-way classification of sales is presented by product and by region. This analysis provides data of three different types. First, it shows the contribution of each product to total sales volume; second, it shows the contribution of each region's sales to total sales; and finally, it shows the contribution of each product in each region.

EXHIBIT 4.6. Sales analysis by product and region for industrial parts.

Product	Total sales	Sales by region			
		Southwest	Southeast	Northwest	Northeast
Grinders	$127,806	$34,606	$27,901	$48,600	$16,699
Drills	238,700	58,731	62,800	54,601	62,568
Drill bits	158,208	39,653	47,288	34,046	37,221
Buffers	252,900	63,985	65,126	54,631	69,158
Sanders	328,500	75,858	84,720	85,952	81,970
Total sales	$1,106,114	$272,833	$287,835	$277,830	$267,616

This type of analysis would be most revealing when first completed because it shows the composition of the total sales volume. This detailed information is needed because decisions are made on the basis of individual products, territories, customers, and so forth, and not on the basis of totals. In fact, the good performance of one product may offset the bad performance of another product, which could be unnoticed if only total net sales are examined. This has been called the "iceberg principle" in that total sales (the top of the iceberg), can cover up the sales by segments (the hidden part of the iceberg). The submerged part of the iceberg usually causes the problems.

Another basic finding in this type of analysis has been referred to as the 80/20 principle or rule. This generalization states that 80 percent of the business is accounted for by 20 percent of the products, customers, or territories. The percentages, of course, will vary, but the point is that there will be an uneven proportionate contribution to total sales by certain segments. In Exhibit 4.6, for example, two products, buffers and sanders, account for 52 percent of sales, and for grinders, three regions account for 87 percent of sales. If a manager is aware of these types of situations, attention and marketing effort can be allocated appropriately in the marketing plan. However, unless this type of analysis has been made, a misallocation of effort usually occurs. This means more effort is directed at a part or a segment—a specific region, for example—than its potential contribution would warrant. If, in the example, 25 percent of the marketing budget and effort for grinders were directed at the Northeast region, too much effort would probably be exerted in that region, given its contribution to sales is only 13 percent.[9]

This type of analysis begins to provide a clear picture of "where we are" for specific products and services and for any other segments that are analyzed. It offers a much sounder basis for planning than merely a general analysis of sales volume. Since these data are not part of a regular accounting system, they must be requested and sometimes generated by the marketing planner. Computer facilities would facilitate detailed analysis of sales volume.

COST ANALYSIS

Sales analysis, even by segments, is only a part of the information needed to understand the nature of a firm's current marketing operations. Sales analysis, when considered alone, can even be misleading. A product low in sales volume may not be low in its profit contribution. Sales and profitability can be determined only through sales and costs analysis.

The three basic types of cost analyses are: (1) analysis of ledger accounts, (2) functional or activity cost analysis, and (3) segment cost analysis. These types of cost analyses are not part of the accounting system, and a manager must request this information and in most cases work with the information supplier in coordinating the analysis.

Analysis of Ledger Accounts

The simplest type of cost analysis involves examining costs, over a period of time, as they appear in the natural accounts used in the accounting system. The interest is in the absolute size and growth of an account, such as the change in sales salaries over time. One tool frequently used in this analysis is the common-size income statement shown in Exhibit 4.7. This statement shows each item as a percentage of sales. When several years are compared, the actual percentage growth and relative value of a given expense can be evaluated. A manager can then begin to question why a given expense has grown or why it represents such a large part of total expenses. Answers to such questions help explain why an expenditure pattern exists and enable planners to increase their understanding of expenditure patterns.

EXHIBIT 4.7. Common-size income statement, 1997.

Net sales		100.0%
Cost of sales		72.0
Gross profit		28.0%
Selling expenses:		
Sales salaries	5.5%	
Travel and entertainment	.9	
Sales supplies used	.5	
Advertising	5.6	
Other selling expenses	.5	
Total selling expenses		13.0%
Administrative expenses:		
Office salaries	4.9%	
Office supplies used	.8	
Office rent	.8	
Taxes and insurance	.6	
Depreciation of equipment	.3	
Other administrative expenses	.1	
Total administrative expenses		7.5%
Total operating expenses		20.5%
Net operating income		7.5%
Less interest expense		.5
Net income		7.0%

Functional Cost Analysis

Functional or activity cost analysis involves allocating cost from the natural accounts to accounts set up for each marketing function or activity. This analysis serves two purposes. First, it provides information on the total costs of performing the various marketing activities, and second, it is an intermediate step to segment cost analysis. Knowing the total cost of performing a function or activity is useful in major strategic decisions such as altering the physical distribution system. This type of analysis is illustrated in Exhibit 4.8. It permits answering questions such as "How much is it costing us for storage?" Then when costs are allocated to a category, such as a product, questions about the costs of storage for a specific product can be answered.

The basis used to allocate functional cost to a specific category is determined by the nature of the function. For example, storage costs would usually be allocated to products on the basis of the number of square feet of warehouse space used to store each product. If storage costs were to be allocated to geographical areas, sales volumes in each area would usually be used as the basis for allocation unless there were storage facilities in each area.

Segment Cost Analysis

Segment cost analysis is illustrated in Exhibits 4.9 and 4.10. The objective in segment cost analysis is to determine the contribution of a segment—products, customers, territories—to total profitability. Two alternate approaches to allocating cost from the activity accounts are shown in Exhibit 4.8 to the three products analyzed in Exhibits 4.9 and 4.10. These approaches are the full cost approach and the contribution margin approach. In the full cost approach, illustrated in Exhibit 4.9, all costs—direct and indirect—are allocated to a specific category, such as a product. This form permits determining the net profit contribution of each product to total profit.

However, this approach also poses a problem. It forces allocation of indirect costs to individual products. Indirect costs are costs that are not eliminated if a given product is dropped. For example, the sales manager's salary is an indirect cost of a particular product because if you eliminate that product you would not eliminate the manager's salary. To allocate indirect costs, a basis of allocation must be selected. Three commonly used allocation methods are: (1) allocate equally to each part of a segment, (2) allocate in direct proportion to sales of each part of a segment, or (3) allocate in direct proportion to the direct cost of each part of a segment. If you choose to allocate the sales manager's salary equally to each product and the salary was $30,000, then each product would be assigned $10,000 as its share of that indirect cost. Although all indirect costs must be allocated to arrive at a net profit figure by product, this process can be misleading. It

EXHIBIT 4.8. Activity cost analysis.

| | | | | | | Activity cost groups | | |
Ledger expenses	Total expenses	Direct selling	Advertising and promotion	Transportation and shipping	Storage	Credits and collections	Financial and clerical	Marketing administration
Sales force commissions	$312,000	$312,000	—	—	—	—	—	—
Sales force salaries	120,000	120,000	—	—	—	—	—	—
Office supplies	13,320	2,400	2,040	1,560	1,200	1,200	4,200	720
Media space and time	120,000	—	120,000	—	—	—	—	—
Advertising salaries	30,000	—	30,000	—	—	—	—	—
Administrative salaries	108,000	19,200	—	8,400	8,400	7,200	16,800	48,000
Rent	16,920	—	1,800	3,840	4,200	2,304	2,256	2,520
Taxes and insurance	13,500	2,040	960	2,760	3,000	1,260	1,260	2,220
Heat and light	7,020	—	960	1,620	1,620	1,020	1,020	780
Depreciation	9,240	960	600	2,040	2,640	480	1,920	600
Miscellaneous	4,560	420	960	600	780	960	660	180
Totals	$754,560	$457,020	$157,320	$20,820	$21,840	$14,424	$28,116	$55,020

EXHIBIT 4.9. Income statement by product: Total cost approach.

	Total	Drills	Drill Bits	Grinders
Net sales	$3,600,000	$1,200,000	$600,000	$1,800,000
Less cost of goods sold	2,520,000	880,000	440,000	1,200,000
Gross margin	$1,080,000	$320,000	$160,000	$600,000
Less operating expenses:				
Direct selling	$457,020	$132,536	$82,264	$242,220
Advertising and sales promotion	157,320	56,635	23,598	77,087
Transportation and shipping	20,820	7,912	5,205	7,703
Storage	21,840	8,955	5,678	7,207
Credits and collections	14,424	4,472	2,596	7,356
Financial and clerical	28,116	8,997	7,873	11,246
Marketing administrative	55,020	18,707	8,803	27,510
Total operating expenses	$754,560	$238,214	$136,017	$380,329
Net profit before income taxes	$325,440	$81,786	$23,983	$219,671

may appear that a product not showing a profit should be eliminated, thereby increasing total profitability. However, if a product is eliminated, only direct costs are eliminated, and the indirect costs have to be reallocated to remaining products.

To overcome this problem, the contribution margin approach is commonly used. With this approach only direct costs are allocated to each part of a segment (see Exhibit 4.9). The contribution margin is the amount each product contributes to cover indirect costs and earn a profit after all its direct costs are subtracted. As long as a product's contribution is positive, the firm is better off having the product (i.e., its sales cover all its costs and make a contribution to indirect costs and profit). This type of analysis does not reveal why costs or contri-

EXHIBIT 4.10. Income statement by product: Contribution margin approach.

	Total	Drills	Drill bits	Grinders
Net Sales	$3,600,000	$1,200,000	$600,000	$1,800,000
Less cost of goods sold, labor and materials only	2,520,000	880,000	440,000	1,200,000
Gross margin	$1,080,000	$320,000	$160,000	$600,000
Less direct operating expenses:				
Direct selling	$370,186	$107,354	$66,634	$196,198
Advertising and sales promotion	99,112	33,698	13,876	51,538
Transportation and shipping	8,328	2,748	2,082	3,498
Storage	7,862	2,359	1,965	3,538
Credits and collections	7,645	2,828	994	3,823
Financial and clerical	10,122	3,037	1,822	5,263
Total direct expenses	$503,255	$152,024	$87,373	$263,858
Contribution margin	$576,745	$167,976	$72,627	$336,142
Less indirect operating expenses:				
Direct selling	$86,834			
Advertising and sales promotion	55,208			
Transportation and shipping	12,492			
Storage	13,978			
Credits and collections	6,779			
Financial and clerical	17,994			
Marketing administrative	55,020			
Total indirect expenses	$251,305			
Net profit before income taxes	$325,440			

butions are the way they are but simply tells the user what is happening in specific aspects of the firm's business.

The analytical methods discussed in this chapter can provide specific detailed data about markets and products. The analyses are not done in many companies because marketing planners may not understand the procedures. Another factor that may limit the use of these analyses is that the planner must submit a detailed request in order to secure the information that is so vital to effective planning. Since the analyses are not part of a typical accounting system, additional expenditures are necessary in order to complete the analyses and make them available for use in planning. This investment in information should produce a very high and quick payback in the form of better marketing plans.

SUMMARY

As the marketing planner begins to analyze the firm's current situation, a factual base begins to emerge from which objectives and strategies can be developed. The first step in the analysis is to identify factors in the environment and market that influence the firm's operations. Consideration of each product/market in which a firm operates includes a study of the customer needs, customer segments, and alternative technologies that define the product/market. Markets can evolve along each of these dimensions. Market analysis also includes a study of market size and growth and the key success factors that the market dictates successful firms must have if they are to remain competitive over time in that product/market. Then the analysis turns inward to the company's internal records to develop trends in company sales. Market share data derived from total sales analysis are especially enlightening because they show a firm's growth in sales in relation to the total market.

More specific analysis of a firm's position is obtained through sales and cost analysis by segments. Such analyses clarify the contribution of individual products, services, territories, and so forth, and are particularly important because this is the level at which decisions must be made. Sales and cost analysis can provide the type of specific data a planner needs.

Chapter 5 deals with consumer analysis, and the focus of marketing planning—on consumer needs—comes clearly into view.

Chapter 5

Consumer Analysis

MARKETING PLANNING IN ACTION:
THE ANTIAGING MOVEMENT

A crowd of mostly middle-age women gathered inside a makeshift television studio to witness the taping of a television special, "The Beauty-Brain Connection." Although this particular taping was for public broadcasting (PBS) television, the speaker that day was Dr. Nicholas Perricone, author of two bestsellers, *The Wrinkle Cure* and *The Perricone Prescription.* He is one of several dermatologists who are becoming celebrities by selling their own line of antiwrinkle creams and nutritional supplements through various types of media. In 2002 his product sales reached $42 million, an increase from $11 million the previous year.

Sales of dermatologist and "clinical brands" have exploded, becoming the fastest-growing segment of department store skin-care business. Several factors have fueled this growth, particularly the number of consumers who are approaching their fifties. According to the U.S. Census data for 2000, the number of people who will be age fifty or over this year will rise to 35 percent of the total population. This group's need to turn back the clock and search for any means to keep them looking and feeling younger, has contributed to the explosive growth of several industries. In 2002, Americans spent $7.7 billion on cosmetic procedures, more than triple the number in 1997. These procedures included 1.7 million Botox injections for facial wrinkles, 495,000 chemical peels, and 125,000 facelifts. Women accounted for 88 percent of these.

However, "cosmeceutical" marketers such as Dr. Perricone are astutely aware that not all consumers who are turning fifty are likely to be part of their target market. With his products selling from $85 for an olive oil cream to $570 for two ounces of his new antiwrinkle cream, his products are clearly marked for a more narrowly defined target segment than by age alone.

Dr. Perricone's appearance on PBS is evidence that he continues to target a more highly educated, higher-income customer. Although his appearance was criticized by those who did not want the program to appear to be an infomercial, one of his broadcasts in 2002 raised $4 million for PBS. He has already created a devoted following. One of his customers commented that she was attracted to the doctor's regimen by his medical credentials. "It definitely made a difference that he was a doctor—he was more credible."[1]

INTRODUCTION

In Chapter 4 we discussed the importance of analyzing the product/market in which the firm intends to compete. This chapter continues that analysis by narrowing the market focus to the groups of consumers that make up those markets. The adoption of a societal marketing orientation implicitly and explicitly requires marketing planners to consider the needs and welfare of those consumers the organization serves. Consumer analysis is also a fundamental prerequisite to the task of identifying a competitive advantage in each product/market, since it is with consumers that you gain an advantage over your competitors. A firm must gain a competitive advantage with each targeted group of consumers—no firm gains a "universal" competitive advantage by doing one thing since different groups of consumers differentially value the firm's marketing offerings and programs.

Thus, nothing is more central to marketing than consumer analysis. This chapter focuses on consumers' needs, which are the pivotal point around which objectives and strategies are developed.

The key words in this chapter are *consumer* and *analysis*. The objective of the process is understanding consumers' needs, which is accomplished through analysis. The word analysis simply means to break into parts. The tools used in this analysis activity comprise the primary focus of this chapter. Selecting the appropriate segments and successfully attracting customers is the basis for a firm's survival and growth.

Once a specific market segment has been identified, its size must be estimated. This estimate becomes a key to assessing opportunity or attractiveness of the segment.

MARKET SEGMENTATION

One fundamental concept that underlies the type of analysis described in this chapter is the idea that what is sometimes referred to as a "market" is actually a composite of smaller markets, each with identifiable characteristics. When we speak of the product market, for example, we are making reference to a large market composed of smaller submarkets or segments. This market can be segmented in several ways to identify the various submarkets. The type of consumer, for example, may be used to identify at least two submarkets or segments: industrial and individual. This process of breaking up a market into smaller parts or segments is usually referred to as market segmentation. The basic premise is that the needs of consumers in one segment are different from those in another segment and therefore, different marketing strategies should be used to reach different segments. The results of the analysis should be an understanding of consumers' needs by segment and some insight into the types of strategies needed to meet those needs. This is the basis of the entire planning process if a societal marketing-oriented approach is to be used in planning.

Perhaps we should stop at this point to make an obvious but somewhat strange-sounding observation: market segments do not actually exist. They are there because we declare them to be there; they have no tangible reality apart from our calling them into existence. Your own experience as a consumer supports this contention. As a consumer you are a member of hundreds, if not thousands, of market segments created by firms both here and abroad, yet you do not define yourself in any way by that membership. Indeed, you are oblivious to the fact that numerous automobile companies, for example, have classified you into segments based on your age and income by one company, lifestyle by another, benefits sought by yet another, etc.

Classification of markets into segments is not like classifying the animal kingdom by genus, subgenus, and species (i.e., the old aphorism "a leopard cannot change its spots"). We do not change our species, but we can be classified quite differently into segments by marketers in different types of companies or even by competitors in the same business, or by the same company at different points in time. Marketers "create" market segments (or, as we prefer to think of it, "identify" market segments) to allow for a more focused marketing plan to reach a particular group of consumers with some homogeneous trait that causes them to respond similarly to a marketing appeal. Hence, the concept of a market segment is a convenient construct for marketing planning purposes, but its importance to contemporary marketers cannot be exaggerated. Market segmentation may be "artificial," but it is an essential part of an analysis of consumer and industrial product markets.

For each segment that is identified, two basic questions must be asked: (1) What are the identifying characteristics of that segment? and (2) What is its size? Answering the first question helps define consumers' needs and helps develop a profile of consumers for each segment—the qualitative side of the market. The answer to the second question provides information on the size or quantitative side of the market.

Once the segments are identified, the firm must decide which ones they want to direct their marketing effort toward. This process is referred to as target marketing. It involves directing marketing efforts at specific identifiable market segments that have been selected because of their size and characteristics.

Bases for Market Segmentation

Segmentation bases can be classified into two broad categories—*a priori* and *a posteriori*. Loosely translated, these refer to segmentations of the market according to bases that you apply before addressing the market's consumers in order or after the result of market research to determine the existence and nature of the segments. For example, some marketers decided that their marketing mix decisions (product, price, place, and promotion) will be made differently for different age categories of consumers. This is an a priori segmentation based on age, unless marketing research studies have determined that consumers' age is the variable most effective in predicting similar responses of consumers within the same segment to marketing appeals. In this example, the marketer, for whatever reason, has determined that age-based market segments will be the most effective way of looking at a market and designing marketing programs to appeal to different targeted age segments. Choosing age or any other variable on an a priori basis is okay as long as the result is that marketing programs can be more efficient and effective in reaching and serving targeted customers.

A posteriori segmentation refers to the process of conducting research to let the market reveal not only the best base for segmenting that particular market, but also to reveal the number and characteristics of those segments. A discussion of how research can be capable of such a revelation is beyond the scope of this book;[2] however, recognize that one source of a competitive advantage in any particular product/market could consist of an in-depth understanding of market segments that can only be obtained by a study of the market. The a posteriori approach of studying the market to let it reveal the existence of segments is another manifestation of a societal marketing orientation approach of letting the market dictate what you will do instead of the selling orientation's approach of dictating to the market.

With these two approaches to identifying a segmentation base in mind, we will now discuss the typical variables that might be used to segment a market.

Several commonly used bases for segmentation include geographic, demographic, geodemographic, usage, benefits sought, stage in the family life cycle, and psychographics. The following section on market grids shows how several of the bases can be combined for analysis.

Geographic and Demographic Segmentation

The most commonly used basis for segmentation utilizes geographic and demographic variables. Geographic segmentation involves use of geographic areas such as county, state, regional, and national as the basis of segmentation. For many firms, this is a logical framework because of differences between areas. They may distribute their products in a few areas and not do anything in others. They are using geographic location to segment the customers they will serve.

Demographic segmentation uses variables such as sex, age, income, race, and educational level as the basis for segmenting a market. These variables are appropriate for many types of products. For example, to reach families with adolescents who were not interested in sit-down, casual restaurants, Bennigan's experimented with smaller portions of adult items as part of a major menu enhancement program directed specifically to young teens and their parents. Bennigan's and other restaurants have found that the "pizza set" is somewhere in between the fast-food preferred by younger children and the older teen market. Adolescents ages ten to fourteen represent about 20 million potential customers as well as future employees. For this group, casual dining usually becomes an option only when they are eating out with families. So far, the experiment has been been successful with both adolescents and their parents, since the smaller portions also are priced lower than the adult menu.[3]

Geographic and demographic characteristics of industrial consumers can also be useful in segmenting industrial markets. In fact, some customers are concentrated both geographically and by industry in certain industrial markets. Tire manufacturers in Ohio and electronics manufacturing in California are two examples.

Geodemographic Segmentation

Despite the name, geodemographic segmentation is not a simple combination of geographic and demographic segmentation approaches. Rather, it is the effort of a handful of firms using the U.S. Census data combined with dozens of other consumer data sources to identify segments within the U.S. adult population that could best be described as lifestyle clusters. Services such as Donnelley's Cluster-Plus, Claritas's PRIZM, and CACI's ACORN have divided the population into forty or more segments which differ primarily by socioeconomic status and which evidence different lifestyles. The databases used to create these segments reveal that there can be substantial differences in lifestyle between two segments that may be otherwise close in average age and income. This fact merely confirms what marketing managers know to be true based on observation and experience—there can be considerable difference in the way people of the same age and income choose to live their lives and spend their money. The creation of these forty or more basic segments of North American society allows marketers to precisely target those segments whose homogeneous lifestyles make them attractive targets for the company's products. When combined with the company's own customer base, it is possible to learn from which segments of society the firm has been successfully attracting its customers. Finding noncustomers who share the same lifestyle as their customers (i.e., belong to the same segment of society), locating them and using this information to reach them with a marketing mix designed specifically with them in mind is a simple step. The geodemographic segmentation approach has also been used to segment the Canadian population into lifestyle segments. This advanced method of segmenting a country's population into distinct lifestyle clusters has proven useful to many companies whose products' sales vary by socioeconomic or lifestyle segments.[4]

Segmentation by Product Usage

Another approach to market segmentation concentrates on the product usage patterns of consumers. Consumers are classified as users or nonusers, and users are further classified as light, medium, and heavy users. In many product categories, a small percentage of the consumers account for a majority of the purchases. Air travel, car rental, dog food, and hair coloring are such products. Thus, usage rates become important as a basis for segmentation for some products.

Benefit Segmentation

Another way to segment markets is based on the benefits the buyers expect to receive upon purchase or use of a product. In one study, the toothpaste market was segmented on such bases as flavor and product appearance, brightness of teeth, decay prevention, and price. Each of these variables represents the principal benefits sought by the purchaser; and each of these benefit segments in turn is composed of consumers with different demographic characteristics.

Segmentation by Family Life Cycle Stage

The *family life cycle* is the process of family formation and dissolution. Using this concept, the marketer combines the family characteristics of age, marital status, and presence and ages of children to develop programs and services aimed at various segments. A multistage family life cycle with several subcategories has been proposed. These stages are shown in Exhibit 5.1.

EXHIBIT 5.1. Family life cycle stages.

1. Young single (under 35)
2. Young married without children (under 35)
3. Other young (under 35)
   a. Young divorced without children
   b. Young married with children
   c. Young divorced with children
4. Middle-aged (35-64)
   a. Middle-aged married without children
   b. Middle-aged divorced without children
   c. Middle-aged married with children
   d. Middle-aged divorced with children
   e. Middle-aged married without dependent children
   f. Middle-aged divorced without dependent children
5. Older (65 and older)
   a. Older married
   b. Older unmarried (divorced, widowed)
6. Other
   All adults and children not accounted for by family life cycle stages

The characteristics and needs of people in each life cycle stage often vary considerably with people in other stages. Young singles have relatively few financial burdens, and are recreation-oriented. By contrast, young married people with young children tend to have low liquid assets and they are more likely to watch television than young singles or young married couples without children. The empty-nest households in the middle-age and older categories with no dependent children are more likely to have more disposable income, more time for recreation, self-education, travel, and more than one member in the labor force than their full-nest counterparts with younger children. Similar differences are evident in the other stages of the family life cycle.

Analysis of life cycle stages often gives better results than reliance on single variables such as age. The family of four, headed by parents in their twenties, usually has a different pattern of expenditures than a single person of the same age.

PSYCHOGRAPHICS/LIFESTYLE SEGMENTATION

Demographic characteristics lack "richness" in describing consumers for market segmentation and strategy development. Consequently, many firms have found lifestyle and psychographics to be a better way to define markets. *Lifestyle* refers to an individual's unique pattern of living, which influences and is reflected by his or her consumption behavior. *Psychographics* has to do with mental profiles of consumers; it allows the marketer to define consumers' lifestyles in measurable terms. By incorporating lifestyle characteristics, in addition to demographics, marketers obtain a better, more true-to-life portrait of target consumers.

Lifestyle-segmentation research examines (1) *activities* consumers engage in, e.g., work, hobbies, social events, vacation, entertainment, and shopping; (2) *interests* they have in such subjects as family, home, job and community, for example; and (3) *opinions* or views they hold about themselves and the world around them, including such things as social issues, politics, business, products, economics, culture, and the future. These three topics on which information is gathered in a lifestyle segmentation study are referred to simply as *AIOs*.

Armed with AIOs, demographics, and the data such as product and media usage, the marketer can construct user profits. The analysis involves relating levels of agreement/disagreement with perhaps 300 AIO statements in a questionnaire (e.g., "I like gardening," "I enjoy going to concerts," "There should be a gun in every house," "I stay home most evenings," and "Our family has a lot of love") with demographic characteristics, product usage, and media exposure. Typically, a pattern emerges in which AIO statements cluster together, meaning that similar respondents are grouped together on a lifestyle basis. The marketer then must determine which lifestyle segment is desirable as a target group and how best to appeal to them with the marketing mix. The following example illustrates how Timex used an active lifestyle target as the focus of its marketing planning.

Case Study: Timex

Timex's $500 million in yearly sales makes it the largest player in the $1.5 billion U.S. watch market. Timex also has the best-selling watch in the country, the Ironman. This $40 watch is designed with a stopwatch for runners, swimmers, and cyclers.

This is a dramatic turnaround from Timex's poor situation in the late 1970s. John Cameron Swayze promoted Timex for years with "torture-test" commercials, which showed that Timex "takes a lickin' and keeps on tickin'." The cheap watches were durable, but consumers had become more interested in flashy style.

Timex then realized that its target group of younger customers was interested in healthy, sporting activities. In the Olympic year of 1984, they introduced the Triathlon watch, the predecessor of the Ironman. It was initially marketed at a discount to athletes in sporting events, a gimmick that appealed to amateur athletes with professional aspirations.

Timex's advertising copy is light, too. An ad in *Ski* magazine read, "A ski watch should fit over your coat," and showed the watch on a polar bear's wrist. Timex is no longer selling just a watch—they are selling fun and fitness. That is what consumers seem to want.[5]

Lifestyle segmentation as described here differs from the geo-demographic lifestyle segmentation in that in the former case the specific product/market is being classified into segments, and in the latter case, the U.S. population is classified into forty or more segments independent of the product/market of interest. For example, a lifestyle segmentation of the men's clothing market may reveal four lifestyle segments: the classic independent who wears tailored wool suits and styled clothing, the trendy casual who wears open-necked leisure suits with gold chains, the utilitarian jeans consumer who is basically a T-shirt and jeans wearer, and a mainstream traditionalist who buys polyester blends when forced to buy clothes at all. These lifestyle segments may hold true only for the male menswear market and not for other product/markets. In contrast, a geodemographic lifestyle segmentation approach might reveal some differences in the clothes-buying habits of men in each of the forty or more segments, but their clothing preferences were not instrumental in the formation of the segments as they were in the former case. If a menswear company had a list of their customers, which they profiled using the geodemographic database, they would probably find some variability in the index of usage of their products from one segment to another, but it would not be as distinctive a difference as when they conducted a research study specifically intended to segment the menswear market. Hence, if you choose to segment the market by lifestyles, the question becomes one of choosing to do a time-consuming, expensive, but customized segmentation study of your product/market to discover its unique lifestyle segments for targeting and marketing planning purposes, or use the standardized segments of the geodemographic approach, which is less costly, but probably less well-suited to your particular needs.

MARKET GRID ANALYSIS

Marketing planners can use data collected from customers and prospective customers to segment their markets, then offer products aimed at specific needs. This is similar to using a rifle, rather than a shotgun, to shoot at a target. Specific products are developed for specific segments.

One basic tool that can be used to segment a market is a market grid. A market grid is a two-dimensional view of a market, which is divided into various segments based on characteristics of potential customers. Grid analysis has two important concepts. First, characteristics of potential customers are used to segment the market rather than product characteristics. This ensures a customer-oriented view of the market rather than a product-oriented one. Second, characteristics of potential customers rather than existing customers are used to focus on customers the organization may not currently serve.

Normally, a series of grids must be used in order to describe a market completely. Therefore, the planner must begin with a set of characteristics thought to be useful in differentiating consumers' needs. Each characteristic must be analyzed to determine its probable effect on consumers' satisfaction.

The types of characteristics used in the analysis may be those described previously: geographic, demographic, geodemographic, usage, benefits sought, family life cycle stage, and psychographics. Using these characteristics to divide a large group into smaller subgroups enables the planner to isolate the needs of a very specific segment and then design products for these segments.

The examples shown are not all-inclusive, but are intended to illustrate the types of characteristics that can be used. A planner may begin with a relatively long list of characteristics. The characteristics chosen from the list are those which not only differentiate among groups of customers (i.e., customers can be grouped by that characteristic into segments that are homogeneous within and heterogeneous between segments), but which also are instrumental in some way in affecting consumer response to marketing programs. For example, company size may vary among customers, but does it matter? That is, will companies have different needs and respond to different appeals based upon factors that vary by company size? If not, then the mere fact that we can group companies by their size is insufficient justification for the use of company size in the grid analysis. Research studies and/or managerial market experience are used to choose characteristics.

Grid Construction

Once a list of potential consumer characteristics has been developed, the next step is actual grid construction. Exhibits 5.2 and 5.3 illustrate the process. Each section within the grid is actually a market segment for accounting services. Notice that as each characteristic is used to identify a specific segment, the nature of the products, place, and promotion most likely to satisfy needs in each segment can be determined.

The two shaded areas in the first grid represent two completely different market segments. Needs of these groups would be different and different marketing strategies must be used to satisfy the clients in each segment.

In the second grid, the needs of users represented by the two shaded areas (segments) would be different. As market segments emerge through the analysis, they represent a potential group of consumers with similar characteristics that the planner can select as a target market—that specific segment whose needs the firm will attempt to satisfy. For smaller firms, only one or a few segments may be of in-

EXHIBIT 5.2. Market grid for individual income tax services.

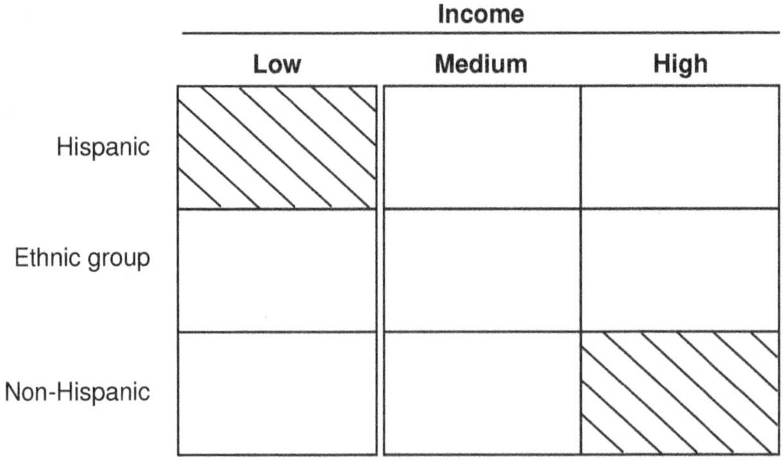

EXHIBIT 5.3. Market grid for corporate accounting services.

Company Size (Sales)

	Under $5 Million	$5 to 100 Million	Over $100 Million
Regional	*(shaded)*		
Location			
National			*(shaded)*

terest, whereas a large firm may develop or already have a complete line of products and therefore select several segments as potential target markets. This type of analysis is needed regardless of whether one or many segments are selected.

Three types of characteristics are useful in the analysis: socioeconomic, behavioral, and psychological. Some examples of each of these types are shown in Exhibit 5.4. Socioeconomic characteristics are concerned with such factors as age, sex, number of employees, and sales volume of ultimate and industrial consumers. These characteristics are helpful in "finding" consumers or customers. Typically media such as newspapers, trade journals, radio, magazines, etc., have profiles of their audience, which use socioeconomic and demographic descriptions. Selection of media for marketing purposes is made based on whether these profiles match those of the target markets. The behavioral characteristics are concerned with what behavioral acts or patterns of behavior are descriptive of consumers. Psychological characteristics help a planner understand and explain behavior in the market.

Psychological variables can also be used to effectively segment the industrial market by looking at psychographics for the company as well as the individual. In this context, the organization's culture is analyzed as a basis of segmentation. In entering new markets, such an

EXHIBIT 5.4. Consumer characteristics by buyer type.

Characteristic	Buyer type	
	Ultimate consumers	**Industrial customers**
Socioeconomic	Age	Size or volume
	Sex	Number of employees
	Income	Number of plants
	Education	Type of organization
	Marital status	
Behavioral	Brands purchased	Decision makers
	Coupon redemption	Growth markets
	Stores shopped	Public versus private
	Loyalty	Distribution pattern
	Hobbies	
Psychological[a]	Activities	Management attitudes
	Interests	Management style
	Opinions	Organizational culture
	Personality traits	

[a]These would include psychographic characteristics.

approach is valuable because it helps identify companies whose culture is receptive to changing suppliers and their motivations for such change before developing a strategy that focuses on attracting customers away from competitors.[6]

The examples shown in Exhibit 5.4 are not all-inclusive of course, but are intended to illustrate the types of characteristics that can be used. Again, the planner must select a specific list of characteristics from the many possible. This is accomplished by assessing the impact of the characteristic on buyer-need satisfaction. Only those characteristics useful in differentiating needs are used in the market grids. A clothing manufacturer might develop a list that includes age, sex, income, geographical location, shopping behavior, and activity engaged in by consumers. The primary impact of each characteristic might be assessed as shown in Exhibit 5.5. The consumer's age would certainly influence his or her needs, e.g., the styles the consumer is interested in, the person who actually is the decision maker, and the types of retail stores shopped.

EXHIBIT 5.5. Consumer characteristics for grid analysis in clothing purchases.

Characteristic	Probable impact on need
Age	Style, who decision maker is, type of retail outlet
Sex	Style, type of retail outlet, motives for purchase
Income level	Price or quality, type of retail outlet, motives for purchase
Geographic location	Style, material used
Shopping behavior	Promotion, type of retail outlet
Product usage	Style, materials used, durability, colors

An alternate approach to the representation of a market is a build-up grid or diagram. This approach involves identifying the individual market segments and then putting them together to represent a market. The result is the same: a recognition of the differences in needs of different consumers.

An example of this approach for an industrial product is shown in Exhibit 5.6. This is a reconstruction of the market for component parts of mud pumps used on oil rigs. In the consumer analysis, it was found that the market was dominated by one firm, which accounted for about 75 percent of the original equipment manufacturers' (OEM) sales in this market; the rest of the sales volume was divided among four other firms. The large manufacturer was designated a *key account,* meaning it was a very significant buyer and, therefore, a different marketing effort would be directed at this segment of the market.

Consumer Profiles

As the process of developing market grids continues, a profile of the consumers in each segment emerges. This profile should be as complete as possible for each segment and should include all three types of characteristics. The results of the analysis can be used in subsequent time periods so they should be easily accessible. In fact, if this type of analysis has already been completed, it can be updated or expanded.

The results of the analysis may be summarized as shown in Exhibit 5.7. This approach allows a comparison of the characteristics for each segment in which a planner is interested.

EXHIBIT 5.6. Market segments for industrial product.

Key account
Apine manufacturing company
75 percent market share
Other accounts
25 percent market share

EXHIBIT 5.7. Consumer characteristics by segment.

Characteristic	Segment 1	Segment 2	Segment 3
Socioeconomic			
Age	26-40	41-65	Over 65
Sex	Male	Male	Male
Income	Upper	Middle	Lower
Location	Southwest	Southeast	Southwest
Behavioral			
Shopping behavior	Specialty stores	Department stores	Discount stores
Purchase rate	High	High	High
Psychological			
Opinions	Fashion-oriented	Comfort-oriented	Economy-oriented
Awareness	High brand-name awareness	Some brand-name awareness	Low brand-name awareness

Much of the information needed for this type of analysis can be obtained through secondary data (data already published). The most difficult data to obtain from secondary sources is psychological data. Unless the firm has previously conducted research to collect these data, a new study will be needed to collect them. For firms without a research staff, outside consultants or research firms may be used.

Consumer Motivations

One important area of concern in consumer analysis is why consumers in a market behave the way they do. Why are some products purchased and not others? Why are some stores shopped and not others? Answers to these types of questions, although difficult to determine, are important in understanding consumer behavior. Entire books are written on this topic, threfore no attempt is made here to present all the theories and their applications to marketing. Our approach is to develop a framework with which planners can organize their own thinking, along with that of others in the organization who are familiar with the market. If available, data provided through research would be an important consideration in this type of analysis.

Needs

Consumer needs are primary factors in understanding behavior. Although human needs can be classified in many ways, a commonly used classification system is Maslow's hierarchy of needs. This approach, shown in Exhibit 5.8, views needs in an ascending order of primacy in which low-level needs must be satisfied or partially satisfied before high-level needs emerge.

Physiological and safety needs represent the lowest levels and self-actualization the highest. Products can be viewed as a way to fulfill or partially fulfill one or more of these needs. For example, the purchase of insurance could be seen as satisfying the need for safety.

In the industrial market, the classification of needs is different since the buyer is not the ultimate consumer of the goods or services purchased. One way to classify the industrial consumer's needs is simply as: (1) *institutional*—the need for goods and services to carry out the functions of the business, and (2) *personal*—the needs of the

EXHIBIT 5.8. Maslow's hierarchy of needs.

Physiological and safety	Need for food, water, air, etc.
	Need for protection, security from elements in the environment
Belonging and love	Need to be accepted by family, friends, and significant others
Esteem	Need for high regard by self and significant others
Self-actualization	Need to reach one's potential in terms of personal values

people involved in the purchase of the goods and services for the company.

Motives

A motive (or drive) is a stimulated need that is sufficiently strong to cause the person to take action that will satisfy that need. Motives may be viewed as the intervening force between a need and behavior undertaken to satisfy it. Two sets of motives are involved in a purchase and both must be recognized to understand behavior. The first set deals with why a specific product or service is purchased in an attempt to satisfy a need, and the second deals with the source from which goods and services are purchased. This second set of motives has been referred to as patronage motives—motives for patronizing a given source. Typical types of motives for both consumer and indus-

EXHIBIT 5.9. Buying motives: Product or service motives.

Ultimate consumer	Industrial consumer
1. Satisfaction of senses	1. Fear
2. Preservation of species	2. Pride
3. Fear	3. Sociability
4. Rest and recreation	4. Striving
5. Pride	5. Handiness
6. Sociability	6. Efficiency in operation or use
7. Striving	7. Dependability in use
8. Curiosity or mystery	8. Reliability of auxiliary service
9. Handiness	9. Durability
10. Efficiency in operation or use	10. Enhancement of earnings
11. Dependability in use	11. Enhancement of productivity of property
12. Reliability of auxiliary service	12. Economy of purchase or use
13. Durability	
14. Enhancement of earnings	
15. Enhancement of productivity of property	
16. Economy of purchase or use	

EXHIBIT 5.10. Source buying motives.

Ultimate consumer	Industrial consumer
1. Convenience	1. Convenience
2. Variety or selection	2. Variety or selection
3. Quality of goods—freshness, purity, craftmanship, etc.	3. Quality of goods—freshness, purity, craftmanship, etc.
4. Courtesy of sales personnel	4. Courtesy of sales personnel
5. Integrity—reputation for fairness in dealings	5. Integrity of sales personnel
6. Services offered—delivery, credit, returned-goods privileges	6. Services offered—delivery, credit, returned-goods privileges
7. Value offered	7. Value offered

trial goods and services are shown in Exhibit 5.9. Exhibit 5.10 gives a list of potential motives for buying from a specific source—a store or supplier.

Behavior

Behavior is what can be observed or inferred in the marketplace. The planner is concerned not only with initial purchase behavior but also with repeat purchase behavior. The former involves the movement of the consumer from a stage of simply becoming aware of a product to actual trial of the product through purchase, whereas the latter involves the establishment of buying patterns. An established buying pattern—repetition of the same type of behavior over time—indicates a different consumer attitude toward a product or source than does initial buying alone.

Applying Motivational Concepts

The marketing planner should be interested in explaining the purchase of specific goods and services rather than consumer behavior in general. All available information should be used in applying these motivational concepts. Some companies have this information available already through their own research efforts, and the problem is one of updating in light of environmental changes. When this information is not already available, information must be collected in formal research projects or on a more informal basis from sales personnel, dealers, and others who have insight into consumer motivation. Information from existing published articles and reports may be available for a specific product application.

MARKET POTENTIAL

Once a market has been divided into various segments, and characteristics and motivations of consumers in each market have been analyzed, the planner can then estimate the size of the market. The term *market potential* is used to refer to the expected sales of a product or service for an entire market over a specific time period. More simply, if everybody who could buy would buy, how many units or dollar sales would occur? The answer is the market potential. Marketers are interested in identifying not only consumers' needs but also those market segments that can be served profitably. For a new product, this analysis would be part of a feasibility study, which should precede introduction of the product. A market segment that does not have enough consumers spending enough dollars does not justify marketing effort, unless a firm is seeking to accomplish some non-revenue-related objective. Market potential is a quantitative measure of a market's capacity to consume a product in a given time period, which is a prerequisite to assessing profitability.

Market potential can be measured in either absolute or relative terms. An absolute measure is one that can be expressed in units or dollars, whereas a relative measure relates one part of a market to another and is expressed as a percent.

The Sales Index Measure of Relative Potential

The sales index method provides a relative measure of potential for products that have passed the introductory stage of their product life cycle. This technique is useful in answering questions about the relative potential of various geographical market areas. Use of this approach requires familiarity with the product in terms of its stage in the life cycle, penetration of distribution in various areas, and sales history.

This technique, using industrial water softeners, is illustrated in Exhibit 5.11. Notice that the resulting figures are percentages of total

EXHIBIT 5.11. Industrial water softeners: Sales index method.

Region	Industry sales	Sales index (%)	Potential (%)
Northeast	$8,500,009	28.8	28.8
Southeast	6,753,090	22.8	22.8
Northwest	6,870,421	23.2	23.2
Southwest	7,430,218	25.2	25.2
Total	$29,553,738	100.0	100.0

industry sales by region, which in effect indicate that industry sales will occur next year in the same proportion as last year's in each region. The potential in the Northwest region is expected to be 23.2 percent of the total—whatever that total turns out to be next year. One region can be compared to another by using this measure of potential.

The Market Factor Method

Relative potential is generally not an adequate approach; therefore, an absolute measure of potential is needed to provide unit or dollar estimates. One technique used to accomplish this is the *market factor* method. This involves identifying the factors that influence sales and relating them to sales in some way. (These sales-growth factors were mentioned in the previous chapter.) An example in which population—the market factor—is related to sales on the basis of sales per 1,000 people is shown in Exhibit 5.12. Notice that absolute and relative potential can be calculated by region. This is accomplished by using the projected regional population as the market factor and using the regional sales rate to relate sales to the market factor in each region.

The potential of a segment can be calculated when the segment is identified and the number of people and expenditure rate in the segment are known. This technique produces an estimate of the absolute potential of a given market. Of course, the planner would have to assume a constant sales rate and accurate population projections. The sales rate would depend on the level of market development and consumer preferences for a given product.

EXHIBIT 5.12. The market factor method.

Region	Sales ($) 1996	Population (000)	Sales rate/1,000
Northeast	$8,500,009	68,570	$123.96
Southeast	6,753,090	38,720	174.40
Northwest	6,870,421	32,810	209.40
Southwest	7,430,218	66,730	111.34
Total	$29,553,738	206,830	$154.78 (average)

Population projection (2000) = 250,847,000
Sales rate (average) = $154.78/1,000
Absolute market potential (154.78 × 250,847) = $38,826,098

The Regression Analysis Method

Regression analysis is another technique used to estimate potential-uses statistics. This technique also uses market factors, but the factors are related to sales in a more mathematically complex manner. Space does not permit a complete explanation of this technique. The purpose here is to show how it could be used in estimating potential. One result of regression analysis is an equation that relates the market factor to sales. If more than one market factor is used, multiple regression analysis is needed. Exhibit 5.13 shows data that have been analyzed by using two market factors. The resulting equation is then used to estimate potential. This approach still requires estimates of the two market factors (independent variables) for the future time period for which the measure of potential is desired. In this example, Y represents total industry sales and X_1 and X_2 represent two market factors related to total industry sales. Estimates of the value of these factors for the next time period are substituted into the equation in order to estimate potential. This technique also permits calculation of a confidence interval for the estimate of sales.

Customer Relationship Management

In addition to estimating the market potential of a particular segment of customers, companies must also effectively manage these segments to assure long-term profitability. Customer relationship

EXHIBIT 5.13. Using multiple regression analysis in estimating market potential (in thousands).

	Industry sales (in thousands of units)		
Year	Y	X_1	X_2
1994	6,860	1,329	40
1995	6,520	1,116	39
1996	6,345	1,041	40
1997	6,710	1,209	37
1998	7,222	1,553	44
1999	6,810	1,296	45
2000	7,005	1,365	44
2001	7,275	1,492	50
2002	7,450	1,641	53
2003	7,250	1,591	59
2004	7,105	1,510	66
2005	6,666	1,196	71
2006	6,900	1,322	72

$Y = a + b_1 X_1 + b_2 X_2$ (general equation)
$Y = 4,641 + (1.70) (1,600) + (-.46) (60)$
$Y = 7,333,000$ (the estimated market potential for this product in 1997)

management (CRM) is a relatively new concept that further analyzes a targeted segment by addressing each customer's potential for profitability. Although many companies have operated on the premise that the best customers are loyal ones and have focused on segmentation by frequency of purchase, traditional loyalty programs have neglected to analyze their profitability.[7] Instead of focusing on loyalty alone, customer relationship management goes one step further in finding ways to measure the company's "cost" to maintain that relationship. Many companies now offer software for CRM programs, which if implemented appropriately, can provide a competitive edge for your company.[8]

SUMMARY

Consumer analysis furnishes the planner with market specifics from a consumer perspective. Approaches based on general information are less effective than a plan based on this type of specific analysis. Consumer analysis can be compared to the use of a rifle, rather than a shotgun, to shoot at a target. If your aim is to get a bulls-eye, you may waste a lot of effort with a shotgun, whereas a rifle permits much more precision.

The two questions that must be answered for each segment (size and characteristics) become the bases for further analysis. The analysis also provides information needed to develop the elements of the marketing mix—product, promotion, price, and distribution.

Once a planner has determined the market potential for a good or service, an estimate of the firm's share of that potential is used to set sales and profit objectives. These will be discussed in detail later.

Chapter 6 presents the concepts and tools needed to complete a competitive analysis for each market segment.

Chapter 6

Competitive Analysis

MARKETING PLANNING IN ACTION: THE PACKAGE DELIVERY INDUSTRY

At the age of eleven, James Casey began to support his family as a delivery boy after his father died. As a teenager, he cofounded the American Messenger Co., a communication and delivery service, with friend Claude Ryan. Casey and Ryan believed in building their business on professionalism, courtesy, and service, sleeping in the office so they could deliver service 24/7, including holidays. By 1915 the Seattle-based company had expanded its delivery fleet to four cars and five motorcycles, which Casey wanted to paint yellow. However, one of his partners insisted that yellow vehicles would be impossible to keep clean, and noted that Pullman railroad cars were painted brown for that reason. Casey's partner won out, and today, "What Can Brown Do for You?" is a well-known advertising tagline.

Casey's business cards were posted near public phones, and carried the company slogan "Best service and lowest rates," a motto that would guide his entire career. As more families began to acquire telephones in their homes, the need for his messenger service declined. Casey responded by partnering with local department stores to deliver packages to customer's homes. He saw the potential for department store package delivery across the country and in 1919 changed the company name to United Parcel Service (UPS). The biggest challenge from competition has been from rival company, Federal Express (FedEx). Fred Smith's FedEx had taken the delivery business to a new standard in the 1980s—that of next-day delivery via air. UPS responded, however, somewhat reluctantly, with its own second-day service, then finally competing directly with FedEx by offering next-day shipping. In the competitive, $47 billion-a-year package delivery industry, FedEx has the majority of the air delivery service while UPS has 60 percent of the ground-market share.

Both companies continue to make operational improvements that shave time off their delivery via both air and ground transportation, blurring the distinction between the two. This is especially important as ground shipments are typically one-third the cost of those transported by air. For FedEx, who has the greatest market share of air transportation, these costs may make it more difficult to compete with UPS based on price or delivery time. In fact, UPS has claimed that it can make at least some next-day ground deliveries to anyone in the country, and FedEx touts that it can do so to about 92 percent. Given that delivery time between air and ground is blurring, the competitive advantage in this industry may come down to "service."[1]

INTRODUCTION

After analyzing the overall market and needs of customers in specific market segments, the next step in the marketing planning process is to analyze competition for each of the specific market segments. For new products that represent innovations, this analysis may be limited to potential competition rather than identifiable competitors. In most cases, however, an established market exists with clearly identified competitors who must be evaluated for their strategies, strengths, and weaknesses.

This chapter presents the concepts and tools needed to analyze competition for existing markets. Especially useful is the marketing mix audit form, which permits evaluation of a competitor on all the basic strategy elements.

THE CONCEPT OF COMPETITIVE ADVANTAGE

To understand the concept of competitive advantage and why it plays such a central role in marketing strategy, one must understand how marketers view competition. The most successful marketers do not have a desire to "beat the competition"; their desire is to make competitors totally irrelevant to their customers. That is, marketers want to establish such a close, satisfying, long-term relationship with their customers that those customers have no interest in considering alternatives. The strength of the relationship makes movement to a competitor so inconvenient, risky, and unnecessary that the customer exercises a "willful suspension of choice" and determines to continue to give the company his or her business. In a sense, what marketers are trying to do is to satisfy the customer so completely that the barriers to exit from the relationship are too high in their minds to justify seeking alternative means of addressing their needs. A marketer successful in establishing such a relationship with a customer has made competition irrelevant. Accomplishing this goal requires the identification and exploitation of a significant competitive advantage.

A competitive advantage is "something special that a firm does, or possesses that gives it an edge against competitors."[2] Four characteristics must be present for a competitive advantage to be exploitable:

1. The advantage(s) must be real. Just wishing it to be there does not make it so. Saying you have the lowest prices does not make it true.
2. The advantage(s) must be important to *the customer*. Competitive advantages exist only when they ultimately translate into a benefit that the customer seeks and values. Merely being different from competitors along some dimension that you, the company, thinks is important does not mean that you have a true competitive advantage. "When the perception of competitive advantage differs between the marketer and customer, the customer always wins" (p. 30).
3. The advantage(s) must be specific. "It is not enough to say, 'We're the best.' The question is, 'The best what?' And why? To the customer nonspecificity translates into mere puffery and is not a competitive advantage" (p. 31).
4. The advantages(s) must be promotable—meaning you must be able to communicate the advantage to the customer in a language which he or she not only understands, but which is also highly motivating. The first three characteristics must be present before this fourth characteristic has relevance; but unless this fourth point is implemented, the value of the first three goes wanting. Also implied in this point is that a marketing budget of sufficient size is in place so that the competitive advantage can be promoted with enough frequency and reach to attract the target market audience.[3]

A competitive advantage may have several different sources (see Exhibit 6.1). Organizations must be extremely objective in determining if they truly have a competitive advantage based on the sources in Exhibit 6.1 or other sources that meet the four criteria previously stated. Adoption of a societal marketing orientation is tacit agreement

EXHIBIT 6.1. Sources of competitive advantage.

Source	Description
The way you compete	Product design, positioning strategy, distribution strategy, and pricing strategy can all be potential sources of advantage over competition.
Basis of competition	The combination of assets and skills, which can deliver more of what the customer values (e.g., higher-quality product, speedy delivery, etc.), can be an advantage if those assets and skills exceed those of the competition.
Where you compete	The careful selection and tracking of a product market as it evolves over time can provide a better match between a firm's distinctive competencies and the product market's key success factors than the match gained by competitors.
Whom you compete against	Positioning your firm as having solutions to problems that cannot be delivered by other firms competing in the same product market can accentuate a competitive advantage. Showing customers your strengths or competitor's weaknesses can provide a competitive advantage, at least temporarily.

Source: Adapted with modification from Aaker, David A. *Strategic Market Management.* New York: John Wiley and Sons, 2001, p. 184.

with the premise that it is consumers who either grant a competitive advantage to the organization or not.

Although obtaining such a strong competitive advantage that competitors are irrelevant remains the goal of savvy organizations, unfortunately most firms have not yet reached a point where all of their customers no longer consider alternative products from competitor firms. Therefore, the remainder of this chapter is devoted to a discussion of how companies can conduct competitive analysis for marketing planning purposes.

PURPOSE OF COMPETITIVE ANALYSIS

Two fundamental questions are answered through the competitive analysis: What is the nature of the forces that shape competition in this market? and Which competitors are going after which market segments with what marketing strategies? The first question focuses on overall competition and the forces that influence the nature of competition in a given product-market situation. The second question focuses on specific market segments that have been isolated through consumer analysis.

At this point, you should already know the size (potential) and the characteristics of each segment, and now the analysis begins to deal with competition on a segment-by-segment basis. It should be clear by now that a firm gains a competitive advantage on a segment-by-segment basis rather than for an entire market. This is true, of course, because, as we discussed in Chapter 5, consumer motives, needs, and desires vary significantly from segment to segment, making a strategy that hits the "sweet spot" of one segment of no consequence to another. What you are trying to uncover in your analysis of the segments are groups of consumers who are not currently being served or segments where competitors do not have clearly identifiable strategies but each seems to be using a strategy similar to the others. Several segments can better be served through strategies aimed directly at their needs. What you are looking for is the opportunity to create a competitive advantage or edge over competition in specific market segments.

Types of Competition

In order to be complete, the competitive analysis must consider both existing and potential competitors. Trying to anticipate the moves of competitors can become the basis for opting or not opting to target a given segment as well as the choice of strategy to use if the segment is targeted. This chapter begins with a discussion of the nature of competition and then develops a basic tool to analyze competitors. First, let's look at different forms of competition.

Pure Competition

One of the earliest types of competition identified by economists is called pure competition. This form of competition is seldom found in the marketplace. However, it is somewhat characteristic of some market environments and serves as a useful concept in analysis. An industry or a local market that could be described as pure competition usually has the following characteristics: (1) a large number of relatively small competitors, (2) little or no differences between strategies, and (3) ease of entry by new competitors. The large number of small competitors means the actions of one competitor may be unnoticed by the others. Differences among strategies may be small, and good location or length of time in business may be of prime importance in attracting customers. The ease of entry may mean new competitors are continually coming into the market or old ones are leaving. Unless a well-financed competitor enters the market and alters the competitive environment, the market tends to be unorganized, even fragmented, with the number of customers and competitors within the geographical bounds of the firm determining both revenues and strategies. Similarities in prices, products, distribution, and promotion are common.

Monopolistic Competition

In the market characterized by monopolistic competition, the individual images of the various firms begin to emerge in terms of more clearly differentiated strategies. Although there may still be many competitors and relative ease of entry, each firm has attempted to differentiate itself in some way from its competitors. It may be a market with much diversity of products, price, distribution, and promotional activities, or it can also be characterized by similarities among two or three variables in the marketing mix and variety in the other—promotion, for example. In this competitive environment, each competitor has more control over the marketing mix variables, and therefore a diversity of strategies is possible.

Oligopolistic Competition

In a competitive environment described as oligopolistic, the number of competitors and ease of entry are both decreased. This market has a few relatively large competitors, and perhaps a few smaller ones. The actions of one competitor are clearly recognized in both nature and impact by other competitors, and their retaliation to competitive moves is anticipated. Strategies are diverse in this type of environment. However, it is more likely to be of the nonprice variety. Price competition can be easily copied and also must be responded to if clients readily substitute one firm's services for another. Price leadership may develop as one firm is allowed to set the scale for others.

Monopoly

A monopoly is a market environment characterized by one seller. Legal restrictions determine entry if it is considered a natural monopoly (e.g., telephone company, electric utility company, etc.). Natural monopolies are regulated by government in terms of prices and distribution. Nonnatural monopolies, if successful, usually attract other competitors who are willing to overcome barriers to entry because of a potentially large return. Therefore, nonnatural monopolies are usually short-lived.

Deciding on the Nature of Competition

Exhibit 6.2 provides a summary of the variations of several factors depending on the type of competitive environment that is appropriate. This chart is useful in understanding the nature of the competitive environment. Instead of trying to define what is meant by "many," in the case of number of firms, and "ease of entry," in the case of how easy it is to enter a market, attention should be focused on the overall nature of the market as described by the factors collectively. Since most of economic reality lies somewhere between pure competition and monopoly, attention should be focused there in the analysis. Identifying the nature of competition helps in understanding not only how firms compete in a market but also whether or not retaliatory actions can be expected.

COMPETITIVE FORCES AND ADVANTAGES

Effective competitive analysis will take into consideration the search for—and need for—differential advantages. Differential advantages are those factors in which a particular organization excels or has the potential to excel over competitive organizations. A differential advantage is different from a competitive advantage in that a differential advantage does not have to meet the four conditions required for having a competitive advantage. A differential advantage exists whenever one firm's strength exceeds that of its competitors along some dimension. Differential advantages may be found in the follow-

EXHIBIT 6.2. Effects of competitive environment.

	Competitive environment			
Factor	Pure competition	Monopolistic competition	Oligopolistic competition	Monopoly
Number of firms	Many	Many	Few	One
Entry and exit	Easy	Easy	Difficult	May be legally banned
Service	Undifferentiated	Differentiated	Differentiated	N/A
Fees	Undifferentiated	Undifferentiated if nonprice competition is emphasized Differentiated if price competition is used by some competitors	Undifferentiated if nonprice competition is emphasized Differentiated if price competition is used by some competitors	N/A
Access	Undifferentiated	Differentiated if nonprice competition is used by some competitors Undifferentiated if price competition is emphasized	Differentiated if nonprice competition is used by some competitors Undifferentiated if price competition is emphasized	N/A
Promotion	Undifferentiated	Differentiated if nonprice competition is used by some competitors Undifferentiated if price competition is used by some competitors	Differentiated if nonprice competition is used by some competitors Undifferentiated if price competition is used by some competitors	N/A
Competitive reactions	Little	Some, depending on type of action	A lot, especially related to prices	N/A

ing areas: (1) production, (2) technology, (3) natural resources, (4) marketing, and (5) management.

> *Production:* A superior ability to turn out a product is a crucial differential advantage that many companies have capitalized on. The advantage may also lie in a firm's ability to maintain superior production quality over its competitors.
>
> *Technology:* Initial innovative research and development, as well as properly managed scientific application, can establish and preserve strong differential advantages over competitors.
>
> *Natural resources:* Valuable or scarce resources are often appropriate assets on which to base a strategy. Tremendous advantage can be given to organizations, cartels, and nations that control natural resources or are located in favorable proximity to them.
>
> *Marketing:* Market advantage usually refers to the advantage one firm has over another because it is more positively positioned in the minds of customers. Those firms having greater customer awareness, higher preference, or stronger loyalty have distinct marketing differential advantage over their competitors.
>
> *Management:* Management advantage takes the form of positive personnel relations, effective planning and information systems, and overall managerial competence.

The forces of competition greatly influence an organization's strategy formation and market-opportunity decisions (see Exhibit 6.3). Although each industry has its own unique characteristics, competitive pressures coming from five main sources represent the actual driving mechanisms of any given industry:

1. Rivalry among existing competitors
2. Consumer/buyer composition
3. Supplier composition
4. Possibility of new entrants
5. Availability of good product substitutes

The rivalry among companies within an industry is constantly involved in dynamic interplay in an attempt to build a successful com-

EXHIBIT 6.3. Competitive forces.

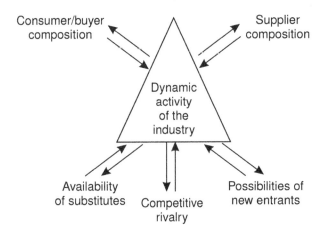

petitive edge over one another. The success of one organization's strategy in accomplishing this is based in large measure on the strategies of the other members. Constant monitoring of these interdependent strategic maneuvers is required to make the adjustments necessary to improve competitive position and achieve market success.

America West Airlines, for example, initiated a price strategy aimed at gaining market share from other low-cost airlines such as AirTran Airways and Spirit Airlines. America West slashed its first-class fares by up to 70 percent, while maintaining both first-class and business-class services such as bigger, more comfortable seats. Competitive pricing can mean market share gains and can decrease the pressure on advertising to bring in customers. It can also mean retaliation from competitors who respond to such actions. America West's move has prompted several other airlines to match its fares.[4]

The consumer/buyer composition can range from a few large-volume purchasers to a large number of low-volume purchasers. In the first instance, losing a few customers can be the difference between success and failure; at the other extreme, losing that same number of customers has virtually no impact. Most firms try to minimize the number of customers that can exert an adverse effect on their business.

The supplier composition also has an important influence on the competing position of individual organizations. The relative importance of the goods or services they supply will determine the strength of their competitive influence over firms in the industry. They can have a positive or negative impact on profit margins, inventory levels, product quality, and prices.

The possibility of new entrants into the market constantly threatens to alter market share, production capacity, and supply distribution within the industry. This threat can be minimal when there are strong barriers to entry, such as strong customer loyalty, large capital requirements, difficulty in establishing distribution channels, and strong response of existing firms. When entry barriers are weak or the expected response of existing firms is weak, then the possibility of entry is stronger.

Volkswagen, for example, launched a new sedan aimed at the midsized luxury car market, particularly to the thirty-five- to forty-five-year-old man. The new all-wheel drive Phaeton has eight air bags and sells for about $70,000—comparable to cars made by BMW or Mercedes.[5]

The fifth force in this five-forces model is the availability of good product substitutes. Existing firms are threatened when high-quality substitutes exist in ample quantity at competitive or comparable prices. Artificial sweeteners and sugar are examples of substitutable products.

In evaluating different competitive approaches, the following need to be considered:

- Current strategy
- Current performance
- Strengths and weaknesses
- Future strategic possibilities

Each major competitor should be studied separately. If this is not possible, then the strategy of the closest competitors should be evaluated.

Analyzing current competitor strategy involves determining how the competitor defines the industry in terms of market segments, product features, marketing mix, manufacturing policy, research and development commitment, growth policy, distribution, and promotion. The marketing mix analysis can take several forms, but perhaps the most useful is the competitive market mix audit discussed in the following.

The Competitive Marketing Mix Audit

Competition in most areas of business is increasingly intense. Therefore, know who your competitors are, what products they provide, where they are located, how they promote themselves, and what price they charge. Such an analysis is what is involved in a marketing mix audit.

The word *audit,* regardless of the business context in which it is used, refers to an unbiased appraisal of what is being done and how it is being done. Thus, an accounting audit refers to an unbiased appraisal of a firm's accounting practices. In the same manner, a competitive marketing mix audit is an analysis of competitors' activities by market segment. The form shown in Exhibit 6.4 is one of the most useful tools available for performing such an audit. It involves the

EXHIBIT 6.4. The competitive marketing mix.

	Audit form		
Evaluation	Competitor A	Competitor B	Competitor C
A. Product offered			
1. Type	_____	_____	_____
2. Quality	_____	_____	_____
3. Assortment	_____	_____	_____
B. Place			
1. Location	_____	_____	_____
2. Channels used	_____	_____	_____
3. Distribution services	_____	_____	_____
C. Prices			
1. Price level	_____	_____	_____
2. Dealer discounts	_____	_____	_____
3. Quantity discounts	_____	_____	_____
D. Promotion			
1. Quality	_____	_____	_____
2. Quantity	_____	_____	_____
3. Budget	_____	_____	_____

planner in an appraisal of every aspect of a firm's marketing mix compared to that of its major competitors. Several steps are involved in using this form to complete the audit.

First, the form should reflect the nature of the marketing mix activities for each market segment analyzed. For example, if industrial segments are being analyzed, the form must reflect the components important to these segments.

Second, the major competitors must be identified by name so that a realistic comparison can be made. This requirement forces the planner to identify the specific competitors going after a market segment and permits the collection of data on those specific firms. Remember that competition is not limited to just other firms of the same type. For example, banks, other financial institutions, and retail companies are providing services that once were handled only by brokers. Therefore, competitors may not be as easy to identify as they once were. Nevertheless, the marketer must identify those major competitors with whom they will be battling to attract customers.

Although it may appear relatively easy to identify a firm's major competitors, that assumption is based upon competition at only the brand level. Competition exists at several "levels." See, for example, competition for Pepsi at multiple levels as shown in Exhibit 6.5. All organizations should compete at the most basic level the target market will allow. This effort is exemplified by Rolls-Royce, when the chairman of the company said that the Rolls-Royce does not compete against any other automobile, but rather against second and third homes, yachts, and private airplanes (i.e., once a potential customer makes a decision to buy an automobile the choice becomes obvious). For Pepsi, if they can get people to think in terms of a choice being made at, say, the generic level for either Pepsi, a fruit drink, or "designer" water (see Exhibit 6.5), then they have effectively eliminated competition at the brand level. Such objectives are obviously the most desirable by organizations, however, consumers are not always willing to make their choices in accordance with those objectives. Organizations may be able to achieve this goal if they can so satisfy their customers that competition at the brand level becomes, as previously described, irrelevant. Marketing plans will necessarily need to be different when competing at the different levels shown in Exhibit 6.5.

Third, sources of data must be identified to complete the audit. Some of the data may already be available from previous analysis or

EXHIBIT 6.5. Levels of competition—Pepsi.

1. Desire competition
   Need: Thirst
   Products:

   Liquor
   Beer
   Wine
   Milk
   Coffee
   Tea
   Water
   Designer water
   Fruit drinks
   Soft drink

2. Generic competitors
   Nonalcoholic beverages
   Products:

   Fruit drinks
   Designer water
   Soft drink

3. Form competitors
   Soft drinks
   Products:

   Root beer
   Orange
   Lemon-lime
   Cola

4. Type competitors
   Cola products:

   Caffeinated/decaffeinated
   Diet/regular
   Flavored/straight

5. Brand competitors
   Regular/caffeinated/straight cola
   Brands: (Pepsi's competitors)

   R C Cola
   Coke
   Shasta
   House brands

research and may merely need updating, or data may have to be collected to complete the audit. For instance, a variety of data sources can be used to identify competition. A manufacturer, for example, may find the Thomas Register of Manufacturing Firms a useful source. Such sources will help you identify who your present and potential competitors are and compile information about such things as what products they sell, where they are located, and price levels. Looking at competitive advertising and obtaining information from media representatives about advertising will also help provide data for the audit. For some types of comparisons, judgment must be used if research or other objective data are not available. However, bias is a possibility in such instances—for the introduction of a "halo effect" when comparing the firm's activities with competitors. One way to avoid bias is to use the judgment of several people rather than relying on that of one person's judgment.

Finally, some system must be developed to "grade" your own company's and competitors' efforts on each aspect of the audit. For new firms anticipating entry into a market, competitors are compared with each other. One ranking system is to give your competitor a plus if it is better than you, a zero if equal, and a minus if the competitor is not as good. Alternatively, you may choose to rank competitors in order using a one to indicate the best, a two the second best, and so on.

Rather than a more general analysis of price levels, this audit would need to be completed for each segment analyzed. The planner is not particularly interested in the generalities here but rather the details about specific groups or segments in the market. Thoroughness is important in this type of analysis. Lack of digging into the details may even be misleading.

In a consumer study done for a restaurant, respondents were asked whether they thought their friends would eat at that particular restaurant. If the answer was no, they were asked why. The most common response was that prices were "too high." Yet the competitive analysis revealed a completely different story. The prices charged by the restaurant were about the same as the other competitors for comparable menu items, which means respondents *thought* the prices were too high. This problem leads to a completely different type of strategy or tactics than if prices were in fact higher than those of competitors.

If a retail operation is being evaluated, the form can be altered to reflect retailing variables. An example is shown in Exhibit 6.6. If other aspects of each variable are thought to be important to the analysis, these should be added to the form.

Competitive Strategies and Resources

Several other factors should be analyzed for a more complete evaluation of competitors in a market. They include competitors' strategic tendencies and resources—marketing, finances, and personnel. The

EXHIBIT 6.6. Retail marketing mix audit.

Evaluations	Competitor A	Competitor B	Competitor C
Product or Service			
1. Customer acceptance			
2. Customer satisfaction in use			
3. Product quality level(s)			
4. Adequacy of assortments			
5. Services provided			
a. Extent			
b. quality			
Place			
1. Customer accessibility			
2. Suitability of site for			
a. Services offered			
b. Attracting customers			
3. Customer traffic potential			
4. Appearance of facility			
a. Outside			
b. Inside			
5. Selling areas			
a. Adequacy of space (capacity)			
b. Attractiveness			
c. Layout			
6. Parking facilities			
a. Adequacy			
b. Customer convenience			
7. Drawing power of neighboring firms			
8. Customer image of facilities			
Price			
1. Comparative price level(s)			
2. Consumers' images of store's prices			
3. Number of price lines			
4. Consistency of price policies			
5. Credit policies and practices			
a. Suitability to customers' wants and needs			
b. Cost to customers			

Promotion

1. Promotional ability
   a. Money available
   b. Money spent
   c. Media available
   d. Promotional know-how
2. Amount and quality of promotional efforts in
   a. Personal selling
   b. Newspaper advertising
   c. Radio and TV advertising
   d. Direct mail
   e. Outdoor advertising
   f. Exterior display
   g. Interior display
   h. Special sales events
3. Ethical standards
4. Consistency of efforts

first factor is concerned with competitors' willingness to change or react to competitive moves; the second deals with their ability to make strategic moves.

Assessing strategic tendencies involves deciding whether competitors' actions tend to be reactive or proactive. Reactive strategies are those that follow the lead of other firms in the market or simply settle into a niche. Proactive strategies involve market leadership or a challenge to the market leader. If market leaders and challengers can be identified, they are the competitors whose actions must be anticipated. In Japan's "beer wars," for example, the Asahi Breweries, Ltd., has apparently taken on the competitive position of the initiator of change in the industry because of the success of its dry beer—so called because of its light taste and high alcohol content. The marketing mix audit of these firms helps identify the exact nature of their strategies.[6]

Assessing competitors' resources involves determining whether specific competitors have the marketing expertise and production capabilities to respond successfully to events in the marketplace, the personnel to respond in terms of both levels of demand and skills, and finally, the financial resources to respond to problems and opportunities that occur. Moreover, since most firms attempt to build on their strengths and nullify their weaknesses, analysis can help you forecast the type of response they are most likely to make. A firm that is strong financially and has underutilized plant capacity and weaker marketing skills is more likely to meet a challenge with lower prices or an increase in promotional expenditures than would a firm with an opposite set of strengths and weaknesses.

As the market moves toward oligopolistic competition, the necessity of this type of analysis becomes more significant. To fail to expect and anticipate competitive reactions is to ignore the realities of the dynamics of the market.

After completing the competitive analysis develop summary statements about each market segment with respect to competition. This provides you with an overview of the competitive forces at work in each segment.

SUMMARY

At this point in the analysis, the planner should begin to see several clear-cut problems and opportunities in the market. Not only have general and specific characteristics of the market been analyzed but so have the responses of competitive firms that are pursuing the market.

For new firms in a market, the competitive analysis has another advantage. Because the other firms have already adjusted to market conditions with their own strategies, their own approaches to the market are suggestive of successful and unsuccessful ways to enter and compete. Their trials and errors should become a guide to avoiding mistakes already made and activities already proven unsuccessful either by their nature or by the way they were carried out by existing firms.

Chapter 7 focuses on opportunity analysis. This is the next major step in preparing a marketing plan.

Chapter 7

Opportunity Analysis

MARKETING PLANNING IN ACTION:
REINVENTING BARBIE

The Bratz pack is bad news for Mattel. Yasmin, Sasha, Cloe, and Jade first burst on the scene in 2001 as an alternative to the squeaky-clean Barbie. The newcomers are multiethnic and sport racy clothing including platform shoes, hip-huggers, tube tops, and fur vests. The dolls, property of the upstart company MGA Entertainment, Inc., have given Barbie the toughest challenge of her forty-seven-year career. Sales of Mattel's Barbie declined to about $1.6 billion in 2001 from their 1997 peak of $1.9 billion, and continue to drop. This is unsettling for Mattel, who counts on Barbie for about one-third of its corporate revenues and even more of its profits. In the fickle toy business, brand management is different than for other products such as cereal or shampoo. The volatile whims of children are attracted by innovative products that are promoted heavily. Mattel has been trying for years to find out how to get the tweenies, girls ages seven to twelve, to play with dolls. Children are outgrowing the traditional toys at younger ages than in previous years; in fact the core market for Barbie is now girls ages three to seven. When they get older they want to move on to something different, more edgy and hip. The Bratz dolls fill the void of the seven- to twelve-year-old teen-wannabees.

The Mattel toy company has responded to the onslaught from Bratz with a new doll line, Flavas. Introduced in mid-2003, they are new friends to Barbie, and have highlighted hair, midriff-baring tops, and low-slung pants. Two boy Flavas sport earrings and cargo pants, with boxer underwear peeking out of the top. Mattel realizes that Barbie may have lost touch with the lives of some girls. "Barbie began as a great girl who was simply a reflection of popular culture, but in the past few years we had sort of put her on a pedestal," says Matt Bousquette, president of the newly created Mattel Brands unit Flavas. "We're taking her off that pedestal."[1]

INTRODUCTION

The analyses described thus far are extended into the decision-making realm in this chapter. At this stage, you must decide which, if any, of the market opportunities represent company opportunities— that is, opportunities the company should pursue. Special attention is given to the factors that must be analyzed in assessing opportunities and the tools needed for this analysis.

PROBLEMS VERSUS OPPORTUNITIES

You must differentiate between problems and opportunities, even though some of the same types of analyses are appropriate for dealing with both. A *problem* is defined as anything that stands in the way of reaching an objective, whereas an *opportunity* is a chance to improve overall performance. In order to know that you are experiencing a problem, you must have identified objectives to be accomplished and have made an effort to accomplish them. Failure to meet the expectations spelled out in a statement of objectives is, by definition, a problem. Assuming that realistic objectives have been established, you must: (1) define the exact nature of the problem, (2) identify alternative courses of action (strategies), and (3) select a course of action (strategy) to solve that problem. When you are dealing with existing problems, resources have already been committed; decisions revolve around continuation of the commitment, the extent of additional commitments, and the nature of the commitments.

Dealing with opportunities is a somewhat different proposition. Here, you have not been involved in the market prior to the analysis— the company is not experiencing a failure to reach objectives. Instead, you are searching for new markets to enter or new ways to improve on current performance.

One distinct feature of opportunity analysis is that it involves alignment of market opportunities with purpose and resources. In many cases, this goes beyond the realm of a marketing decision because it involves a new commitment of resources. It may be that the types of analyses described thus far are the basic inputs into a capital budgeting decision, which may be beyond the scope of the market planner's job description.

INTERNAL FACTORS

To evaluate opportunities successfully, you must combine the external analysis with internal analysis, which directly influences a firm's willingness and ability to respond to opportunities. Internal factors include purpose or mission and company resources.

Purpose

The presence of marketing opportunities is a necessary but not a sufficient condition for action. Management must decide whether it wants to take advantage of the existing opportunity and whether it has the resources to exploit the opportunity successfully. That is, it must decide whether the opportunity in the marketplace represents a *company* opportunity. Opportunities are always available, but not all companies are equally prepared to handle them. The purpose of the organization has a direct bearing on which market opportunities are pursued. A company's statement of purpose or mission should be used to evaluate market opportunities. Market activities and purpose must align. The organization wants to pursue only those ventures that will help it fulfill its overall mission; it should reject those that do not.

If, for example, a firm's mission is defined as developing high-quality products, then the identification of a market segment that needs a low-quality product at low price levels should not be viewed as a company opportunity regardless of how attractive that segment appears in terms of market potential and lack of competition. Trying to serve the needs of such a segment is in direct opposition to what the company has stated as its mission; such an opportunity must be rejected.

Company Resources

Given that an opportunity is consistent with purpose, the firm's resources must be analyzed to determine its ability to respond to an opportunity. The ability to capitalize on an opportunity will depend upon whether the firm can find and exploit *a competitive advantage* in the market under investigation. Although this concept was introduced in Chapter 6, we should stress here that the ability to leverage a competitive advantage can help to determine the extent of the market opportunity. A good opportunity would be distinguishable from an inferior one by the ability of a firm to exploit an advantage over competition along some dimension that delivers benefits and value consumers deem important, and which cannot be duplicated by another competitor without a substantial investment of time and/or resources.

Consideration should be given to at least four types of resources to determine if they provide an ability to meet the requirements of a potential opportunity.

Marketing Resources

A firm's ability to take advantage of opportunities requires personnel with the marketing skills necessary to develop and execute effective marketing strategies. A good product does not guarantee success. The old adage "Build a better mousetrap and the world will beat a path to your door" is just not true. Good marketing is the result of good marketers. Many firms that were successful in previous time periods have failed in the new environment because of a lack of marketing know-how. If a firm does not have adequate marketing skills available within its own organization, its financial resources must be sufficient to acquire the marketing personnel or it must seek the acquisition of a successful firm which is already positioned in the market and which has strong marketing abilities.

An example of the influence of marketing resources on a firm's success is illustrated by a large chemical company's experience with a new consumer product. For years, this company was a leader in manufacturing and marketing chemical products aimed at the industrial market. Several years ago, the firm developed a new cleaning compound and decided to sell it in the consumer market. The attempt was unsuccessful because of a lack of experience in marketing consumer products. The product was sold to a consumer-goods firm, which marketed the product successfully. Thus it was the original firm's inexperience in marketing consumer goods that caused its failure, not the absence of an opportunity, nor the quality of the product and its ability to deliver customer satisfaction.

Another example of the consequences of lack of marketing skill was the failure of Sony's Betamax video recording and playback system to dominate the video market. Arguably a superior technology to VHS, and over its life cycle able to provide better performance and more features for the money, Beta still failed to generate staying power in the market. Here again, the failure to fully exploit the market opportunity was not because of insufficient consumer demand or low product quality. Sony's failure was one of poor marketing (failure to license the technology and convince consumers of Beta's superiority) and this from a company widely regarded as having considerable marketing skill.

These examples illustrate that the demands each market opportunity places on the firm must be considered sui generis. The market will not necessarily always reward the pioneer more highly than the follower, and past success is no guarantor of future glories. IBM can testify to these truths in the personal computer market. Marketing expertise and resources are tested every day in the highly competitive markets at the turn of the century, and no firm can afford to avoid asking the harsh question of whether its marketing resources are sufficient to handle the unique challenges presented with each new market opportunity.

Production Resources

Several distinctly different production resource elements affect a firm's ability to handle new opportunities: production capacity, synergies, cost structure, technology, and labor skills. Production capacity is influenced by previous commitments to acquire production facilities. In the short run, this capacity is usually fixed, but it can be altered, over time, for new strategic opportunities. The skills of labor available during the short run are also considered fixed. Therefore, a firm must have both the capacity and the labor skills on hand or it must have the financial ability to acquire them. The cost structure of a firm can be a determining factor for some opportunities. The ability or lack of ability to be a low-cost producer closes opportunities in some markets. Synergies of production may be possible when the demands of potential production of a new product make good use of existing production technologies, skills, resources, by-products, etc. Technological capabilities must also be considered. Some new products may require production technology not currently available in the company. If the technology cannot be acquired at a reasonable cost, some opportunities will have to be foregone.

Financial Resources

The total amount of financial resources a firm has available and the process through which these funds are allocated influence the firm's ability to enter a market effectively. For some opportunities insurmountable financial barriers may exist. Not only are capital needs extensive, but marketing expenditures are at a high level. In addition, some opportunities may appear attractive, but the return on investment may be too low. Adequate financial resources must be available to ensure the provision of adequate production and marketing capabilities or the firm must have easy access to financial markets before some opportunities can be undertaken.

Adequate financial resources are needed to operate in many markets for the first few years—years necessary to build enough customers to sustain a profitable operation. Low revenue levels and high operating costs during the first few years must be anticipated. Unless the financial resources to permit continued operation are available, failure is imminent. Thus, a firm's current financial position, plus its ability to successfully obtain financing, directly influence its ability to pursue opportunities. The trend of charging "slotting allowances" to retailers means substantial cash advances may be needed just to obtain shelf space for products. Slotting allowances refers to the fees paid by a manufacturer to a retailer for slots on the retail shelf. These allowances are frequently up-front transfer payments from manufacturer to retailer when the manufacturer launches a new product. Typically, the amount of slotting fees paid is lower for those who have a strong market-share position. For large chains, such fees can reach $100,000 or more to get a truckload of products into a fifty-store chain.[2] For example, wholesale magazine distributors have paid as much as $15,000 per store to display their magazines and those who refused to do so lost chain store customers.[3]

Previously, manufacturers gave retailers additional merchandise to obtain shelf space. Retailers found that such merchandise did not pay the cost of rearranging shelves, turned to slotting fees as a way to offset cost and also increase profits. This means companies without the financial resources needed to buy distribution would simply be unable to get their products distributed.[4]

Managerial Resources

The other important part of the resource base that must be analyzed is managerial resources. This was referred to in Chapter 2 in terms of matching skills and opportunities. Management's willingness to take risks, and their values, skills, age, and experience are all important aspects of an organization's ability to respond to opportunities.

Financial resources can be used to offset personnel shortcomings if new managers are hired for opportunities that represent a distinct departure from current operations. The skills of the newly acquired managers are used to supplement skills of existing managers.

Exhibit 7.1 illustrates one format for evaluating market opportunities by taking into consideration organizational resources. Each factor—capacity, personnel, marketing, finance, and management—is rated in relation to an opportunity on a quantitative basis.

An alternate approach is to analyze these resources in relation to the opportunity as a strength or weakness. This approach is shown in Exhibit 7.2. For each strength and weakness identified, strategy implications are drawn.

Analysis of strength and weakness flows logically from the identification of the resources relative to the opportunity. Each resource, when evaluated within this framework, can be labeled as a strength or weakness, and the implications of that strength or weakness for a specific opportunity can be evaluated.

OTHER FACTORS

Other factors should also be analyzed in choosing opportunities. The importance of such factors as economic conditions, technology, political/legal, and cultural/social conditions will vary by opportunity and should not be overlooked in the opportunity analysis. In a technologically driven industry, such as personal computers, the inability to develop new technologies or to incorporate new technologies into products can severely limit or even prohibit a company's entrance into a market. On the other hand, new and better technologic breakthroughs can become the means by which market entrance is achieved. These factors were referred to as key success factors in Chapter 6.

EXHIBIT 7.1. Company resource evaluation matrix.

	Rating				
	Very good (5)	Good (4)	Fair (3)	Poor (2)	Very poor (1)
Production					
Production capacity					
Cost structure					
Technology					
Labor skills					
Production					
Production score					
Marketing					
Marketing skills					
Distribution facilities					
Channel availability					
Marketing score					
Finance					
Fixed capital requirements					
Working capital requirements					
Return on investment					
Finance score					
Managerial					
Number					
Depth					
Experience					
Managerial score					
Total score					

Source: Adapted from Rewoldt, Stewart H., James R. Scott, and Martin R. Warshaw. *Introduction to Marketing Management.* Homewood, IL: Richard D. Irwin, Inc., 1977, pp. 257, 261.

EXHIBIT 7.2. Analysis of strengths and weaknesses.

Factor	Opportunity Implication
A. Marketing resources	
1. Strengths:	
Established facilities	New service could use the same facilities
2. Weaknesses	
No in-house advertising and dependence on agency relationship	Service needs strong advertising effort—must use ad agency
B. Financial resources	
1. Strengths:	
Good cash position and strong earnings record	Offer customers payment plans
2. Weaknesses:	
Higher than average debt/equity ratio	Must fund through internal sources
C. Productive capacity	
1. Strengths:	
High-quality production	Go for quality end of market
2. Weaknesses:	
Low labor availability	Must offer limited quantities
D. Managerial resources	
1. Strengths:	
Strong research and development staff	Cost-effectiveness in operation
2. Weaknesses:	
No experience with new product	Hire new manager

RANKING OPPORTUNITIES

Develop a comprehensive view of each opportunity by looking at all the various elements that have been analyzed, rather than examining one element—market potential, for example—and then making a decision on the basis of that factor alone. It is not one factor by itself that determines the attractiveness of an opportunity, but the composite effect of all the factors.

To help quantify the attractiveness of the various opportunities, numbers can be assigned to each opportunity for each factor evaluated. For example, if four opportunities are evaluated, the numbers one through four can be used to rank each opportunity on a specific factor. If two opportunities appear to be equal on a given factor, the same number is assigned to each opportunity. If lower numbers are used to indicate higher rankings—that is, if one represents the highest rank—the opportunity with the lowest overall score represents the most desirable opportunity for the firm.

As pointed out earlier, it is not a matter of choosing only one opportunity. A firm with adequate resources may choose several and develop strategies appropriate for each. The result of this analysis is recognition of the differences between opportunities and what this implies in terms of the strategies and resources required by a given opportunity.

SUMMARY

The opportunity analysis is decision-oriented work that synthesizes all of the analysis into a choice framework. The marketing planner must not only evaluate but order the various opportunities to ensure the correct choice of the most attractive opportunities. Most companies have more opportunities than they have resources to pursue and must therefore select only those that provide the best fit with purpose, objectives, strategies, and resources.

Once an opportunity is selected, the next tasks involve setting objectives and developing the marketing strategies needed to accomplish these objectives. Chapter 8 focuses on the first of these tasks, establishing marketing objectives.

PART III: OBJECTIVES

Chapter 8

Marketing Objectives

MARKETING PLANNING IN ACTION: KODAK

Once one of the most identifiable brands in the world, Kodak is now facing an uncertain future. The company that virtually brought us photography over a century ago and remains the world's largest maker of photographic film must now make decisions about where to focus its efforts. Several factors have contributed to the company's uncertainty, not the least of which is the advent and popularity of digital cameras and media. In 2003, digital cameras outsold traditional film cameras in the United States for the first time. With 70 percent of its revenue coming from traditional film and photography, Kodak has experienced financial loss that has translated in considerable job cuts at the company. This strategic move will result in a cost savings of about $1 billion annually and will allow Kodak to invest funds into other ventures, technologies, and markets.

Although Kodak is a globally recognized name, its strategies are adapted for the needs and wants of specific markets. Kodak has seen the majority of recent profits from film cameras in Asia, Eastern Europe, and Latin America, and plans to introduce several new models of traditional film cameras in those markets during the next few years. However, the company has recently announced that it will stop selling its reloadable film-based cameras in the United States, Canada, and Western Europe. It will focus its efforts in those areas on digital technology with its new EasyShare digital camera, at the lower-priced end of the market. Its EasyShare sales in the United States during 2003 were second only to those of Sony Corp.

In addition to changing its focus toward film and digital cameras, Kodak has also turned toward technology in the ink-jet printer market and in digital imaging for health care. Kodak Chief Executive Daniel Carp cites the decline in its core business, the traditional film market, as a reason to redirect its investments toward digital technology. "It's just smart business in a business that's shrinking," Mr. Carp said.[1]

INTRODUCTION

After completion of the market, consumer, competitive, and opportunity analyses, the next step in the development of a marketing plan is to set objectives. The basis for setting the specific objectives is the qualitative and quantitative data gathered from previous analysis. The objectives, in turn, become the basis for the development of the marketing strategy. Realistic objectives cannot be established without consideration of the operating environment and the specific consumer segments to which the marketing effort is to be targeted.

This chapter presents the concepts and illustrations needed to aid you in this difficult task. An example is given of how data from the situation analysis is used to set objectives.

WHAT ARE OBJECTIVES?

Marketing objectives can be defined as clear, concise, written statements outlining what is to be accomplished in key areas in a certain time period, in objectively measurable terms that are consistent with overall organizational objectives. Objectives are the results desired upon completion of the planning period. In the absence of objectives, no sense of direction can be attained in decision making. As is often stated, "If you don't know where you are going, any road will get you there."

In marketing planning, objectives answer one of the basic questions posed in the planning process: Where do we want to go? These objectives become the focal point for strategy decisions.

Another basic purpose served by objectives is in the evaluation of performance. The objectives in the marketing plan become the yardsticks used to evaluate performance. Evaluating performance without some standard with which results can be compared is impossible. The objectives become the standards for evaluating performance because they are the statement of results desired by the planner.

Objectives have been called "the neglected area of management" because in many situations there is a failure to set objectives, or the objectives that are set forth are unsound and therefore lose much of their effectiveness. In fact, MBO emphasizes the need for setting objectives as a basic managerial process.

ALTERNATIVES TO MANAGING BY OBJECTIVES

One way to be convinced of the usefulness and power of managing by objectives is to consider some of the alternatives.[2]

Managing by Extrapolation (MBE)

This approach relies on the principle, "If it ain't broke, don't fix it." The basic idea is to keep on doing about the same things in about the same ways because what we are doing (1) works well enough and (2) has gotten us where we are. The basic assumption is that, for whatever reason, "our act is together," so why worry?; the future will take care of itself and things will work out all right.

Managing by Crisis (MBC)

This approach to administration is based upon the idea that the forte of any really good manager is solving problems. Since crises are abundant enough to keep everyone occupied, managers ought to focus their time and energy on solving the most pressing problems of today. MBC is, essentially, reactive rather than proactive, and the events that occur dictate management decisions.

Managing by Subjectives (MBS)

The MBS approach occurs when no organization-wide consensus or clear-cut directives exist on which way to head and what to do. Managers translate this to mean they should do their best to accomplish what they think should be done. This is a "do your own thing the best way you know how" approach. This is also referred to as "the mystery approach." Managers are left on their own with no clear direction ever articulated by senior management.

Managing by Hope (MBH)

In this approach, decisions are predicated on the hope that they will work out and that good times are just around the corner. It is based on the belief that if you try hard enough and long enough, things are bound to get better. Poor performance is attributed to unexpected events and the fact that decisions always have uncertainties and surprises. Much time, therefore, is spent hoping and wishing things will get better.

All four of these approaches represent "muddling through." Absent is any effort to calculate what effort is needed to influence where an organization is headed and what its activities should be. Managers who reject these approaches in favor of managing with objectives are much more likely to achieve targeted results and have a sense of direction.

CHARACTERISTICS OF GOOD OBJECTIVES

For marketing objectives to accomplish their purpose of providing direction and a standard for evaluation, they must possess certain characteristics. The more of these characteristics possessed by a given objective, the more likely it will achieve its basic purpose.

Objectives Should Be Clear and Concise

Cleary state what results are sought in a given objective. Avoid the use of long statements with words or phrases that may be defined or interpreted in different ways by different people.

Objectives Should Be in Written Form

This helps solve two problems: effective communication and altering unwritten objectives over time. Everyone who has played the game of "gossip" realizes that oral statements can be unintentionally altered as they are communicated. Lawyers, perhaps better than any other group, realize this. Written statements avoid this problem and permit ease of communication. A second problem with unwritten objectives is that they can be altered to fit current circumstances.

Objectives Should Name Specific Results
in Key Areas

The key areas in which objectives are needed will be dealt with later, but usually included in a marketing plan are billable hours and revenue objectives. Specific results, such as $100,000 in net profit rather than a "high level of profits" or "an acceptable level of profits," should be used to avoid doubt about what result is sought.

Objectives Should Be Stated Within a Specific Time Period

Intermediate objectives may need to be specified in a different time period because their accomplishment is a prerequisite to other objectives. The time period specified becomes a deadline for producing results and also sets up the final evaluation of the success of a strategy.

Objectives Should Be Stated in Measurable Terms

Concepts that defy precise definition and quantification should be avoided. "Goodwill" is an example of an important concept, but which in itself is difficult to define and measure. If a planner felt goodwill was a concept that needed to be measured, a substitute measure or measures would have to be used. An objective related to goodwill, which would be capable of quantification, might be stated as follows: "To have at least eighty-five percent of our customers rate our firm as the best firm in the area in our annual survey." Phrases such as "high sales volume" are unclear and unspecific, and cannot be measured. Does high mean first, second, or third in sales; a specific number; or percent? If the statement is quantified as "Increase sales volume by ten percent by December 1, 2005," it can be objectively measured. The accomplishment or failure of such a stated objective can be readily evaluated.

Objectives Should Be Consistent with Organizational Objectives

Marketing objectives must meet with overall company objectives and purposes. This idea has been previously stated, but must be continually reemphasized because of the need for organizational unity.

Objectives Should Be Challenging but Attainable

Two problems can be avoided if this characteristic is achieved. One is the avoidance of frustration produced by objectives that cannot be attained, or which cannot be attained within the specified time period. If an organization already has an unusually large market share, the desirability and likelihood of substantial increases in market share are doubtful. The other problem is setting objectives that are so easy to attain that only minimum effort is needed. This results in an unrealistic performance evaluation and does not maximize the contribution of a given marketing plan. Thus, objectives should stimulate effort.

One approach to writing marketing objectives that contain these characteristics is to apply a set of criteria to each statement to increase the probability of good objectives. One such list follows:

1. *Relevance.* Are the objectives related to and supportive of the basic purpose of the organization?
2. *Practicality.* Do the objectives take into consideration obvious constraints?
3. *Challenge.* Do the objectives provide a challenge?
4. *Measurability.* Are the objectives capable of some form of quantification, if only by order of magnitude?
5. *Schedule.* Are the objectives so constituted that they can be time-phased and monitored at interim points to ensure progress toward their attainment?
6. *Balance.* Do the objectives provide for a proportional emphasis on all activities and keep the strengths and weaknesses of the organization in proper balance?

Objectives that meet such criteria are much more likely to serve their intended purpose. The resulting statements can then serve as the directing force in the development of marketing strategy. Consider the following examples:

> *Poor:* Our objective is to maximize profits.
> *Remarks:* How much is "maximum"? The statement is not subject to measurement. What criterion or yardstick will be used to determine if and when actual billable

hours are equal to the maximum? No deadline is specified.

Better: Our net-profit target for 2006 is an average of 20 percent return on investment.

Poor: Our objective is to increase sales.

Remarks: How much? A one dollar increase will meet that objective but is that really the desired target?

Better: Our objective this calendar year is to increase sales from $300,000 to $500,000.

Poor: Our objective in 2006 is to boost advertising expenditures by 15 percent.

Remarks: Advertising is an activity, not a result. The advertising objective should be stated in terms of what result the extra advertising is intended to produce.

Better: Our objective is to boost awareness of our firm's name from 8 to 10 percent with the help of a 15 percent increase in advertising expenditures.

Poor: Our objective is to be the best firm in the business.

Remarks: This is not specific enough. What measures of "best" are to be used? Sales volume? Profits? Return on investment?

Better: We will strive to become the number one firm in the industry in terms of sales volume in 2006.

TYPES OF OBJECTIVES INCLUDED
IN A MARKETING PLAN

Marketing plans for a firm should contain three types of objectives: sales, profits, and consumer objectives. Short-term objectives are stated for the operating period only, normally one year, whereas long-term objectives usually span five to twenty years. Examples of both types will be given in this section.

Sales Objectives

Sales objectives relate to an organization's impact on an industry, and are a basic measure of the level of activity for a firm. Sales objectives are closely tied to products offered, production, budgeting, and so on.

Sales objectives may be stated numerically or as a percent of the total number. If the objectives are stated in percentages, they also need to be converted to numbers for budgeting and estimating the financial impact. Examples of sales objectives are given in Exhibit 8.1. The way objectives are stated must reflect what the organization can realistically expect to attain under a given plan. Also, the steps of setting objectives and developing strategy in preparing a marketing plan should be viewed as interactive. In setting objectives, they are first stated in terms of what we want to accomplish, but as we develop the strategy we may discover that we cannot afford what we want. The available resources committed to a given program or service may not be sufficient to achieve a stated objective, and if the planning process is resource-controlled, the objectives must be altered. It must be remembered that objectives are not fate, but they are direction. They are not commands, but commitments. As a planner, you must not fall into the trap of thinking that once objectives are set they cannot be altered.

Profit Objectives

Profits are a vital part of any business. Profit objectives force the planner to estimate the resources needed to meet company objectives, both in terms of sales and costs. For new products, the profitability of the product should have been analyzed before introduction. For existing products, sales and costs can be analyzed to project continued levels of profits. Sales projections, combined with estimates of costs involved in implementing the marketing strategy, provide a basis for statements of objectives about profits.

Sample statements are shown in Exhibit 8.2 as illustrations of profit objectives. Again, nebulous statements such as "acceptable profit levels" or "reasonable profits" should be avoided because of the possible variations in definition and the lack of quantifiability. The objective of a percentage increase in profits is the only one requiring additional information for its evaluation. The total previous

EXHIBIT 8.1. Examples of sales objectives.

1. Achieve sales volume of 200,000 units by the end of 2006.
2. Increase sales by 10 percent by December 31, 2006.

EXHIBIT 8.2. Examples of revenue objectives.

1. Produce profits of $180,000 by December 31, 2006.
2. Generate a 20 percent increase in profits by the end of 2009.
3. Produce a net profit of $20 million for the new product by May 15, 2006.

profits would be required to determine whether this objective has been reached.

Again, the interactive processes of setting objectives and developing strategies must be used to set objectives that are realistic. The costs of many aspects of strategy cannot be estimated until a written statement of strategy is developed. If the marketing strategy calls for a new ad campaign, for example, that strategy must be spelled out in detail before production and media costs can be estimated.

Customer Objectives

Customer objectives may seem unusual to some, but their inclusion should be obvious. They serve as enabling objectives in determining sales and profits and they also represent specific statements of customer behaviors and/or attitudes an organization would want customers to have toward its products. Examples of these types of objectives are shown in Exhibit 8.3. Customer objectives are especially important in providing direction to the development of the promotional strategy section of the marketing plan. They specify results desired of customers in terms of behaviors and attitudes, and should have the same characteristics as other objectives. They must be stated in objectively measurable terms and should be evaluated in relation to their accomplishment as a part of the monitoring and control system used in the plan.

Short-Term and Strategic Objectives

The time period covered in operating-level marketing plans is usually a year or less, and it is sometimes worthwhile to include statements of strategic objectives in the short-term plan. As discussed in Chapter 1, the short-term marketing plan is a subset of a strategic plan, and therefore, the objectives of each short-term marketing plan must be consistent with the strategic objectives of the organization.

EXHIBIT 8.3. Examples of customer objectives.

1. Create at least an 80 percent awareness of the existence and nature of our firm by the end of the fifth week of operation, October 15, 2006.
2. Have at least 80 percent of our customers favorably rate our products in our next survey of August 15, 2006.

One way to help ensure this congruency is to include statements of strategic objectives in the short-term operating plan. For example, the strategic objective of an organization might be to achieve a 20 percent market share from a given customer group. If its current share is only 3 percent, the next short-term marketing plan may state a 5 percent objective, the next an 8 percent share, and so on. The accomplishment of the individual objectives, which are short-term, can be related to the strategic objective in each plan to help create an awareness of the interrelationship between the two types of objectives.

USING SITUATION ANALYSIS DATA TO SET OBJECTIVES

The objectives of a given plan are based on the data provided in the situation analysis. In this section, a specific example of this process is illustrated to show how it is accomplished.

Assume a law firm is considering offering legal services through an office in a new shopping mall in order to reach residents of a suburban area. About 350,000 shoppers per month visit the mall to shop.

Consumer research identified a specific segment of consumers who said they would like legal services available at the mall and would be willing to pay reasonable rates to talk to any attorney about legal problems they had. A survey of these shoppers revealed that about 1 out of every 1,000 shoppers said they would use the services if available.

Based on this information a calculation of the size of this segment was developed along with a specific objective. These figures are shown in Exhibit 8.4.

Objectives derived through such a process represent the realities of the market and also the firm's willingness and ability to commit itself to such objectives. This example should also reemphasize the logic in the marketing planning format. The analysis precedes setting objec-

EXHIBIT 8.4. Market potential for shopping mall office.

1. Number of adult shoppers who visit the mall each month. Total: 350,000.
2. Estimated percent who say they are interested in legal service at the mall. Percent: .001.
3. Estimated market potential: 350,000 × .001 = 350.
4. Objective: attract an average of 50 clients per week or 200 per month.

tives, because realistic objectives must be derived from the results of the analysis. Also note that if the response were smaller in the survey, say 1 out of 10,000, the size of the market would probably be too small to serve profitably.

SUMMARY

Setting objectives is the second major part of a marketing plan. The necessity for objectives and their characteristics were presented to lay the groundwork for identifying the three basic types of objectives: sales, profits, and customer objectives. The statements of objectives given as examples in this chapter possessed the basic characteristics needed to serve both as a source of direction and in evaluation of the strategies developed in the plan.

PART IV:
STRATEGY, STRATEGY VARIABLES, AND FINANCIAL IMPACT

Chapter 9

Marketing Strategy Development

MARKETING PLANNING IN ACTION:
MERCEDES

A billboard above a busy urban freeway depicts the Mercedes M-Class for around $30,000. TV commercials for the car have hip, edgy photography and music that is more Dave Matthews than Amadeus Mozart. In an effort to appeal to a younger, less affluent buyer, Mercedes has repositioned its product to reflect more of a metrosophisticate than a luxury profile. Mercedes has also introduced models that are smaller and less expensive than the company's traditional cars, and are meant to sharply alter customers' perspectives of the kinds of vehicles that Mercedes produces. In an effort to expand its market base and attract a more price-conscious customer, Mercedes plans to introduce its A-Class crossover vehicle in 2006 with a price tag of about $24,900.

Taking charge of the Mercedes passenger-car division in 1989, Jurgen Hubbert responded to competition in the luxury-car market by making several changes. He led the company in developing less expensive models, in part by restricting engineers and holding them to design cars to meet certain price points rather than handing them carte blanche as in the past. Unfortunately, this was not without a cost. In a J. D. Power study that measures defects within the first three months of ownership, Mercedes has steadily declined over the past six years, to fourteenth place in 2003, finishing behind makes such as Buick and Chevrolet. Declines in customer satisfaction have also begun to affect the resale value of the Mercedes, especially when compared to other luxury models such as Lexus and BMW.

The introduction of the newer, less expensive A-Class further risks tarnishing the rest of the Mercedes lineup, as well as having a financial risk. Hubbert admits that the A-Class, still in its first generation, is marginally profitable at best. So why jeopardize a company whose profit of 7 percent is among the highest in the auto industry? Market expansion. Paul Halata, who runs Mercedes' U.S. operations, looks forward to the new A-Class and Smart vehicles. "Smart gives the company a chance to serve a new segment of the population that is younger, hipper, more fashionable. It fits their lifestyle as a second or third vehicle."[1]

INTRODUCTION

After developing a set of objectives for the time period covered by the marketing plan, the marketing strategy needed to accomplish those objectives must be formulated. First, an overall strategy must be designed. Then, the details of that strategy, as it relates to product, place, promotion, and price, must be planned to guide the firm's marketing efforts. This chapter introduces the concept of strategy and describes strategy elements and approaches to strategy development.

WHAT IS STRATEGY?

The word *strategy* has been used in a number of ways over the years and especially so in the context of business. When *objectives, policies, procedures, strategies,* and *tactics* are discussed, some uncertainty develops about the precise meaning of these terms. *Strategy* is derived from a Greek word meaning leadership and may be defined as the course of action taken by an organization to achieve its objectives. In a marketing context it refers to marketing actions and marketing objectives. Strategy is the catalyst or dynamic element of managing that enables a company to accomplish its objectives.

Similar to management itself, marketing strategy development is both a science and an art and is a product of both logic and creativity. The scientific aspect deals with assembling and allocating the resources necessary to achieve a company's marketing objectives with emphasis on opportunities, costs, and time. The art of strategy is mainly concerned with the utilization of resources, including motivation of the workforce, sensitivity to the environment, and ability to readjust to counterstrategies of competitors.

Marketing strategies provide the direction to marketing efforts. The alternate strategies considered by management are the alternate courses of action evaluated by management before commitment is made to a specific course of action outlined in the marketing plan. Thus, strategy is the link between objectives and results. It answers one of the basic questions posed in a marketing plan: How are we going to get there?

ELEMENTS OF MARKETING STRATEGY

Previously we made a distinction of planning activities and outcomes at the corporate, SBU, and product/market levels. The focus of our strategy also varies by planning level, although we can identify five components of strategy that define strategy at each of the three levels. The five components of strategy are described in the following, and Exhibit 9.1 illustrates the different strategic issues that should be addressed for these five components at the corporate, SBU, and product/market levels.[2]

1. *Scope.* The scope of an organization refers to the breadth of its strategic domain—the number and types of industries, product lines, and market segments it competes in or plans to enter. Decisions about an organization's strategic scope should reflect management's view of the firm's purpose, mission, and value discipline. This common thread among its various activities and product/markets defines the essential nature of what its business is and what it should be and how it contributes value to its customers.

2. *Goals and objectives.* Strategies should also detail desired levels of accomplishment on one or more dimensions of performance—such as volume growth, profit contribution, return on investment, and customer satisfaction—over specified time periods for each of those businesses and products/markets and for the organization as a whole.

3. *Resource deployments.* Every organization has limited financial and human resources. Formulating a strategy also involves deciding how those resources are to be obtained and allocated—across businesses, product/markets, market segments, functional departments, and activities within each business or product/market.

4. *Identification of a sustainable competitive advantage.* The heart of any strategy is a specification of *how the organization will compete* in each business and product/market within its domain.

How can it position itself to develop and sustain a competitive advantage over current and potential competitors? To answer such questions, managers must examine the market opportunities in each business and product/market and the company's distinctive competencies or strengths relative to its competitors (i.e., its differential advantage). Real competitive advantages exist only when all four qualifying conditions are met (see Chapter 6).

5. *Synergy.* Synergy exists when the firm's businesses, product/markets, resources deployments, and competencies complement and reinforce one another. Synergy enables the total performance of the related businesses to be greater than it would otherwise be: the whole becomes greater than the sum of its parts.

As can be seen in the "allocation of resources" and "sources of competitive advantage," components at the product/market level, the basic strategic elements for the operating marketing plan are the product, price, promotion, and place (channels of distribution) or *marketing mix* of the company. Therefore, marketing strategy in the product/market level's operating marketing plan primarily consists of *targeting a specific customer segment with a marketing mix that capitalizes on a competitive advantage the firm has with that target market in order to achieve the firm's goals and objectives and take advantage of sources of synergy across product/market entries.* Such a strategy should be guided by the societal marketing orientation and be consistent with the firm's value discipline and mission at the corporate level and the decisions regarding the product/markets the firm wishes to compete in at the SBU level.

When you evaluate the various strategies that can be used in marketing, you are asking what combination of these variables could be used to satisfy customer needs and accomplish the plan's objectives. Once a strategy is chosen it may be followed for several years, being altered only in response to counterstrategies of competitors or changes in other relevant environments. If you are working with an established product, the question of strategy becomes: Do we need to change our strategy to respond to new conditions in the environment, and if so, in what ways?

EXHIBIT 9.1. Strategic elements by planning level.

Strategic component	Corporate strategy	SBU strategy	Product/market strategy
Scope	Corporate domain—"Which businesses should we be in?" Corporate value discipline Corporate development strategy Conglomerate diversification (expansion into unrelated businesses) Vertical integration Acquisition and divestiture policies	Business domain—"Which product/markets should we be in within this business or industry?" Business development strategy Concentric diversification (new products for existing customers or new customers for existing products)	Target market definition Product line depth and breadth Branding policies Product/market development plan Line extension and product elimination plans
Goals and objectives	Overall corporate objectives aggregated across businesses Revenue growth Profitability ROI (return on investment) Earnings per share Contributions to other stakeholders	Constrained by corporate goals Objectives aggregated across product/market entries in the business unit Sales growth New product or market growth Profitability ROI Cash flow Strengthening bases of competitive advantage	Constrained by corporate and business goals Objectives for a specific product/market entry Sales Market share Contribution margin Customer satisfaction

EXHIBIT 9.1. *(continued)*

Strategic component	Corporate strategy	SBU strategy	Product/market strategy
Allocation of resources	Allocation among businesses in the corporate portfolio Allocation across functions shared by multiple businesses (corporate R&D MS)	Allocation among product/market entries in the business unit Allocation across functional departments within the business	Allocation across components of marketing plan (elements of the marketing mix) for a specific product/market entry
Sources of competitive advantage	Primarily through superior corporate financial or human resources; more corporate R&D; better organizational processes or synergies relative to competitors across all industries in which the firm operates	Primarily through competitive strategy; business unit's competencies relative to competitors in its industry; careful selection of product/markets in which to compete	Primarily through effective product positioning; superiority on one or more components of marketing mix relative to competitors within a specific product/market
Sources of synergy	Shared resources, technologies, of functional competencies across businesses within the firm	Shared resources (including favorable customer image) or functional competencies across product/markets within an industry	Shared marketing resources, competencies, or activities across product/market entries

Source: Adapted from Boyd, Harper W., Orville C. Walker, and Jean-Claude Larreche. *Marketing Management.* Chicago, IL: Irwin, 1995, p. 28.

If no changes in overall strategy are needed, your chief concern is the changes, if any, that are needed in the marketing effort used to implement the strategy. Some may prefer to use the term *tactics* when considering changes in the implementation of a given strategy. Regardless, you must be aware of the strategy alternatives available in marketing.

ALTERNATE MARKETING STRATEGIES

The development of alternate marketing strategies can be viewed in many ways, but three approaches will be discussed in this chapter. First, the overall way a firm approaches the markets it is attempting to serve. Second, one firm's strategy in relation to competitive strategies. The third approach deals with the position of a product or firm in relation to competitive offerings.

Product/Market-Oriented Strategies

The product/market approach to strategy development is illustrated in Exhibit 9.2. Three approaches can be used under this strategy development concept: *undifferentiated strategy* basically offers one product aimed at all market segments. Even if differences in market segments are recognized, these differences are not incorporated into the firm's marketing activities. Ford Motor Company used such a strategy in its early days when its only model was the Model T. As Henry Ford would say, "You can have any color you want as long as it's black."

Such strategies only work when faced with little or no competition. New competitors entering the market using a differentiated strategy or a concentrated strategy soon begin to erode the market share of an

EXHIBIT 9.2. Product/market strategies.

Undifferentiated marketing Ford Motor Company in 1925			Differentiated marketing Ford Motor Company in 2005			Concentrated marketing Rolls Royce in 2005	
Model T	Model T	Model T	Taurus	Thunderbird	Crown Victoria	Rolls Royce	
Model T	Model T	Model T	Mustang	Explorer	Expedition		
Model T	Model T	Model T	Contour	Windstar	F150 Pickup		

undifferentiated strategist. Ford had to drop the strategy in the late 1920s because competitors began to offer more models, more colors, and different product features. (In a contemporary example, Honda's introduction of the Acura to compete with BMW and Mercedes-Benz has led to counterstrategies by Toyota, Nissan, and Volkswagen, who have all introduced competing models selling for about $40,000. Volkswagen has upped the ante by introducing its new Phaeton, a sedan with a price tag of $70,000+. The number of luxury sedans now on the market will cause further strategy changes due to increased competition for customers and dealerships.[3])

A firm using a segmentation marketing strategy recognizes differences in the needs of each market segment and responds by developing a unique marketing mix for each segment pursued. Of course, not all segments have to be pursued, but at least two are required to use the term *segmentation strategy*. When a company develops mixes aimed at different segments, it can also be referred to as a market segmentation strategy. A firm using this approach usually offers a wide variety of products to meet the needs of customers in many segments.

Focused marketing strategies pinpoint one segment of the market and concentrate all their efforts on it. A financial firm specializing in mergers/acquisitions would use this strategy as would firms specializing in financing new ventures. Firms using this strategy option develop a distinctive competence for doing one thing well. Focus strategies are based on finding growth segments with unique requirements the firm can meet. Tandem's Failsafe computer system approach for applications, where continuous computer monitoring and control are needed, such as emergency services or power generating, is an example of a focus strategy based on unique and user needs.

The basic difference in the segmentation marketing strategy and the focused marketing strategy is the number of segments the firm attempts to serve. Firms following a focused strategy target their efforts on one segment. The factors that influence the choice of a particular strategy will be discussed in another section of this chapter.

Ford Motor Company is following such a segmentation currently with many different car and truck products, promotional themes, and prices. Procter & Gamble, Inc., maker of Head & Shoulders shampoo, also follows a segmentation strategy. They introduced a new version of the basic product by adding a conditioner to the original formula, thus segmenting the dandruff shampoo market.

A focus strategy concentrates on one segment of the market and directs all its efforts to that one segment. Volkswagen of America followed this approach for years in the small-car market with its Volkswagen Beetle. However, it now has expanded its strategy to several segments, with a product line that includes a moderately priced SUV (sport utility vehicle), the Touareg, and the new luxury Phaeton.[4] Retail stores selling to "big and tall" men's clothes have followed a similar strategy in segmenting the clothing market and concentrating on one specific segment.

Competitive Marketing Strategies

Another approach to strategy development is in relation to competitive marketing strategies currently used in the market. Exhibit 9.3 classifies the strategies that may be used by a company, based on its market position. Market position is defined in terms of one firm's share of the total market and its relation to competitors in the industry. Exhibit 9.3 identifies four market positions and suggests some possible strategies for each.

Market leaders are the recognized leaders who have the largest market share of the relevant market. Although their position of dominance may be widely recognized, their success may be constantly challenged by other firms. The strategies used by market leaders focus on expanding their own control of the market and warding off or countering the activities of aggressive competitors. The leader's strategy becomes the pivot point around which other competitors adjust their own strategies.

Market challengers are constantly trying to increase their market share in head-on competition with the leader, attacking the leader at its weak points or merging with smaller competitors. Market challengers are usually large firms in terms of revenues and profits, and may be even more profitable than the leader. The challenger usually tries to identify weaknesses in the leader's strategy and either confronts or goes around the leader or concentrates its efforts on taking over smaller firms. Pepsi's challenge of Coke's leadership position clearly demonstrates how the challenger's strategy can affect the strategies of other competitors. The New Coke, which was closer in taste to that of Pepsi than Classic Coke, was clearly a competitive strategy response.[5]

EXHIBIT 9.3. Competitive marketing strategies.

Market position	Possible strategies
Market leader This is the firm acknowledged as the leader, and it has the largest market share of the relevant market.	1. Expand total market: Develop new uses, new users, or more usage by existing customers. 2. Protect market share: Use innovative marketing tactics or retaliate against challengers.
Market challenger This is the second, third, or fourth firm in market share, and may be quite large, though smaller in a relevant market than the market leader.	1. Direct attack strategy: Meet leader head-on with aggressive promotion and/or prices. 2. Backdoor strategy: Go around leader options through innovative strategy. 3. Guppy strategy: Increase market share by going after smaller firms.
Market follower This is a firm that chooses not to challenge the leader and is content with market conditions.	1. Copy leader: Match as closely as possible leader's strategy without directly challenging. 2. Coping strategy: Adjust to strategies of both leader and challenger without direct confrontation.
Market nicher This is a smaller firm that operates in a geographic or client niche without directly clashing with competitors. Specialization is key to its success.	1. Geographic niche: Specialize by offering quick response to customers. 2. Product niche: Offer products that are unique to the customers served.

Source: Adapted from Kotler, Philip. *Marketing Management: Analysis, Planning, and Control,* Fourth Edition. Englewood Cliffs, NJ: Prentice-Hall, Inc., 1980, pp. 273-285.

Market followers and "nichers" adjust to the strategies of the market leader and challenger without making challenges. Nichers try to specialize geographically or by products offered, and basically avoid direct confrontation with other competitors. The followers simply copy the leader's strategy or adjust their strategy to cope with both the leader and the challenger's strategies, again without calling attention to their own activities. Rent-A-Wreck, a car rental service, attempts to target the niche created by higher rental fees charged by most rental companies.

Thus, competitive strategies must be considered in developing the marketing strategy to be used by a firm where established markets are at stake. You are striving to develop a strategy that will give you a competitive advantage over other competitors and provide long-run profitability.

Positioning Strategies

Positioning strategies usually evolve when several well-defined competitors are present with fairly unambiguous images. This situation permits placement of a firm or a new product relative to existing firms or in some instances, the repositioning of a firm or product. The firm or product is positioned in the market based on customers' needs and the firm's own distinctive competencies, that is, what the firm does well.

For firms that have gone through the strategic planning process, this approach is an extension of the work done in answering such questions as "What kind of firm are we?" and "What kind of firm do we want to become?" Such a strategy encourages the firm to focus on what it does best relative to other competing firms and clearly defined client markets.

The positioning of Acura Lexus and Infiniti are examples of the use of a positioning strategy. These newer market entrants have been positioned against two popular luxury cars: the Mercedes and the BMW. The positioning map shown in Exhibit 9.4 demonstrates this approach.[6]

General Motors also used a positioning strategy in the design of the Saturn, a mid-priced sedan designed to compete with such cars as the Honda Accord and the Nissan Maxima. When few competitors occupy a position, it becomes attractive for other companies to position products in the same quadrant. This, in turn, creates more markets and forces firms to concentrate on differentiating their products from each other.

FACTORS INFLUENCING THE STRATEGY SELECTED

At least four factors influence the choice of a strategy selected by the firm: corporate strategy and resources, the firm's distinctive com-

EXHIBIT 9.4. Example of a positioning strategy.

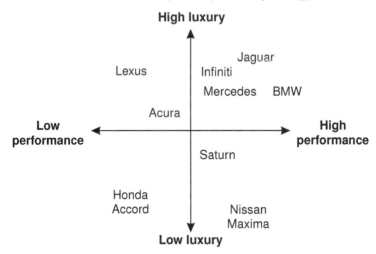

petencies, stage in the market's and product's life cycle, and competitive strategies. No one strategy will always prove successful. Instead, the strategy chosen must be the one that is best for the firm, given the nature of these four factors. A firm's resources, for example, may limit the company to a relatively low position in the market, and a nicher strategy may be the only feasible alternative to follow. The firm may even be an innovator in terms of product ideas but not have the financial, marketing, or personnel resources to compete for the mass market.

As was emphasized in Chapters 1 and 2, the marketing strategy must be derived from the corporate strategy. If the corporate strategy is focused on diversification through funds generated by a specific product or product line, then the strategy used for the product must be one that generates maximum cash flow. If the firm wants to harvest a product, the marketing strategy needs to reflect the need to generate short-term cash and eventual elimination through reduced research, promotion, etc. Also, the organization's value discipline provides a context within which the strategy should fall. For example, it would be inconsistent for a firm whose business is grounded in customer intimacy to pursue a strategy that reflects a desire to be a low-cost "one-size-fits-all" producer.

The distinctive competencies of the company have a direct bearing on the strategy selected. Distinctive skills and experience in marketing, production, or finance influence strategy choice. These distinctive competencies are the basis of targeting marketing effort and developing a competitive advantage.

The product's life cycle stage and competitive strategies are two additional factors influencing strategy selection. The influence of competitive strategies was discussed earlier. The firm's or specific product's stage in its life cycle also distinctly influences strategy. For example, a firm that has had its market share erode over time due to a failure to alter strategy may need to take an aggressive turnaround strategy stance. Repositioning the firm by introducing new products or going after new markets would be a pivotal point of its strategy.

As the product and its market go through their stages, many alterations in strategy may be necessary to adjust to the growth or decline in the size of the market and the entrance or departure of competitors. Note the many strategy element changes that may need to be made to remain competitive in the market. Likewise, the evolving stages of the market also require adjustments to strategy.

The strategy selected must be given sufficient time to be implemented and affect consumers, but an obviously ineffective strategy should be changed. This concept should be understood without mention, but the resistance to change in many companies is a common phenomenon.

SUMMARY

This chapter has outlined the basic approaches to strategy development in marketing. Although each of these approaches is an aid in evaluating options, the positioning approach appears to be the most comprehensive.

The factors influencing strategy selection were also identified. The strategy selected by an organization must reflect these factors since no one strategy will always be successful.

The next four chapters concentrate on the decisions to be made concerning each strategy variable. Chapter 10 examines the area of decisions about products offered to customers.

Chapter 10

Product Decisions

MARKET PLANNING IN ACTION: DUPONT

Paul Tebo used to run DuPont's petrochemical division, worth $3 billion to the company. Although profitable, this division probably put DuPont on the map as America's worst polluter. Those days have changed however, and now Tebo is a social responsibility advocate and DuPont's corporate vice president for safety, health, and environment. His goal is to transform DuPont from an oil-and-chemicals company to a eco-friendly firm. His most recent venture is in soymilk.

In an effort to create sustainable growth, DuPont began pledging a decade ago to reduce waste, emissions, and energy usage. Its goal then was to curb pollution and cut costs, but its new goal is to own businesses that can grow infinitely without depleting natural resources. With its start in the early 1800s making gunpowder, it has now turned to producing soy protein and biodegradable materials for plastic tableware. They hired Paul Gilding, the former executive director of Greenpeace, as a consultant.

Tebo believes that both the world and DuPont are better off because of the progress the company has made. It has dramatically reduced greenhouse gas emissions and hazardous waste. The company plans to divest its oil-based textiles and interiors unit which make nylon, polyester, and Lycra, instead turning to a new stretchable fabric, Sorona, made from corn. It is also making high-tech products such as Tyvek, a type of housing insulation that saves far more energy than is used to make it, Super Solids, a paint that can be applied to cars without discharging toxic solvents into the air, and Solae, a soy protein that goes into more than 1,000 food products, including 8th Continent soymilk. Looking to the future, DuPont wants to generate 25 percent of revenues from renewable resources by the year 2010 (they are currently at 14 percent). "The closer we can align with social values," Tebo says, "the faster we'll grow."[1]

INTRODUCTION

To this point in our discussion we have discussed how societal-marketing-oriented planners begin the planning process by taking an "outside-in" approach to determining their market offering. The first step of developing a marketing plan is to conduct a thorough situation analysis, which will help the organization better see the nature and scope of any opportunities available in the marketplace. In the process of conducting such an analysis, the marketing planner will naturally begin to formulate a set of objectives and the outlines of a strategy as the firm's response to the market opportunity(s). Thus, before this consideration of product decisions you will already have given considerable thought to how the products and/or service(s) must be configured to carry out a strategy centered around exploiting a competitive advantage with a specific target market.

Some of a product/market's key success factors may include specification of certain product/service features or benefits that must be present if the product/service is to generate satisfied customers. We will turn our attention in this chapter to specific decisions the marketing planner must make with regard to the product in order to put that part of the marketing strategy into action.

PRODUCT: THE FIRST COMPONENT
OF THE MARKETING MIX

Planning the marketing mix begins with the product or service to be offered. Pricing structures, promotional mixes, and channels of distribution are all based on the product or service that is offered to the consumer. The consumer's viewpoint of a firm's offering must be taken in order to understand fully what is meant by the term *product;* likewise, this approach must be taken in order to develop products with the right attributes.

This chapter is concerned with product concepts and the decisions that must be made about new and existing products. The decisions on product and service attributes are discussed, along with decisions on product line, branding, and packaging. These are the major decisions faced by a planner in developing marketing strategy for products.

Nowhere is the interaction of marketing, finance, and production personnel more necessary than in product decisions. All three areas are directly affected, and input from each is a prerequisite to successful product planning.

WHAT IS A PRODUCT?

Although at first glance this question may seem naive and obvious, reflection begins to unveil many alternate answers, depending on one's perspective. A few examples will help illustrate the broad meaning that product can have from a consumer or marketing viewpoint. A famous name-brand men's dress shirt sells for $50. This brand has always been top-of-the-line and is usually carried by retailers who specialize in dealing with high-income consumers who are willing to pay more for quality goods. If the label in the shirt were torn out it would be functionally unchanged. In fact, most people never see the label anyway. But would consumers still pay $50 for the shirt without the label? Probably not. The product is more than its functional value.

When Honda Motors introduced the Acura Legend in the United States, it had already been selling them in other countries as the Honda Legend. However, U.S. consumers associated the Honda brand with economy cars. Rather than try to change the image in the consumers' minds, Honda launched them under a new brand name, Acura. The brand has been successful and has been extended to several models.

A product is more than just the materials that go into it, and a service is more than just its end results. From a marketing perspective, a product or service may be defined as the sum total of all physiological, psychological, aesthetic, and spiritual satisfactions derived from the purchase and/or use. This means that a product or service must be conceived from a total perspective and not just a narrowly defined one of physical elements. The package of the product, the brand-name or symbol, the color, who else might purchase it, and where it is purchased are all part of a consumer's perception of a product. Not to understand this point can cause failure to reinforce buying satisfaction at more than one level. For example, a consumer purchasing a car battery that is guaranteed to last four to five years is interested in both price and warranty. But not to consider the color of the battery is to miss a chance to add symbolic satisfaction to the purchase. Since black is associated with death in this country, using a different color—white, red, or green—may add symbolic meaning to the claim of long life.

For the retail store, this is an extremely important concept since a retailer carries many products—perhaps as many as 10,000 different items. What is the retailer's product? It is really the customer's perceptions of the whole store—products, personnel, layouts, smell, color, and so on. Again, the total offering must be considered, not just the narrow view of a product in a purely physical context.

In effect, each firm's product is composed of two parts: a core product and a total product. The core product/service is the essential ingredients that constitute the product. A hotel's core product is a bed, dresser, chair, bathroom with towels, and usually a television and a telephone.

The core product can be augmented by the additions of features or amenities. In the case of a hotel, the augmentation may take the form of room service, a pool, a restaurant, valet/laundry service, a prime location, exercise equipment, etc. Thus, the core product plus the additions to it are used to create a total product that is the sum total of all the satisfactions derived from purchase of the product or service.

The augmentation of the product produces the opportunity for a firm to differentiate its total product from that of competitors. Offering more or different additions to a product or providing the same additions as competing products at lower prices creates a superior value for the customer, which becomes the basis of the product's position against competitors.

PRODUCT POSITIONING STRATEGIES

One of the most obvious ways in which the previously conducted situation analysis affects the development of a product strategy is in the positioning process. The term *positioning* refers to the place the product occupies in the minds of customers relative to a set of criteria the customers use to think about the product and relative to a group of competitors that the customers have as an evoked set when considering the product. Such a position using this dimension was illustrated in Exhibit 9.4 for luxury cars. Here luxury and performance are the criteria used in differentiating between the various makes in the customers' minds. Although a product's position is achieved through the use of the entire marketing mix (i.e., the product design, pricing, promotion, and place decisions), it is generally referred to as product positioning because it reflects the decisions made when developing product strategy.

The process used to determine the product positioning strategy reveals the reliance on information gained during the situation analysis phase of the marketing planning process:

1. Determine the product features/benefits used by members of your target market to evaluate product offerings.
2. Determine what positions existing competitive products occupy along those dimensions.
3. Identify those niches where customers have desires for a product with that combination of features/benefits where you can deliver the desired combination better than can competitors who occupy that space (i.e., where you can deliver satisfaction of their needs at a competitive advantage).
4. Write a positioning strategy that spells out how the product should be configured and promoted to occupy the targeted position.
5. Do not lose sight of your intended position when developing and marketing the product.

This last point is emphasized because on some occasions the actual product has strayed from the intended position due to compromises made in its development or in the marketing mix used to establish its position. Such deviation from the objective can be unintentional and subtle, but can contribute to the dilution of the planned positioning strategy. The actual positioning pursued may be based upon several possible approaches:[3]

1. *Attribute.* Using one or more product attributes, features, or benefits that the brand can deliver better than its competitors. An airline touting the fact that it has the best on-time arrival record exemplifies this approach.
2. *Price/quality.* Indicating the brand's place on the price/quality continuum can position it firmly in the minds of customers. This has been successfully executed at both ends of the continuum (for example, at the high end with Corum watches and Nieman-Marcus stores, and at the low end with Timex and Wal-Mart).
3. *Use or application.* Here the product is positioned by how it is to be used or applied. The Samsung E715 Camera Phone is an example of this type of positioning. The cell phone has a built-in camera, along with flash.

4. *Product user.* This approach associates the product with a particular type of user. Some athletic and outdoor wear is positioned for the "serious" amateur or professionals only.
5. *Product class.* Positioning with respect to product class involves
   association with a specific group of products, usually different
   from what might be the conventional association. Examples
   would be positioning Caress as a bath oil product and Neutro-
   gena as a beauty bar instead of as soaps. Olay, which usually is
   associated with skin care, has a new line of vitamins that are positioned as beauty supplements.
6. *Competitor.* Here the attempt is to distinguish your product from
   its competition by directly positioning it against that leading
   brand. The famous Avis slogan, "We try harder," is an example
   of this approach.

Whatever approach is used in executing the positioning strategy, the
end result must be a strategy that reflects both the market realities revealed by the situation analysis (i.e., Will your target market segment
favorably respond to your positioning message because it addresses
an unsatisfied need of theirs?), and the firm's distinctive competencies (i.e., Can you deliver the promised benefits better than competition?). A positioning strategy can not be a way to "hype" your product. It is the way to stake out your territory in the market, and you
must be able to hold that ground against competition and generate
satisfied customers along the dimension by which you have established your position.

QUALITY- AND VALUE-BASED MARKETING

One of the most significant trends in marketing at the turn of the
century has been the emphasis on value—the right combination of
product quality, service support, and timely delivery at a reasonable
price. This concern with value by customers has forced many firms to
reconsider their views of product quality and customer service in order to meet the demands of a global marketplace. For example, consider the differences between the traditional view of product quality
and the view the TQM (total quality management) approach provides
in Exhibit 10.1.

EXHIBIT 10.1. Traditional view versus total quality management view.

Traditional view	Total quality management view
• Productivity and quality are conflicting goals.	• Productivity gains are achieved through quality improvements.
• Quality is defined as conformance to specifications or standards.	• Quality is defined by degree of satisfaction of user needs.
• Quality is measured by degree of conformance.	• Quality is measured by continuous process/product improvement and user satisfaction.
• Quality is achieved through inspection.	• Quality is determined by product design and is achieved by effective process controls.
• Some defects are allowed if the product meets minimum quality standards.	• Defects are prevented through process-control techniques.
• Quality is a separate function and focuses on evaluating production process and output.	• Quality is part of every function in all phases of the product life cycle.
• Workers are blamed for poor quality.	• Everyone is responsible for quality.
• Supplier relationships are short-term and cost-oriented.	• Supplier relationships are long term and quality-oriented.

Source: Adapted from Hunt, V. Daniel. *Quality in America.* Homewood, IL: Business One Irwin, 1992, p. 76.

Marketing plans must reflect the emphasis on value demanded by the market with respect to the quality of product and level of customer service.

Quality Strategy

Firms adopting a societal marketing orientation to their markets are interested in understanding how their customers perceive and define quality as well as making sure that their products are fully capable of generating customer satisfaction in both the short- and long- term.[4] Thus, product quality is not primarily internally determined, but is rather centered around customer perceptions and evaluative criteria. The Strategic Planning Institute's procedure for assessing perceived quality may be instructive:

1. A meeting is held, in which a multifunctional team of managers and staff specialists identify the nonprice product and service attributes that affect customer buying decisions. For an office equipment product, these might include durability, maintenance costs, flexibility, credit terms, and appearance.
2. The team is then asked to assign "importance weights" for each attribute representing their relative decisions. These relative importance weights sum to 100. (For markets in which there are important segments with different importance weights, separate weights are assigned to each segment.)
3. The management team creates its business unit's product line, and those of leading competitors, on each of the performance dimensions identified in Step 1. From these attribute-by-attribute ratings, each weighted by its respective importance weight, an overall relative quality score is constructed.
4. The overall relative quality score and other measures of competitive position (relative price, market share, etc.) and financial performance (return on investment, and return on sales) are validated against benchmarks based on the experience of "look-alike" businesses in similar strategic positions in order to
   • check the internal consistency of strategic and financial data.
   • confirm the business and market definition.
5. Finally, the management team tests their plans and budgets for reality, develops a blueprint for improving market perceived quality, relative to competitors', and calibrates the financial payoff.[5]

In many cases, the judgmental ratings assigned by the management team are tested (and when appropriate, modified) by collecting ratings from customers via field interviews.

The key to successful implementation of a quality strategy is teamwork and cooperation. Everyone should see their job, whatever their functional area, as a value-adding role in the delivery of a quality product. People must be cognizant of what constitutes quality in the customer's mind, feel that quality is everyone's responsibility, and be empowered to make decisions that affect the value delivery chain. Keys to successfully achieving world-class quality include the following:

- Receive the unequivocal support of top management for the quality program.
- Maintain a close liaison with customers in order to fully understand their needs.
- Fix the business process if gaps exist in meeting customer needs.
- Reduce the amount of time it takes to react to changing definitions of product quality to avoid untimely delays.
- Empower people to allow them to utilize their best talents.
- Assess and adjust the performance measurement and reward system to recognize efforts consistent with quality objectives.
- Total quality programs must be seen as a continuous concern throughout the organization.

SERVICE STRATEGY

Companies have been concerned with delivery of a satisfactory level of customer service for decades, but the level of concern has increased during the past decade. Competitive forces and the more demanding nature of customers have combined to put customer service at, or near, the top of most marketer's lists of important issues. Research has revealed five dimensions used by customers to define the quality of service they perceive they are receiving (see Exhibit 10.2).

Further research has revealed that although respondents rank all five toward the "very important" end of the scale in defining service quality, they, when asked, said that reliability was the most critical. This result suggested that firms must accomplish the following tasks with regard to their service strategy:

1. Determine the specific service expectations of the target market.
2. Design a service strategy grounded in meeting or exceeding those expectations.
3. Deliver on those promised service levels consistently when dealing with customers.
4. If steps 1 through 3 are done better than competitors, a competitive advantage exists in the area of customer service and should be exploited as such.

EXHIBIT 10.2. Dimensions of service quality.

Tangibles	Appearance of physical facilities, equipment, personnel, and communications materials
Reliability	Ability to perform the promised service dependably and accurately
Responsiveness	Willingness to help customers and provide prompt service
Assurance	Knowledge and courtey of employees and their ability to convey trut and confidence
Empathy	Caring, individualized attention the firm provides its customers

Source: Zeithaml, Valarie A. and Mary Jo Bitner. *Services Marketing: Integrating Customer Focus Across the Firm,* Third Edition. McGraw-Hill Irwin, 2003, p. 93

IMPROVING CUSTOMER PERCEPTIONS OF SERVICE QUALITY

The most vexing challenge for management, given the importance of reliability in defining service quality, is to close any gap that exists between expectations and ultimate delivery of service to customers. Four particular service-related gaps should be of concern to marketing planners:

1. *Gap between customers' expectations and management's perceptions.* Research into what customers are actually thinking is needed—we cannot just assume that absent such research we know with clarity what those expectations are with conducting the proper research.
2. *Gap between management perception and service quality specifications.* Knowledge of customer expectations is but the first link in a chain of steps leading to customer satisfaction with service delivery. Specifications of policies and tasks of service delivery must be developed based on that knowledge, communicated to employees, and that employees that see their job performance will be based in part or in whole on meeting those specifications.

3. *Gap between service quality specifications and service delivery.* Highly motivated, trained, and well-informed employees are needed to actually perform the tasks specified as necessary for delivery of quality service. Control systems that are capable of measuring any gap between desired and actual service delivery should be in place to indicate where excellence or shortfalls are occurring.

4. *Gap between service delivery and external communication.* Excellent delivery of service specifications can still disappoint customers if marketers have caused those customers to have unrealistically high expectations of service. For example, photos that suggest the accommodations at a resort are more spacious or luxurious than they really are will likely raise expectations higher than can be delivered upon, resulting in disappointed customers.[6]

Product quality and customer-service decisions should be the cornerstone of product decisions in the marketing plan for existing products.

NEW-PRODUCT DEVELOPMENT DECISIONS

Developing successful new products is the key to continued success for most companies. Old products eventually reach a sales decline stage, and unless new products are forthcoming, sales stagnation or decline is inevitable. Research into product failures and successes and the experiences of many marketing executives have led to the idea that development of a new product or service should be viewed as a series of stages. The completion of one stage leads to a decision of "go" or "no-go" concerning the next stage. Each additional stage undertaken represents more investment in time and money, and should not be taken unless the outcome of the previous stage has been positive. At any stage, a product or service that fails to measure up to predetermined standards should be dropped or altered before moving to the next stage. The six stages in new-product development are the following:

1. Idea generation
2. Feasibility analysis

3. Product development
4. Consumer tests
5. Test marketing
6. Full-scale commercialization

If the marketing strategy calls for new products or services, these developmental stages should be followed in the order specified when possible. However, there may be some exceptions. Some projects—a theme park, for example—cannot be placed in consumers' hands or test marketed. Since these types of situations involve a great deal more risk, a compensating higher rate of return should be required.

Idea Generation

Ideas for new products and services come from many sources. Customers, dealers, salespeople, competitors, and company employees are some of the most common. Sometimes the creation of a new product can simply involve repackaging of existing products. Capital-EMI Music Inc.'s executives discovered that consumers who were asking for music from the movie *The Witches of Eastwick* actually wanted an aria from the opera *Turandot* by Puccini. In response, the company dug out several movie theme songs and created *The Movies Go to the Opera,* which was so successful that it spawned several other movie-associated classic recordings. Some firms consciously set out to create new ideas, and others do not. It usually depends on the importance of new product ideas to a company's success and the imaginativeness of management. Some firms have a research and development staff for creating new products and improving old ones. The ideas for new products must be evaluated by comparing the product or service with company resources, as discussed in Chapter 7. This analysis should end with the decision to proceed to the next step, drop the idea, or gather more information.

Feasibility Analysis

Products, or services, passing the idea stage are taken to the next stage—a feasibility study. Feasibility analysis involves a three-step approach using secondary data to (1) estimate demand or market potential and the company's anticipated share, (2) estimate cost of producing and marketing the product or service, and (3) determine a return on investment (ROI). Steps 1 and 2 are used to develop a pro forma income statement for the project, and the net profit is then divided by the investment in fixed and working capital to determine potential ROI. If the company has an established "hurdle rate" (a rate below which projects are dropped), a decision is made to drop the idea, proceed to the next stage, or collect additional verifying data.

Product Development

Given that the product or service meets initial ROI requirements in the feasibility analysis, the next stage is actual product development. The objective here is to initiate development of the product or service in order to determine if there are any insurmountable production problems. In addition, working models of the product are available for further testing. An important question at this point is whether to invest in production facilities or try to subcontract for production models at this stage. Limited resources would dictate the latter. However, if at all possible, the firm should attempt the development to "get up on the learning curve." The production experience allows the firm to progress along this learning curve and also maintains control of information about the new product.

The marketing planner's input in this process is to help research and development personnel define important product attributes and how consumers make judgments about them. If, for example, consumers judge the quality of a bicycle by its weight, attention must be given to the weight of the product. If the prototype is too light, then filling tubular or plastic products with waste materials may add the necessary weight.

Consumer Tests

If the developmental process proceeds to this point, you are ready to bring in the consumer in a direct way. Consumer testing can range from a laboratory test to placement of the product in the consumer's home for actual use. Placement tests are especially beneficial because the product is tested under consumer conditions of use, which can lead to the discovery of salient features that may have been overlooked as well as those that should be emphasized. In a placement test of a fabric softener it was discovered that using the right amount of softener was directly related to satisfaction with the product. Although some consumers used a measuring cup to determine exact quantities, most just poured in what they considered to be the right amount. To avoid this problem, the cap was redesigned as a measuring cap. This ensured that the right amount could be easily determined by the consumer. When Corning Glass Works developed a new form of their Pyrex-brand measuring cup to make it more usable for consumers, a placement test was conducted with 1,000 homemakers who used Corning products. These tests confirmed the acceptability of the new product by those who would buy it.

The results of placement tests may lead to other ideas for product attributes or may indicate substantial changes in the product necessary to overcome consumer resistance. Correcting problems is much easier at this stage than after the product is on the market. The rush to get a product on the market may cost a company dearly in lost sales. Products that fail to live up to expectations cannot take advantage of one of the best-selling tools for any product or service—it works!

Test Marketing

After completion of the placement test and any alterations in products, the next stage is test marketing. In a test market, the product is put into the market on a limited basis in a form as close as possible to the final one. This stage offers an answer to a question vital to a product's success: Will consumers buy the product in sufficient quantities to justify full-scale commercialization? This can be considered the acid test for new products because no matter how well a product or service is conceived or designed, the final choice is with the consumers. Their votes in the marketplace are the determining factor of success. Regardless of how promising the earlier stages have been, this stage should not be omitted unless test marketing is an impossibility. Again, the company has an opportunity to move along the learning curve, but this time in marketing. Given the high failure rate for new products, information from test marketing must be available for adjusting the marketing variables in order to produce a successful strategy.

Revelations Entertainment, a company headed by actor Morgan Freeman, is teaming up with Intel Corporation to distribute movies directly to homes, bypassing both theaters and DVD releases. Revelations and Intel began test marketing the service in 2005, which pipes movies into homes via secure Internet transmission, and then onto TV screens via home networks that link computers and TVs. Mr. Freeman cites the movie industry's problems for several years with pirated copies and illegal downloads of movies as a reason for investing in the service. Intel is involved in the hopes of selling more high-end chips that go into these home networks.[7]

In addition to a more realistic estimate of sales provided by test markets, alternate combinations of the strategy variables can be tested to determine their impact. For example, testing alternate prices in various markets can aid in estimating consumer price sensitivity and the demand curve for the product. Such information is invaluable in determining the best price.

Full-Scale Commercialization

Substantial investments have already been made in the product prior to reaching this stage. However, if the earlier stages have been followed, the chances for success have been substantially increased. The remaining marketing tasks are still substantial, since products must be managed over their life cycle. The decisions at this stage hinge upon when to introduce the products into how many markets, and with what strategy. The answers to these questions depend on seasonality of the products, company resources and policies, and results of the test markets. Some companies, for example, have a policy of introducing new products in a market-by-market fashion. Borden uses this approach for many of its products. Insights gained in one market are used to improve entrance into the next. This roll-out approach is used by many companies who use resources from sales in one market to underwrite efforts in another.

Once products are introduced, they go through a cycle referred to as the product life cycle. This cycle includes introduction, growth, maturity, and decline. Thus, they must be managed over their whole life cycle. New products enter the market, others drop out. Demand and consumer preferences may also change. These may require adding new features to augment the product. Changes may also be required to respond to competitors' changes in their product offerings.

CHANGING EXISTING PRODUCTS

Although ideas for changing existing products can come from any source, two specific sources are consumers and competitors—the best source is the consumer. Problems consumers have with existing products or services satisfying their identified needs should be the focal point of any analysis designed to improve current products.

Sometimes this concept is so obvious it is overlooked. For years, anyone who was familiar with hydraulic jackhammers could tell you that the noise and vibrations resulting from their use were major problems. Most users require a relief after about four hours even when using earplugs. Only recently has a new type of jackhammer been marketed in Europe that has overcome the problems. Talking with users would have produced the information on problems in five minutes. Just seeing one in use would not be enough to answer any questions!

Anyone who has struggled with a key-type device to open a metal can could have described the problems with the design. Consumers using shampoo or conditioner in the shower relayed to manufacturers their difficulty with removing and replacing traditional caps on the product. This led to the flip-top packaging on most major brands. Thus, the consumer should be the major source of information for altering existing products.

Activities of competitors can also be a sure signal for needed changes. The problem here is that reacting to a competitor's product change places you in an undesirable position. However, in most cases, their successful altering and/or repositioning of an existing product or service will require some reaction from other firms in the market.

A good approach is to continually try to improve your product offerings. This is similar to having a strategy of making your own products obsolete. In some competitive environments, if you do not, a competitor will. Firms in the market for personal shaving products appear to follow this approach, and it has led to not only improved products but to new ones as well.

PRODUCT LINE DECISIONS

Although many firms may start out by offering only one product or service, most companies develop a line of products. The products may complement or even compete with each other. The Dallas Cowboys, Inc., owns a subsidiary that is responsible for marketing the many promotional football-related items sold by this company. Procter & Gamble markets several detergents under different brand names that compete with each other as well as with brands of other companies.

Several reasons for developing a line of products rather than concentrating on just one are:

- Growth in sales volume
- Spread of fixed cost over several products
- Increase in a firm's importance in the marketplace
- Reaction to a competitor

Two problems must be addressed in developing a product line—cannibalization and diversification into areas beyond the company's abilities. Cannibalization occurs when a new product or service is added to the product line and takes away sales from one of the firm's existing products. In some cases, this is unavoidable, but cannibalization must be evaluated in estimating sales of a new product. When Ford Motor Company introduces a new model, for example, some people may not see it as an alternative to a Chevrolet but as an alternative to another Ford model.

The other problem occurs when a company fails to evaluate its ability to handle a new product. The desire for new products may be so strong that it forces the company into products it is ill-equipped to deal with. The desire for growth in sales must always be balanced by the firm's ability to market a new product successfully.

Just as products may be added to a firm's product line, they may also be dropped. When products fail to accomplish sales and product objectives or positively influence the sales of other products, they must be deleted. Product deletion does not necessarily decrease profitability. The products already may be unprofitable or that the attention focused on other products can more than offset any sales decline caused by deleting a product.

BRANDING DECISIONS

A good brand name is not only a necessity for consumer recognition but also a valuable asset to a company. A brand name is important because consumers can associate satisfaction with a brand, thereby repeating their purchase or recommending it to others. A brand is anything used to identify a product, whereas a brand name is that part of a brand that can be pronounced. A trademark is a brand name that has been registered and becomes the property of one company.

Three basic attributes of a good brand name are: easy to pronounce, easy to recognize, and easy to remember. Consumers must be able to pronounce the brand name in only one way. Nissan Motors of Japan had this problem with the Datsun automobiles. Some people pronounced it Datsun with an a, and others pronounced it Dotsun with an o. The brand name should also be suggestive of the product's use or have some attribute of the product. Kleenex and Sear's Craftsman are examples of brand names that are easy to pronounce and suggest a product attribute—clean for Kleenex and quality for Craftsman.

When international markets are involved, choose a name that is pronounceable in other languages and also one that does not have a negative connotation. "Body by Fisher" translates to "corpse by Fisher" in Flemish.

Another branding decision is whether to use a family brand name or an individual one for new-product additions. Family branding means using one brand name for many products, for example, Heinz Tomato Paste, Heinz Ketchup, and Heinz 57 Sauce. With individual brands, each new product receives its own distinctive brand name. Procter & Gamble uses this approach with Cheer, Tide, Gain, Crest, Gleem, and so forth.

Individual brands cost more to market because the identity of each must be established, but there are also several positive reasons for this choice. If a differentiated or segmentation approach is used, with different brands developed for different segments, the identification of which products are designed for which segments is improved. If a firm is moving outside its established product type, individual brands might be more advisable. General Electric is well established in electrical appliances and other electrical products, but if it started to market cake mixes, for example, the use of the General Electric family brand might be detrimental. Pillsbury might have similar difficulties in developing a line of electrical appliances.

When family brands are used, a transference of the favorable image of one product to another is possible. This is especially true when a new product represents the extension of an existing line—such as another flavor of a candy product—or a complementary product such as icing for cakes. Also, retail shelf space may be easier to attain when a new product bears the name of current products already stocked.

Another branding decision revolves around manufacturer, dealer, and generic brands. A manufacturer must decide whether to produce its own brands, private brands for dealers (wholesalers and retailers), or generic brands. The decision to produce dealer and/or generic brands usually boils down to a "Do we need the volume?" question, since a manufacturer can assume that if it does not make the product, someone else will. However, the manufacturer is losing its identity in the process. Large retailers such as Sears, A&P, and JCPenney market many products under their own private brands. This gives them control over the product and builds store loyalty in the process. Generic brands have met with very limited success in the United States, although they have been popular in Europe for several years. Generic brands have no brand names and are characterized by plain labels, no advertising, and prices of 25 to 35 percent less than brand name products.

Private brands are more common in some industries, groceries and shoes, for example, but appear to be spreading to all industries. Although some manufacturers still shun private and generic brands, both have made substantial inroads in some industries.

PACKAGING AND LABELING DECISIONS

The package and the label may be important in increasing consumer satisfaction. In addition, they aid in protecting and promoting the product. The packaging of many products has been the key to success for many companies. Rapid Shave's entrance into the shave cream market with the aerosol can and Chiquita bananas with their tropic-packed strategies are just two examples. The package performs several functions. The most obvious is protection of the physical product from damage and deterioration. Another is the storage of the product both before and after purchase.

One of the best techniques for designing an effective package is to "follow a product" from a manufacturing process to the garbage can. This permits identifying the package needs in manufacturing, shipping, handling (on the shelf or through the vending machine), in the customers' hands and home, until the product is used and the package discarded. Noting that consumers like to store coffee in the can led many manufacturers to the use of the plastic sealing cap. Marking the computer scan code in an appropriate spot for ease in checkout operations is another example of how this step-by-step trail of a package aids development.

Evaluating the affect of packaging on the environment is also very important. The continued problems of garbage disposal and environmentally safe packaging create challenges but also opportunities for creative marketing. More and more companies are using recycled paper products, designing products with biodegradable packages, and testing refillable packages. Procter & Gamble offers refill pouches for household products such as fabric softener and detergent.

The label of a product is also an important concern for many product applications. The label, which has now become a part of the package for most products, both informs and persuades. The information contained, the colors used, the use of the company logo, the picture shown are all part of a total packaging approach that attempts to maximize the contribution of each element. Both government regulations and the avoidance of liability suits are major reasons for proper labeling. A good label must meet requirements for content listing and also promote safety and correct use of the product.

SUMMARY

The products and services offered by a company are what produce consumer satisfaction. This strategy element requires careful planning in both developing new products and altering existing ones. Well-conceived products and services ease the burden for the other marketing variables. Although a good product will not make people beat a path to your door, it may be what brings them back—again and again.

This chapter focused on the decisions related to product positioning, quality, and service decisions; altering products and packaging; branding; and labeling products. The next chapter discusses decisions that must be made to get the product and services to the target markets.

Chapter 11

Place Decisions

MARKETING PLANNING IN ACTION: THE CHANGING FACE OF RETAIL STORES

The retailing industry has seen considerable changes during the past two decades. Most families are now two-income households, with the majority of women working full- or part-time and still handling most of the family chores. In addition, consumers have more savvy, are more educated, and are more demanding than in the past. They look for what they want, where they want to buy it, and at what price they are willing to pay.

Pressed for time, consumers are either shopping online, at specialty stores for a precise item selection, or are visiting large malls where there are various stores, restaurants, and entertainment opportunities. Capitalizing on the mall traffic and price-conscious consumers, Wal-Mart is now moving to the inner city, especially into mall properties. It recently opened a two-story store in a mall in New York City and a three-story store in Los Angeles. The mall, once the domain of department stores such as Sears and Macy's, is now becoming home to discounters who have moved into properties left vacant from icons such as Montgomery Ward. Discounters see these properties as a way to enter a densely populated urban market, often the only physical space available to them. Both Wal-Mart and Target are taking advantage of these opportunities, where the benefits include good real estate deals from vacant stores, well-established infrastructures, parking, and lighting, and a large number of people in their consumer segment. Mall managers not only get to fill the empty space, but see it as a way to increase sales for their other tenants. "At the very least, the newcomers might 'slow down' the death rates of some department stores," predicts retail consultant Burt Flickinger III of Strategic Resource Group. "In the brutal world of retailing, that's as close as you get to a win-win proposition."[1]

INTRODUCTION

Place decisions involve building relationships with wholesalers, retailers, and through these intermediaries, customers. The relationships may take years to develop, and even in the face of conflicts among channel members, are difficult to change. Products and services must be at the right place, in the right amounts, and at the right time in order to be consumed. This involves physical movement of the product and in most cases, storage. Physical distribution is costly and may account for as much as 50 percent of the marketing costs associated with a product. Many marketing managers considered these activities one of the last frontiers for cost reductions.

Probably the best way to perceive place is to think of the flow of products from manufacturers through intermediaries to the consumer or user. This flow can be thought of as a pipeline or channel used to move goods and services. Because we are following a societal marketing orientation in this planning guide, it could be anticipated by the reader that our first concern in planning the marketing decision regarding such a pipeline or channel is to focus on the customer. In fact, three basic questions should be foremost in the marketing planner's mind when making channel planning decisions:

1. What kinds of services have to be provided to end users by marketing channels in order to assure end user satisfaction, regardless of the specific channels employed?
2. What kinds of marketing and/or logistical activities or functions will have to be performed to generate those services?
3. Which types of institutions or agencies are in the best position to perform the activities, taking into account their effectiveness and their efficiency at doing so? Should potential channel members (e.g., manufacturers, wholesalers, and retailers) divide distribution labor with one another or would vertical integration likely be more successful in accomplishing the objectives established by the focal organization?[2]

Answers to these questions, and indeed answers to questions such as these for all the four components of the marketing mix, should be grounded in the previous stages of the planning process, which provided the planner with insights into the firm's value discipline, product/markets and targeted audience, sources of competitive advantage, objectives, etc. Planners at this stage of the process want to translate that previous analysis and subsequent decisions into a plan for a channel system. This channel plan, along with product, price, and promotion, will successfully enact the overall marketing strategy that sprang from that previous analysis.

WHO WILL BE CHANNEL CAPTAIN?

One aspect of channel management involves determining who has control over the decisions about distribution. The concept of a channel captain evolved to help explain that when several independent firms are involved, someone within the channel must take charge of the decisions to be made. The answer to this question has changed over time and depends on the market strength of the individual firms.

Historically, wholesalers were the early channel captains. Before the industrial revolution, wholesaling companies bought goods from overseas and moved them to retailers and frontier trading posts. As U.S. manufacturing developed with industrialization, these trading companies began losing power. The economic and market power of manufacturing firms and the limited size and power of most wholesalers and retailers meant that the manufacturers made the marketing decisions about where goods would be sold, the number and types of wholesalers and retailers that would be involved, and in general, the nature of the marketing process for their products. For many products, retailers have more recently become the channel captains.[3]

The growth of the chain retail stores that started in the 1930s has caused the control of some channels to shift to these large retail firms. Companies such as Sears, JCPenney, A&P, and Safeway maintain market control of most of the goods and services distributed through their stores. Many manufacturers even give up their identity in the channel because the goods carry the retailers' own brand names. In some instances, these retailers have integrated vertically and bought out manufacturing facilities.

In the future, it may be that consumers' desires to feel more in control of purchase options may radically alter the idea of a channel captain. Weiner and Brown talk of a consumer movement called *disinter-mediation,* where consumers' desire to gain more control of their marketplace choice and purchase options by asserting their power to remove the institutions that traditionally mediate the consumer's access to the desired product or service.[4] For example, more than a third of all retail sales are now out-of-store sales (e.g., direct, via catalogs, TV shopping, and the Internet), where consumers have "dismissed" the intermediators. The Internet has become a viable shopping vehicle where consumers can buy everything from prescription drugs to used automobiles through eBay. Virtually all major retailers now offer Web sites, contributing to the growth in Internet sales, which are expected to double during the next three years.[5] The following factors feeding the consumer's desire for control were suggested by Weiner and Brown:

- Advances in communications and information technology that are constantly and drastically reducing the cost of information
- Availability of more information through expanded media
- Substantially higher levels of education
- A widespread distrust of experts—and of authority in general
- A strong consumer-advocacy movement
- A resistance to arbitrary pricing practices

These trends, according to consumer-trends analyst Daniel Yankelovich, have resulted in the consumer demand for *alternatives*. When unsatisfied with available choices, consumers will create a demand for innovative solutions to their consumption problems. Hundreds of thousands of new services and goods firms are springing up as a response to this consumer drive toward disintermediation. Even traditional professional services such as law and medicine must innovate in the offering of specialized retail businesses (e.g., storefront dentistry, optometry, divorce consultants, will preparers), to satisfy the demand for alternative channels for their services. All types of organizations must carefully consider the shifting bases of power within the supplier-to-consumer channel for goods and services when developing the place decisions for their marketing plan.

In the final analysis, the level in the channel with the greatest degree of market power controls the channel of distribution. Decisions regarding distribution are made at a level. An understanding of where this power lies within a given channel is a great aid in the channel's decision-making process. Failure to understand how a given channel system works can create conflicts rather than cooperation within the channel.

WHICH TYPE OF CHANNEL SHOULD BE USED?

One basic decision in channel management is whether to use direct or indirect channels to distribute products. In a direct channel, the manufacturer deals directly with the consumer, whereas in an indirect channel, independent middlemen are used to reach the consumer. Both types of channels can be used. When different target markets are sought, different channels may be needed to reach them.

Most services (e.g., those offered by barbers, beauticians, and doctors) must be distributed directly because of the need for interaction between the provider and the recipient. However, some services are distributed through middlemen. For example, travel agents are middlemen for airlines, hotels, and other service providers. Some services, for example H&R Block tax service, have developed franchise systems. But still, the franchisees must create and distribute the service directly to consumers.

The basic channels of distribution that a marketer may use for consumer and industrial products are presented in Exhibit 11.1. Direct distribution of consumer products may be accomplished in a number of ways—through telephone sales, direct mail, door-to-door sales, party approaches (e.g., Tupperware, Discovery Toys), or company-owned retail outlets. Indirect channels may simply be through a retailer or the channel may be longer, using one or more wholesalers as well as a retailer. Similar approaches are available for industrial products. However, with industrial goods, middlemen are more likely to be called distributors. Four distinct factors influence the decision of the type of channel to use: (1) target markets sought, (2) nature of product, (3) availability of middlemen, and (4) financial resources. The combination of these factors usually determines which channels will be used, rather than any one factor alone. The decision should not be made until all these factors in their relevant combination have been evaluated extensively for a given situation.

The nature of the target market is a major influence. An appliance manufacturer may use a direct channel in dealing with large housing contractors (an industrial market) but use retail firms to reach the con-

EXHIBIT 11.1. Common channels of distribution.

Consumer goods			Industrial goods		
M	M	M	M	M	M
		W			W
				D	D
	R	R			
C	C	C	C	C	C
Direct	Indirect		Direct	Indirect	

sumer market. Direct channels—company-owned stores—may be used in geographical areas of high potential, and franchises may be used in other areas. When customers are geographically concentrated or an established market is involved, a direct channel may be used; however, indirect channels may be used to break into new territories or to reach geographically dispersed markets. Many industrial manufacturers, for example, will use their own sales force (direct channel) to reach customers in established territories and manufacturer's agents (indirect) to get into new territories. The manufacturers' agents build up business in the territory to the point where it will support a company salesperson.

The nature of the product is another influential factor in this decision-making process. Generally, a product must possess one of two characteristics (or both) in order for direct channels to be used: high unit value or broad product line. In other words, certain products will have a high volume of sales derived from one unit of high value, and others will generate dollar sales as part of a broad product line of relatively low-value items sold to one customer. Avon not only has a variety of women's cosmetics, but also a line of men's and children's products. This increases the chances of a larger individual order. Electrolux has maintained its own field sales force because of the high unit value of its items and also because of the philosophy of the need to demonstrate the product in use to increase sales. Highly perishable products are also more likely to be distributed directly.

The availability of existing middlemen is another factor. If the better wholesalers and/or retailers are already distributing competing brands or simply do not exist, a manufacturer may be forced to sell directly to consumers. In international markets, the strength of import-export companies and their access to markets are so compelling that this channel is normally used even when direct channels are common in domestic markets. A franchiser may prefer to have a franchise unit in a given area, but if no one wants to purchase the franchise and operate in that area, the franchiser may open a company-owned store. This is a common procedure.

A final factor is the financial strength of the firms in the channel. Direct channels may involve capital outlays beyond the scope of operations of the manufacturer. In this situation, indirect channels are used because of the lower financial demands on the manufacturer. Retail firms, on the other hand, may integrate horizontally, and as the number of stores increases, put pressure on manufacturers to deal directly with them. In this case, the financial strength of the retailer would force a manufacturer to use a direct channel.

Combinations of these factors may produce channel decisions that would not be made if only one factor was considered. For example, a manufacturer of a product with a high unit value may prefer to use direct channels but its limited financial resources force a different decision.

WHICH KIND OF MIDDLEMEN SHOULD BE USED?

If indirect channels are used, another decision concerns the kinds of middlemen to use to distribute the product. When several levels of middlemen are involved, this may involve the choice between different kinds of wholesales and retailers.

Two basic types of wholesalers can be used: agents or brokers and merchant wholesalers. Agents or brokers are used when the main need of the manufacturer is help with the selling function. Agents or brokers do not take title to the goods they deal in, and the main function they perform is providing market representation for the manufacturer.

Merchant wholesalers—which are what one commonly thinks of when referring to wholesaling—are more numerous and do about the same dollar volume as agents and brokers. They perform the functions of agents and brokers and they usually perform other functions as well—storage, delivery, and credit. They also take title to the goods. Performance of these additional functions usually entails higher expenses and higher gross margins.

At the retail level, the choice of firms to handle the product involves knowing in which kinds of stores (supermarkets, drug stores, and so on) the consumer expects to find different products, and within a given kind of store (drugstores, for example), the types of stores in which the product would be sold. This second area involves the image projected by the stores and their compatibility with the image the product projects to customers. If an overall strategy involves positioning a product as a luxury item in the jewelry line, the kinds of appropriate stores may be the higher-priced jewelry departments of exclusive department stores and limited-line jewelry stores appealing to upper-income customers. Two decisions were involved in this example: (1) to use jewelry stores or jewelry departments and (2) to use the more exclusive types to appeal to the high-income segment. Thus, the retail stores that carry the products are a part of the strategy design and not just an arbitrary choice. Since the retail facility is seen and experienced by the consumer, it must complement the overall strategy.

The indirect-direct and middleman decisions discussed here are merely a few of the long list of possible channel choices available. An Arthur Andersen study described more than fifty alternative channel choices available to firms seeking to develop systems capable of best answering the third question in this chapter's introduction.[6] Other alternatives, as yet underdeveloped or unthought of, may be needed to provide channel systems capable of delivering completely satisfying goods and services to end users. Marketing planners must constantly challenge themselves to find that competitive advantage in their strategy, which could potentially be found in the place decisions, which deliver superior customer value to target market customers.

MARKET EXPOSURE DECISIONS

The degree of market exposure refers to the number of retail outlets in a given geographical area that carry a product or service. Three basic degrees of market exposure are: intensive, selective, and exclusive. The decision on the degree of market exposure is closely related to the classification of the product.

Intensive distribution means that the product is carried by all acceptable outlets for the product type. It does not mean that all stores carry the product, but rather that all acceptable stores carry it. What makes a store acceptable is that the consumer expects to find the product at that type of store. This expectation changes over time, however, and departure from the usual can be an important strategy variable. Consequently, the consumer must learn to shop for different products at different stores. Consumers do not go to an automobile dealer to buy bread because they do not expect to find it there. Thus, consumer shopping patterns determine what acceptable outlets are in a given time period. Intensive distribution is usually used for convenience goods because consumers want to spend little time and effort acquiring these products. Bread, beverages, candy, and grocery products are distributed intensively in most areas and in a variety of outlets.

Selective distribution involves selecting only a few outlets in a market area to carry a product. Selection is usually based on the retail firm's ability to do a good marketing job with the product. This distribution policy is normally used for shopping goods because consumers are willing to put forth more effort to acquire them. The number of outlets in a market area is determined by the size of the market in terms of potential and the availability of retail firms that could carry the products. Thus, a given area may support only two Chevrolet dealerships but twenty outlets for suits because of the potential in units for the two products, yet both manufacturers may be using a selective distribution policy.

Exclusive distribution is limiting the products to one middleman in a given market area. Exclusive distribution has not received favorable treatment in the courts because it represents monopoly power on the part of a manufacturer who can refuse to sell to potential distributors. New products or companies who are new to an industry are permitted to do so. "New" has been interpreted to mean only six months. In some instances, what may look similar to exclusive distribution is in reality only a failure to find other suitable outlets for a product. The decision to use exclusive distribution may be the result of limited market potential for the product rather than the most desirable choice.

TRANSPORTATION AND STORAGE DECISIONS

As the planner develops the place part of strategy, he or she should consider who will transport and store the products in the channel and who will pay for the performance of these functions. Physical distribution, the hard side of marketing, involves the functions that physically move and store the products as they are distributed to consumers. As stated at the beginning of this chapter, place decisions involve establishing long-term relationships. This means that other firms involved in marketing similar products for which the plan is being developed have already established transportation modes and storage arrangements. Examining how these functions are currently being done is the first step in understanding the problems and processes involved in physical distribution.

Transportation

Five transportation modes are available. Listed in order of volume of ton miles moved, they are railroads, pipelines, trucks, inland waterways, and airways. For many products, more than one mode is used in moving goods to consumers, so the decision is one of relative emphasis.

Railroads

Railroads represent the workhorse of the transportation industry in terms of ton miles moved. They dominated the movement of commodities such as sand, coal, and lumber, which are bulky and heavy and can be transported at relatively low cost by the railroads. Although railroads have had many financial difficulties, they have made some comebacks with piggyback, which involves carrying loaded truck trailers long distances on railroad flatcars and fast freight service for perishable products.

Pipelines

Pipelines are used mainly to move petroleum products to refineries from the oil fields. In some cases, refined products are shipped to terminals by pipelines. These products are then carried to their final destination by truck or rail.

Trucks

The trucking industry often claims that "If you got it today, it came by truck," to emphasize that truck transportation is involved in the movement of most goods. Even when products are shipped by rail they usually reach their final destination by truck. Trucks have flexibility in terms of surfaces they can move on and are not limited, as with other carriers, to fixed physical routes. They not only provide fast service but also may have rates comparable to railroads and airlines for high-value products.

Inland Waterways

Movement of goods by water is one of the least-expensive methods of transportation. Nonperishable bulky commodities are shipped on barges that move both up- and downstream. One major problem is that their use is seasonal because of winter ice.

Airways

Airways usually are the fastest yet most expensive method of transportation. However, for many high-valued products, such as orchids, the added costs are justified because of the importance of speedy delivery. In some instances, the reduced packing costs for air shipment may offset some or all of the transportation costs.

Storage

Storage of products is necessary to deliver time utility—that is having the product available when the consumer wants it. Storage compensates for differences in growing or producing seasons and consumption periods. While toys are produced all year long, Toys-R-Us reports that almost half of its annual sales occur during the last two months of the year. In 2004 the company introduced its new Birthday Club in an effort to stimulate sales year-round.[7] Storage is used to keep products until the time they are wanted by consumers.

Two basic storage methods are available: private and public warehouses. Private warehouses, owned by individual companies for their own use, are feasible when large quantities of goods are stored on a regular basis. Although buying or building warehouse space increases fixed costs, it may reduce operating costs in the long run if public warehousing facilities were to be used extensively.

Public warehouses are a good alternative for firms that have seasonal needs for storage and cannot justify owning their own warehouses. Most public warehouses provide a variety of services and can offer widespread storage facilities for a company without the large capital outlays involved in private warehouses. They also can issue warehouse receipts for use as collateral for banks' loans.

THE PHYSICAL DISTRIBUTION CONCEPT

In recent years, physical distribution has received more attention because of the promise of reduced distribution costs. Part of this attention has resulted in what is called the physical distribution concept. Simply stated, this concept focuses on the total physical distribution process rather than on individual elements. It has involved new organizational positions, such as a distribution manager. It has also brought about the consolidation of some physical distribution functions and caused management to concentrate on total costs of distribution rather than on the costs of performing individual functions. This concept avoids the problem of achieving optimization in some individual functions and suboptimizing from a total approach. Using low-cost and slow transportation, for example, may create increased costs for storage. But, if a higher-cost and speedier transportation mode is used, these costs may be more than offset by lower storage costs, therefore yielding lower total distribution costs. This decrease cannot be realized unless an approach that focuses on the total and not just the individual functions is used.

Another aspect of this approach is that it concentrates on the needs of all those involved in the distribution of goods rather than just the manufacturer or carrier. Knowing that middlemen have palletized their warehousing operations, for example, may lead manufacturers to ship their products on disposable pallets if this is more compatible with both the middlemen and the carrier. This approach should help reduce conflicts in the physical distribution of goods and can lead to lower overall physical distribution costs.

Transportation charges can be borne by the seller or the buyer. If they are to be borne by the buyer, all shipments are sent free on board

(FOB) the point of origin. However, when the seller is going to pay for the transportation one of two alternatives is available: (1) charge each buyer the exact costs of transportation or (2) charge an average transportation cost for each order. The second method produces freight overcharges for some and undercharges for others. This method is usually used when thousands of small orders are involved and the cost of calculating individual transportation charges is not feasible. A variation of this approach is zone rates, where all buyers in a given zone are charged the same rate.

SUMMARY

Place decisions represent a crucial area for planners because of their long-term nature and the difficulty in altering them once established. Many new firms fail because of their inability to get distribution of their products. This is not only a difficult task but one that requires time and money. Consumers cannot buy products that are not available to them where and when they want them. Because place decisions move the products to the customers, they can be the key decision in a marketing strategy.

Traditional problems in distribution—the lack of available middlemen, for example—can be viewed as an opportunity for the creative. Timex was marketed through nontraditional outlets because the traditional outlets were "taken." This became a key to a successful strategy. Thus, place must be viewed from a broad perspective that considers the many dimensions covered in this chapter.

Chapter 12 discusses promotion, the third strategy variable and the communication part of the marketing mix.

Chapter 12

Promotion Decisions

MARKETING PLANNING IN ACTION: PRODUCT PLACEMENT

Crocodile Dundee and a friend pull into the drive-through of a Wendy's restaurant in his latest movie. In his usual flippant style, Dundee places an order and says, "Thank you, Wendy." He then chats with his friend about the availability of late-night cuisine. This scene is written into the script so that viewers hardly notice that they have just seen an advertisement for Wendy's restaurants. Product placement, the act of directly mentioning or displaying a product's brand name in a movie or television program, is now one of the fastest-growing forms of promotion used by advertisers. Marketers see the format as a way to more closely target the segments they want to reach. Although they cannot be assured that their potential customers will see a particular television commercial due to remote controls and TiVo, when someone is watching a movie or television program where the product is written into the script, it is difficult to escape. Movie producers see the format as a way to offset some of their production expenses. *Minority Report* with Tom Cruise received $25 million in product placement fees, which represented one-quarter of its total production cost. In the James Bond movie *Die Another Day,* Ford Motor Company reportedly entered into a $35 million marketing deal with MGM to promote three of its brands. Apparently the format has great success. In *Goldeneye,* James Bond drove a BMW Roadster, replacing his usual Aston Martin. Sales of the BMW Roadster were reported to have significantly increased after the movie was released.

The product placement trend is so popular that major companies such as Whirlpool Corporation have staff based in Los Angeles that serve as movie and TV agents for its brands. In a recent study, almost every television channel contacted had seen a rise in the use of product placement. However, advertisers are increasingly clever in their use of the promotional tool. In the beginning, they merely put the product's brand name or label in sight of the viewer. Now that is changing. Melissa Alcruz, VP-trade marketing at Universal Networks' USA Network says smaller advertisers are even getting into the act. She adds, "A few years ago people were saying, 'I just need my product there on the set.' But now they realize it needs to be integral and make sense for the show."[1]

INTRODUCTION

Promotional efforts are the most visible manifestation of the strategy at the heart of a marketing plan. Some observers might think of the promotional strategy as the marketing strategy. However, as evident from the location of this chapter in this book, much planning and strategizing must necessarily precede promotional decisions. As we have seen, the four elements of the marketing mix (product, place, price, and promotion) are the strategic and tactical tools by which we implement a positioning strategy, which is in turn the product of an extensive situation analysis. Until a solid positioning strategy is articulated to reach a clearly defined target audience, considering promotional decisions is not appropriate.

Promotional decisions center on what is to be communicated, to whom, through what methods and media, and at what appropriate costs. Promotion is necessary to inform, persuade, and remind consumers that a product exists and that they can benefit from the purchase of the product. For a market to exist, exchange must be possible, which necessitates buyers and sellers be able to meet together at a particular place to engage in an exchange of information. *Promotion* may be defined as an organization's activities that are designed to inform, persuade, or remind consumers about the organization and the products it offers.

Insight into the types of decisions involved in promotion can be gained by viewing it as a communication process (see Exhibit 12.1). In the communication process, a source (firm) sends a message by using a certain method or medium. This message reaches a receiver (consumer), who, by his or her words and actions, sends a message back to the source about what was received and his or her willingness

EXHIBIT 12.1. The communication process.

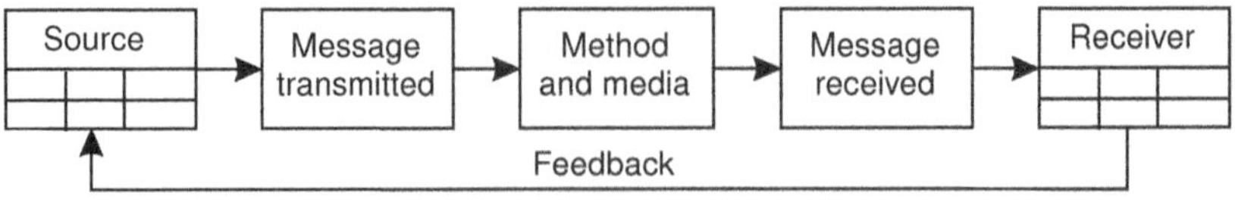

to respond to that message. This process is always goal oriented. The sender is communicating to get a response from the receiver. The response may internal, such as learning certain information or having certain attitudes, or it may show itself in more overt behavior through immediate or precipitant acts. Regardless, a response is desired.

The checkered areas in the sender's and receiver's boxes represent common frames of reference. A common frame of reference is a prerequisite to effective communication. Unless a common area of understanding is established between the sender and receiver, no communication takes place. One example is a language barrier. If the message is sent in English and the receiver understands only Spanish, no communication takes place. The symbols (words) used to communicate are not common to the two parties in the process.

One point that must always be included in the planner's thinking is that promotion from a planning perspective involves sending the right message to the right audience through the right medium by using the right methods at the right costs. Deciding what is "right" constitutes the marketing planner's work in the communications part of the marketing plan.

TARGET AUDIENCE DECISIONS

Two potential audiences to target communication efforts toward when indirect channels are used are: middlemen and consumers. When the communication is directed toward middlemen, and when products are "pushed" through the channels of distribution, it is referred to as a push strategy. A pull strategy is used when the effort is directed toward the consumer or user in an attempt to "pull" the products through the channels of distribution by stimulating demand from the final consumer. Normally, a firm promotes its products to both middlemen and consumers, so it is not an either-or decision but one of relative emphasis.

A push strategy is commonly used by firms with limited financial resources because of the difficulty in supporting a large-scale promotional campaign aimed at the ultimate consumer. In this situation, the key to a firm's success lies with the marketing skills and power of the middlemen. In effect, the task of promoting the product is turned over to wholesalers and/or retailers who are expected to communicate with consumers. If the product is readily accepted by consumers or is fairly important to the middlemen, they will put forth considerable effort. For example, little or no consumer advertising is undertaken for many grocery items. The manufacturers' salesmen call on wholesalers and retailers and get them to stock the item, which is in turn made available to consumers in the store. The shelf space, location, package, and price must complete the job of communicating to consumers who are in a "search mode" for products when they enter a store. The major problem with a push strategy is that if middlemen are carrying many different competing brands, any given brand may receive little direct attention.

A pull strategy promotes the products to the consumers or users. Thus, many brands are "presold" before the consumer reaches the retail store. Although this strategy does require large cash outlays when national markets are sought, it also provides the greatest degree of control over the product's promotion. The company can be sure not only that its products are being promoted to consumers, but also that they are being promoted as the company desires.

PROMOTIONAL METHODS DECISIONS

A company can use two basic methods to promote its goods and services: personal selling and nonpersonal selling. Nonpersonal selling includes advertising, sales promotion activities such as trade shows and displays, and publicity. Because most firms use more than one method, they develop a promotional mix to provide a complete communications program. The relative emphasis on personal selling and nonpersonal selling is determined by the type of product and its value.

Industrial products are normally promoted more heavily by personal selling. The characteristics of the industrial goods market, for example—geographic concentration of customers and large purchases—are conducive to emphasis on this method. Although nonpersonal selling may be used to build consumer awareness and provide information on a company and its products, the complete sales message is usually delivered by a salesperson. This is especially true when there are long lead times between plans for purchases and actual purchases or when products are designed specifically for the industrial consumer. If an extremely large and diverse target market exists, the importance of nonpersonal communications may increase; however, personal selling is still the main method of promotion. For example, Xerox advertises on national television to build company image and product recognition, but sales are made through a highly trained sales force that tailors the information to the individual customer.

For consumer goods, the major emphasis is on nonpersonal selling because of large diverse markets and the need to presell consumers on products and services before they get to a retail store. Even though the cost of an individual advertisement may be $100,000, if 50 million consumers were reached by the message, the cost per 1,000 would only be $2, and the cost per advertising impression would only be $.002—less than a penny per impression. Compare this to the cost of one personal sales call in the range of $25 to $125. Personal selling is still involved for most consumer goods, even for low-value items such as candy bars, but it is directed at middlemen rather than consumers.

The higher the value of the product and the more complex it is, the more likely the role of personal selling will increase. For homes, cars, washing machines, lawn mowers, and so on, the role of personal selling is increased because consumers want more information and need individual help.

Thus, the mix is determined by the nature of the product and the value of the product to the consumer. Although both methods are needed and used, one is usually emphasized more heavily in a particular strategy.

MEDIA DECISIONS

Advertisements must reach consumers through some medium. Selecting the most appropriate one is an important strategy decision. Although the details of the specific medium used, messages sent, timing, and frequency are usually spelled out in the operating marketing plan, the planner must evaluate various promotional alternatives because of the costs involved and the resulting impact on profitability. In many strategies, promotional expenditures represent the largest single marketing cost.

The two broad alternatives in media selection are: print media and broadcast media. As with many other decisions in marketing, choosing the right mix is essential rather than choosing one alternative and not another.

Even within a category—print, for example—a mix of various print vehicles are used rather than just one. The advantages and disadvantages of media types are shown in Exhibit 12.2.

EXHIBIT 12.2. Relative costs, advantages, and disadvantages of major kinds of media.

Media type	Typical cost range	Advantages	Disadvantages
Newspaper	$5,000-$20,000 for one page, weekday	Flexible Timely Local market Credible source	May be expensive Short life No "pass-along"
Television	$2,000-$100,000 for a thirty-second spot, prime time	Offers sight, sound, and motion Good attention Wide reach	Expensive in total "clutter" Short exposure Less selective audience
Direct mail	$35-150 per 1,000 names plus material and postage	Selected audience Flexible—can personalize	Relatively expensive per contact "Junk mail"—hard to retain attention
Radio	$100-200 for one-minute drive time	Wide reach Segmented audiences Inexpensive	Offers audio only Weak attention Many different rates Short exposure
Magazine	$5,000-20,000 for a one-page, four-color ad	Very segmented audiences Credible source Good reproduction Long life Good "pass-along"	Inflexible Long lead times
Outdoor	$4,000-5,000 (painted) prime billboard, thirty- to sixty-day showings	Flexible Repeat exposure Inexpensive	"Mass market" Very short exposure

Several firms have focused on a form of promotion called *experiential marketing,* which combines relationship marketing, sampling, and public relations into a new type of event marketing. Companies take their products on the road, literally. During a recent summer, Home Depot paid college interns to drive an orange Volkswagen Beetle across country, emblazoned with the Home Depot logo. Towing a light-weight trailer that contained several pop-up type exhibits, the interns did training programs for consumers on several new products in parking lots across America. Chevrolet also used the experiential marketing technique to market its newly transformed 2004 Corvette. The company collected thousands of responses via e-mail about interest in the Corvette. It used this information to take the Corvette on the road, conducting minirallies in towns with the greatest interest in the car.[2]

Media selection begins with the characteristics of the consumers to be reached. Different media have different audience characteristics, and therefore a matching process must take place. The characteristics of the media audience must match the characteristics of the market segments to which effort is directed. This maximizes reach—the number of different people or households exposed to a particular medium at a given time. For television, the audience varies depending on the time of day, day of the week, and the specific programs shown. Thus, current audience analysis data for specific times and programs are necessary for effective reach.

In addition to reach, frequency and impact of various media must be analyzed. Frequency refers to the number of times an audience is exposed to a particular message in a given time period; impact is the quality of the exposure in a given medium. The importance of additional exposures to the same message or type of message, and the impact of each exposure together with reach, determines media effectiveness; various media costs determine efficiency. The planner is searching for a media combination that is both effective and efficient.

The kind of analysis shown in Exhibits 12.3 and 12.4 must be completed for various media alternatives to develop the best media mix. Although this exhibit compares only magazines, the same approach can be followed for other media. This approach permits a comparison on the basis of reach, frequency, impact, and costs. All these factors together determine the most appropriate medium.

EXHIBIT 12.3. Media analysis worksheet—Radio audience characteristics by station.

Characteristic	KROC	KLAZ	KJAZ	KOUN
Age	13-25	40+	35-55	18+
Sex	Male 75%	Female 60%	Male 75%	Male 60%
Education	High school/ college	College	College	College
Location	Metro area	Metro area	Metro area	Metro south
Music style	Rock	Easy listening	Jazz	Country
Cost per one-minute spot 7:30-8:00 a.m.	$125	$150	$110	$135
Audience size	10,000	20,000	9,000	16,000
Cost per contact	$.0125	$.0075	$.0122	$.0084

Note: Artificial data and names are used.

The media planner must also be aware of new technology developments that create new forms of media. The widespread availability of facsimile (fax) machines has had companies evaluating their use as an advertising media.[3] Other companies are using wireless technology to broadcast advertising messages through customers' cell phones.[4]

In addition to analyzing individual media types the planner must also consider combining several media types into a promotional campaign. In recent years, more and more companies are finding that a telemarketing campaign, which generates leads, can be followed by a direct mail campaign to put promotional material in the hands of consumers who have already been screened by the telemarketing calls.

MESSAGE CONTENT DECISIONS

Although the sender is the initiator of the communication process, the process really begins with the receiver—the customer. This should be obvious, but is often overlooked because of an organization's desire to tell its "story." Effective communication involves sending the right message, and the right message is the one that will produce the

EXHIBIT 12.4. Media analysis worksheet—magazines.

Characteristic	Consumer Segment	Better Gardens	Green Thumb	Gardener's Journal
Age	35	34	30	46
Sex		Male 50% Female 50%	Male 60% Female 40%	Male 75% Female 25%
Education	College	College	College	High school
Occupation	White collar Blue collar	WC 40% BC 60%	WC 70% BC 30%	WC 30% BC 70%
Marital status	Married Single	M 70% S 30%	M 60% S 40%	M 90% S 10%
Location	South	South 78%	South 60%	South 35%
Hobbies	Gardening Sports Crafts	Yes Yes No	Yes Yes No	Yes No Yes
Gardening interest type		Serious	Light	Serious
Skill level	High	High	Medium	High
Prestige rating		1.7	1.8	2
Readership subscriptions		38,000	40,000	26,000
Pass-along readership		2	1.5	2
Total		76,000	60,000	52,000
Life		6 months	3 months	5 years
Publication times		Bimonthly	Monthly	Monthly
Cost/full page color		$6,000	$4,000	$3,800
Cost/1,000		$0.79	$0.67	$0.73

Note: Artificial data and names are used.

response desired by the organization from the customer. This is not manipulative but integrative. The needs and wants of customers for certain types of information are integrated into the messages that are sent. Here again the planner benefits from the direction provided by a societal marketing orientation—i.e., the "outside-in" perspective. If the marketing plan to this point has been developed by carefully considering the nature of the product/market and the targeted segment, the message content has already begun to take form. The question then is how to put the positioning strategy with its emphasis on exploiting a competitive advantage into words that will hit the target audience's "sweet spot." Variations in the message will need to take into account where the consumer is in the adoption process of the product. A simple way to approach this concept is to look at the individual adoption process for new products. This process is made up of the stages a consumer goes through in learning about and using a service. These stages and the questions a consumer wants answered are shown in Exhibit 12.5.

As individual consumers move through these adoption stages in larger numbers, the program begins to move through its life cycle, which brings about the need to align the messages with the stages in the life cycle. In the introductory stages, promotion messages must inform potential customers of the offering. In the growth stage, mes-

EXHIBIT 12.5. Individual adoption stages and information needs.

Stage in adoption process	Questions consumers want answered
1. *Awareness:* Consumer first learns of product, service, or store.	What are you all about? What do you do?
2. *Interest:* Consumer is stimulated to get more information.	Why would anyone buy your products? What benefits would they get?
3. *Evaluation:* Consumer considers trying the product.	Why should I buy your firm's products?
4. *Trial:* Consumer tries product.	Will it really deliver those claimed benefits? Can I risk trying the product?
5. *Adoption:* Consumer decides to use the product on a regular basis.	Did I make the right decision?
6. *Repeat:* Customer may reevaluate decision.	Should I use the same product again or are there better alternatives?

sages must encourage them to use a specific product rather than competing products. The maturity stage brings the need for reminding customers of the products to build repeat use/referrals. Thus, messages stressing the firm's competitive advantage must be developed to answer consumer's questions and to reflect the nature of the service at a given time.

Since different consumers will be at various stages of adoption and levels of knowledge and experience, a variety of messages conveying different types of information is usually necessary to communicate effectively with different consumers. Although most customers are concerned about the benefits received from a product, some are interested in the detailed information that produces those benefits. Such detailed information should be available to consumers who request it. Exhibit 12.6 details how advertising messages should differ based on the type of audience for products in slow-growth markets.

The information from the consumer analysis is vital in communications decisions on message content. The needs and motives of con-

EXHIBIT 12.6. Advertising implications for slow-growth markets.

Target audience	Implication for advertisers
Nonusers	This group is less likely to attend to advertising. Effective advertising suggests new uses that nonusers can begin to see as solutions to the problems. Generally, this is the least important group to reach with advertising.
Loyal customers	Advertising does not perform as an awareness or persuasive function, but more as reinforcement of this group's "wisdom" and to increase frequency and occasions of usage. The objective is to discourage consideration of switching. Advertising to loyal users of competitive brands should focus on leveraging your competitive advantage.
Brand switchers	If switching is based on price, advertising should promote price difference. If it is convenient availability, remind the audience where it can be purchased. Create strong brand personality with people whose choice is primarily based on familiarity.
Emerging new users	Advertising should create awareness and build brand image to generate product trial. Messages and media must be appropriate to the emerging users' subculture.

Source: Adapted from Stewart, David W. Advertising in a Slow-Growth Economy. *American Demographics,* September 1994, pp. 40-46.

sumers become the center of content decisions. Information from testing, where alternate messages are evaluated, and other research to test the message content and probable consumer responses are extremely valuable. If time and money permit, messages should be tested before use, and response measures indicative of consumer responses should be evaluated in the decision-making process.

PERSONAL SELLING STRATEGY DECISIONS

Regardless of the emphasis on personal and nonpersonal selling, every firm has someone who is assigned the responsibility for dealing with customers and taking them through the selling process shown in Exhibit 12.7. These people are the company's sales force. Sales force decisions revolve around four key areas: quality, number, organization, and compensation.

Quality

The quality of the sales force refers to the level of education and experience of its members. The first step in determining the quality needed is to examine the job description to identify the tasks to be performed by the salespeople. If the sales task is basically order taking, a high level of skill is not necessary. On the other hand, where the sales job is complex, selling a word processing center to a large company, for example, a higher-caliber salesperson is needed. The quality of the sales force is determined basically by the nature of the job to be performed and the importance of the individual salesperson to the company. The greater his or her importance to the company's success, the higher the quality needs to be.

Number

The number of salespeople needed in a given time period can be determined two ways. One is a "bottom-up" approach and the other a "top-down." The bottom-up approach begins by identifying the number of customers, the amount of time to be spent with each, the number of calls to be made on each customer per period, and from this information, the number of customers each salesperson can handle. This number is divided into the number of customers to determine the

EXHIBIT 12.7. The personal selling process.

Step 1: *Customer identification.* The purpose of this step is to identify specifically who will be contacted. Information such as spelling and pronunciation of names, addresses, and telephone numbers should be verified at this stage.

Step 2: *Preapproach.* This step is used to collect information that would be helpful in relating to customers: their prior contact with the firm, their personal background, their firm's business activities, etc.

Step 3: *Approach.* This step refers to how to begin the conversation with the consumer. Approaches include the following:

(1) *Referral.* "Mr. Jones said you were interested in . . ."

(2) *Reminder.* "You telephoned previously . . ."

(3) *Question.* "Would you be interested in hearing how . . . ?"

Step 4: *Telling your story.* This step is where you tell the story of your firm. It includes information on what the organization is, what it does, and what benefits the consumer would receive from buying your firm's products. Many organizations give printed material to prospects. This ensures consistency in the information they distribute. It also provides something specific to say about the organization.

Step 5: *Answering questions.* The communication process must not be one-way. The prospect must be given the opportunity to ask questions and make comments. The questions and comments are feedback that enable you to respond to questions the consumer is interested in.

Step 6: *Closing.* This step gives you the opportunity to make closing statements. These statements may be used to set up another visit or to elicit some specific action from the consumer such as giving an order for the product.

Step 7: *Follow-up.* The final step is often overlooked. A card, letter, or telephone call can reap great rewards in terms of stressing interest in consumers or just letting them know how much you appreciate their time.

size of the sales force. For example, if each salesman should spend an average of one hour with each customer, call once a month, and average six calls a day, a salesperson could handle 120 customers—six calls a day, five days a week, four weeks a month. When 120 is divided into the total number of customers, the size of the sales force can be determined.

The top-down approach begins with the total market potential of the firm divided into an equal number of territories. It then determines the number of salespeople needed to cover these territories. If total potential were 100,000 units and territories were designed with 5,000 potential units each, 20 salespeople would be needed.

A combined approach would consider both the workloads of the sales force in terms of number and type of sales calls and the potential represented by the market areas in which customers are located. This approach would relate both customers' needs and sales potential to the size of the sales force.

Organization

A sales force can be organized three ways: by products, geographical territories, and customer type. A fourth possibility would be to combine two or more of these approaches. The most commonly used organizational structure is territorial. This approach is in line with a movement to the concept of territorial management by salespersons. The territorial approach is best used when the salesperson sells all products to all customers, which avoids duplicated coverage of the territory, customers, or both. Duplication of coverage is a common problem when the sales force is organized by customers or products. More than one salesperson from the same company is calling on the same customer or is in the same territory.

Where the complexity of a company's products or the breadth of the line do not permit organizing by territory, a product organizational structure is used. In this approach, a separate sales force is hired to sell different products or parts of the product line. If some customers buy products from several lines, duplication of effort cannot be avoided. This approach is justified by the greater depth of product knowledge possessed by each salesperson.

When the needs of customers are completely different, a sales force can be organized by customer type. A common breakdown in the sales force is between industrial users and the ultimate consumer. A variation is key account selling. Certain accounts, the larger or more complex, are designated as key accounts and salespeople are assigned to cover them. Central buying offices for retail chains are typically considered key accounts, and a separate sales force may be assigned to these accounts. Another variation of this structure is to divide by government, institution, and business.

These approaches can be combined so that some salespeople call on only government accounts in a certain region. Thus, a combination of customer and geographic structures are used.

Compensation

A company can compensate its sales force in both financial and nonfinancial ways. Nonfinancial compensation refers to opportunity, recognition, and advancement. Financial compensation is monetary in nature and can be direct—monthly pay—or indirect—a paid vacation.

Three compensation plans are used for direct financial compensation. One plan is to pay salespeople a straight salary. In this instance, the firm is paying for a unit of time—week, month, or whatever. This plan is commonly used when the sales job is technical in nature and/or long negotiation periods are involved in the selling process. It provides maximum security but may not offer much incentive for above-average performance unless it is carefully administered.

By contrast, a straight commission is used to compensate the sales force for units of accomplishment or performance rather than units of time. This plan is commonly used when a great deal of stimulus is needed to motivate the salespeople and when it is preferred by the sales force. It provides maximum stimulus but may not provide much security unless a drawing account is used.

The most commonly used compensation plan is the combination plan. This attempts to combine elements of the other two plans—security and incentive. Under this plan, a base salary is paid and additional compensation is tied to performance. Most salespeople prefer this plan because it gives them an opportunity to increase their income through additional effort and at the same time provides for basic necessities during a personal or economic slump.

SALES PROMOTION DECISIONS

Sales promotion activities are used to coordinate personal selling and advertising or to increase their effectiveness. Although nonrepetitive in nature, when one type is successful it may be continued for years. The Macy's Thanksgiving Day Parade is an example of a special promotional event that has become a tradition. Sales promotion activities are diverse in nature, but the most common types are shown in Exhibit 12.8.

These promotional activities can have a significant influence on sales. The use of an in-store product display that complements and/or reinforces advertising can effectively make the transfer from what is seen on television at home to the product display in the retail store where sales occur.

PUBLICITY DECISIONS

Publicity, when properly managed, offers another opportunity to promote a company's offering but in a way unlike those discussed thus far. Publicity involves mass communications transmitted through the media in editorial space rather than paid space. Any time a company or its products and services create news through the media, the firm is using publicity. Publicity could be called "the velvet hammer

---

EXHIBIT 12.8. Common sales promotion activities.

Point-of-purchase advertising: In-store promotion, such as life-size figures, hanging signs or figures, and displays is common.

Specialty advertising: Token coins, pencils, match covers, yardsticks, balloons, etc., carry a product or store name and message.

Trade shows and fairs: Product or company displays, set up for channel members or consumers, at boat shows, antique car shows, and equipment exhibits are common examples. Trade shows are especially useful for industrial products.

Samples, coupons, and premiums: Samples of products, coupons for discounted prices, and additional products are commonly used to stimulate sales. Coupons are widely used as a purchase incentive.

Contests: Firms often sponsor contests to build traffic by bringing customers back or offering special prizes to entrants.

Trading stamps: Although they have declined in popularity to some extent, stamps are distributed to consumers who redeem them for products.

Miscellaneous activities: These are the wide variety of promotions used in store openings, anniversary sales, and other special events. They may involve complimentary products—soft drinks, for example—or popular characters in costume who roam through the store to entertain children.

of promotion" because it can drive home a point in an unobvious manner.

When Cities Service Company changed the name of its petroleum marketing division to Citgo it was part of a significant change in its marketing program. The result of the carefully planned publicity was national news space in magazines, television, radio, and newspapers. Thus, many customers were informed about the company's new brands and programs through the media, and the time and space did not cost the company anything.

Publicity can also be negative since mistakes in products, court cases, oil spills, failures, and so on also make the news. For example, the Exxon oil spill caused the company to receive a great deal of negative publicity. Publicity is usually managed by a public relations department because a company must communicate with many people and this activity needs to be managed to be effective.

PROMOTIONAL BUDGETING DECISIONS

The question of how much to spend on promotion of a product or service is one of the most difficult decisions to make. The reason is the difficulty of knowing when you are spending too much or too little. One company president quipped that he knew 50 percent of his promotional budget was wasted—he just did not know which half. Several alternative ways can allocate promotional budgets, the most common being: (1) a percent of sales, (2) an amount per unit, (3) a match of competitive expenditures, (4) as much as can be afforded, and (5) the task objective.

The task objective method is a concept similar to zero-based budgeting. It begins with a complete definition of exactly what is to be accomplished—the objective or task—and then proceeds to determine what must be spent to accomplish that task. When this approach is used, two assumptions are made. One is that the amount needed to accomplish a given task or objective can be determined. The second is that the objective or task is important enough to warrant whatever levels of expenditures are necessary to accomplish it. The first assumption is the more difficult to justify because relationships between promotional expenditures and results are hard to validate. Thus, in most cases it is a matter of spending what is thought to be necessary to reach the objective. Until valid methods with wide applications are developed to quantify the relationships between promotional expenditures and results, this may be the best that can be done.

SUMMARY

Promotional decisions deal with the communications aspect of the marketing strategy. Many areas are involved, and in most cases a blend or mix of methods, media, and techniques is used rather than singular approaches. A promotional approach is developed in the strategic plan to communicate the firm's offering to both consumers and middlemen.

The many variations in promotional tools and techniques provide a great deal of latitude for the strategist, and in most cases help is available and advisable from advertising departments and agencies to develop a total promotional effect.

Chapter 13 presents the price variable, the last variable to be covered as a part of the marketing mix.

Chapter 13

Price Decisions

MARKETING PLANNING IN ACTION:
HOTEL PRICE GUARANTEES

Americans have changed the way they travel. A sagging economy, the wealth of information on the Internet, and cutbacks in business travel have all contributed to the less-than-bustling hotel industry. Corporations now curtail their employees' frequent trips out of town, opting instead to conduct business via the telephone and Internet. Hotels target leisure travelers to fill that gap and increase occupancy rates. One tool they are using is the price guarantee.

The hotel industry knows that price is a salient factor in leisure travelers' choices of where to stay. Add to that the easy access via the Internet to prices of hotels around the world, and customers are able to bargain shop online in a matter of minutes. Several major hotel chains are attempting to fight back with price guarantees that state that if a customer finds a lower price on an Internet discount site such as Expedia.com or Travelocity.com, the hotel will match it. Choice Hotels International, the parent of hotels such as Comfort Inn, Comfort Suites, and Econo Lodge, offers to undercut any price found on the Internet by 10 percent. However, what may sound like a significant benefit to the customer also has its limits. Some hotel chains refuse to honor the guarantee unless the rooms are *exactly* the same, down to the minutia—such as whether the room has an Internet connection. In addition, the hotels refuse to honor the guarantee to customers who find the lower rates on sites such as Priceline.com or Hotwire.com, where many of the lowest discounts are found. Hotels are eager to steer customers to their own online sites, since they lose as much as 40 percent in profit when rooms are booked by online travel brokers. Currently 9 percent of all hotel rooms are booked through online independent travel sites.

It remains to be seen if the guarantees will bring business in, or alienate the customer through the refusal to honor such. Perhaps this is why sites such as Hotels.com and Expedia.com are not worried about the hotel chains' price guarantees. "The way people shop Hotels.com is, what's the best rate for my location and in the category I'm looking for," says Bob Diener of Hotels.com. "It's not who's got the best rate on a specific hotel."[1]

INTRODUCTION

Pricing decisions have gained importance in recent years because of increased competition and increasing concern over budget management by both firms and households. Also, when de-marketing is used to reduce the demand for a product or service because of scarcity of product supplies, the price is one variable that can bring about immediate market response. Price may not be the determining factor in a decision for a consumer, but it is usually at least a qualifying factor. Price is always a consideration for consumers and, therefore, for marketing planners.

This chapter deals with the pricing decisions that must be made and the approaches used to make those decisions. The factors influencing the decisions and approaches will also be identified and discussed. A section on pricing policies is included because of the consistent nature of some of the questions concerning price for which a firm must develop a policy statement.

PRICE LEVEL DECISIONS

Pricing decisions provide the most visible example of the need for a firm to consider both internal (costs and profit objectives) as well as external (customer demand and competition) factors when making decisions. Although the level of influence of these and other factors will vary from firm to firm, some factors may dominate the price-setting process. For example, one approach to price decisions is pricing a product in relation to its competition. Three alternatives are possible for that decision: above competition, equal to competition, and below competition.

When the product or service is substantially above competition, the quality and/or prestige of the product must be such that consumers are convinced that the value represented is worth the higher price. In some cases, this is due to higher product quality represented by better engineering or better quality raw materials being used in production. In the case of services, this may be higher skill levels passed by the provider. Curtis Mathes, Inc., advertised for years that it was the most expensive television on the market because of the quality materials and workmanship involved in production. Although most consumers cannot judge quality differences in televisions during purchase, Curtis Mathes has a four-year warranty on the product, which is longer than that normally given by other companies. The warranty backs up the claim of better quality.

Pricing with the market does mean very similar prices. When prices are set in this manner, price is in effect neutralized and nonprice components of the marketing mix must be used to differentiate a product from its competitors. Firms use this approach because price changes are the easiest for competitors to copy. If a unique product or a successful advertising campaign is developed, competitors may never duplicate these efforts. If price is the same between alternatives, the consumer must make a choice on the basis of other factors, and planners alter these factors to differentiate their offering in the marketplace. This approach is also used in oligopoly situations because of fear of retaliation from competitors if prices are altered.

Pricing below the market implies that price will be used as the active variable in the marketing mix. If lower levels of quality are used, this may be the average price in a different market rather than a lower price for competing products. Firms often use below-market pricing when entering a new market or when trying to capture a large market share. Demand for the product must be elastic enough to offset the lower price per unit with increased volume or a lower level of profits will result. Since many consumers associate price with quality, a price substantially below the market may suggest reduced product quality. When this happens, lower prices produce lower levels of volume—a positive sloping demand curve.

PRICE DETERMINATION

When a firm sets the price at which it wants to sell its products or services, a balance must be struck between what the company wants to charge and what middlemen and consumers will accept. To put it another way, price determinations usually reflect both demand and supply considerations.

Cost-Oriented Pricing

One approach to determining price emphasizes the cost of manufacturing and marketing and the rate of return desired by the pricing firm. Two cost-oriented approaches commonly used are cost-plus and break-even analysis. The cost-plus approach emphasizes unit cost, whereas break-even analysis emphasizes total cost.

Exhibit 13.1 illustrates the behavior of several average cost curves over a production range. Fixed costs remain constant in total, but as the quantity produced increases, average fixed costs (AFC) decline. Average variable costs decrease at first but then begin to increase at higher production levels because of diminishing returns. Average costs, the sum of average fixed costs and average variable costs, follow a pattern similar to that of the variable costs curve. When the cost-plus approach is used, the average unit cost is determined to which is added as an amount per unit to cover marketing costs and profit. This amount can be determined in a number of ways. It could represent a set rate—percentage per dollar of sales—or it could reflect the profit per unit needed to reach a total profit desired by the company. Thus, unit production and marketing costs would represent a base to which a profit contribution per unit is added.

One obvious problem with this approach is that the outcome of the pricing formula actually depends on how stable demand is going to

EXHIBIT 13.1. Cost curves by production levels.

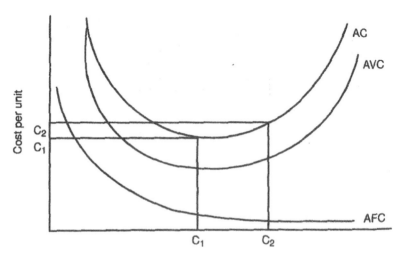

be. If volume is different from that used to set the price, cost per unit will be different and a given price could produce losses. Regardless of the variations that appear in this approach, it is not going to be as effective as one that directly considers demand in setting price.

Wholesalers and retailers customarily use a cost-plus approach when a standard markup is used storewide or when an average markup is used by departments. The wholesaler's cost is the price paid to the manufacturer for the product. In turn, the retailer's cost is the price paid to wholesalers. If a markup is added to this basic cost, the cost-plus approach is being used. The reason for the continued use of this type of pricing is the large number of items carried and the difficulty of pricing each item separately. Manufacturers should realize that markups in the price used by channel members will directly influence the price consumers pay. Different channels will require different markups, depending on services performed, and therefore channel selection influences price.

Another cost-oriented approach is break-even analysis, which concentrates on showing the relationship of total cost to total revenue for a given price (see Exhibit 13.2). This approach is often used in analyzing price-volume relationships.

To generate a break-even chart, total fixed costs are plotted. These costs by nature do not vary in total; therefore, for any given level of output they represent the same level of costs. Variable costs are assumed to be constant per unit and to vary in total. They would be zero with no production and are positive throughout, varying with levels of output. The total revenue line is generated by assuming a price and multiplying it by alternate levels of output. The break-even point is that point where the total revenue (TR) line and the total costs (TC) line intersect and profits are zero. To the right of the break-even point, TR is greater than TC and profits result. To the left of the break-even point is the area of losses, since total cost exceeds total revenue. Three obvious weaknesses in this approach to price determination are: (1) variable costs do not remain constant per unit; (2) price per unit is not constant for various levels of output unless pure competition is assumed; and (3) a price had to be assumed to calculate TR when the objective was to use the analysis to determine price. The first two assumptions can be accepted if a "relevant range" is employed to consider narrow movements along a total revenue or total cost curve, since exact points on a curve could be estimated by a

EXHIBIT 13.2. Break-even analysis.

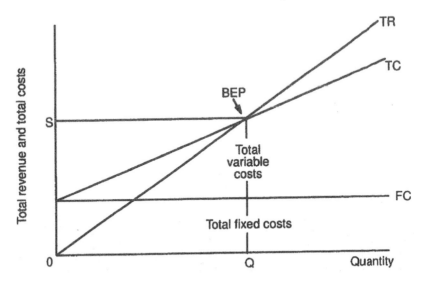

straight line for small movements. However, the last assumption means break-even analysis is more useful for looking at the consequences of a pricing decision than in determining price. The actual position in which a firm finds itself on the break-even chart depends on the level of output bought in a given time period. Thus, the quantity demanded at a specific price determines total revenue.

Demand-Oriented Pricing

The most vivid shortcoming of cost-oriented approaches to price determination is that the level of demand determines the success of these approaches in reaching a predetermined level of profit. Demand must be worked into the analysis to develop a market-oriented price structure. Three approaches to demand-oriented pricing will be discussed: flexible break-even analysis, demand-backward pricing, and demand-cost curve analysis. Flexible break-even analysis uses the break-even chart with two alterations. First, several total revenue lines are generated by assuming alternate prices. A second change is that the quantity demanded is estimated at each alternative price. Each point on each TR line represents an estimate of the quantity that could be sold at each of the prices. Connecting these together generates a curve that shows the areas of profitability for various prices. A flexible break-even chart is shown in Exhibit 13.3.

The quantities demanded at various prices could be based on: (1) historical data, if prices have changed little over time; (2) test market data using alternate prices; or (3) surveys of consumers, middlemen, and/or sales personnel. This approach permits estimating the most profitable price and other profitable prices, which can be used if objectives other than profit maximization are sought.

Another approach that directly considers demand is called demand-backward pricing. In this approach, the retail price is set first and then the product quality and marketing costs are adjusted to this price. For example, a manufacturer of microwave ovens may decide that a substantial market exists for microwaves that would carry a retail price of about $200. As a result, the quality and marketing effort are adjusted to this retail price. In other words, the price is set first and then the costs that could be tolerated for production and marketing at that price are determined. This approach may be especially useful when a positioning strategy is used and price is the key variable in positioning. An accurate estimate of demand must still be provided to use this approach successfully.

EXHIBIT 13.3. Flexible break-even analysis.

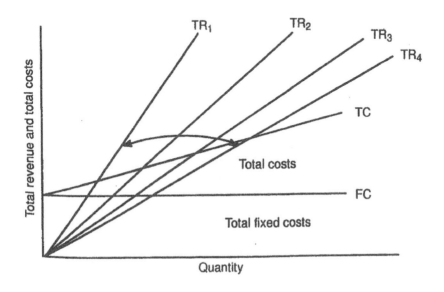

One of the most comprehensive approaches to pricing is a demand-cost curve. Prices set reflect considerations of both demand and costs (see Exhibit 13.4). Although this approach is theoretical in nature and many problems are involved in applying it to a given pricing decision, the major benefit is a consideration of both demand and costs in price determination.

The most difficult problem is estimating the demand curve. The approaches to estimating demand were previously identified, but each approach produces only an estimate. It might appear that estimating the demand curve could easily be attained by simply locating two points on the curve and connecting them together. If only two points on a demand curve are estimated, an assumption is needed if they are connected by a straight line. This approach assumes a linear relationship between price and quantity demanded. If the relationship is not linear but curvilinear, the marginal revenue line shown in Exhibit 13.4 is undefined.

If the linear demand curve is assumed, the profit-maximizing point is where marginal costs (MC) and marginal revenues (MR) are equal. For quantities to the left of that point, each unit adds more to revenue

EXHIBIT 13.4. Demand cost-curve pricing.

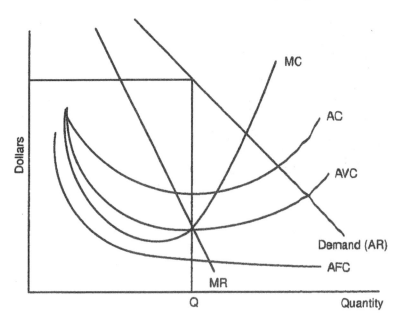

than to costs, so any increase in units sold will increase total profit. To the right of that point, each unit adds more to costs than to profits and fewer should be sold.

The MR = MC intersection is the profit-maximizing quantity. To determine price, the average revenue or demand curve must be used to find the price at which that particular quantity could be sold. If the profit-maximizing point is determined, alternate prices can be analyzed to take into consideration other objectives.

NEW PRODUCT PRICING DECISIONS

Pricing new products is an extremely difficult process unless substantial marketing research using surveys and/or test market data has helped identify consumer expectations about prices. When test markets are used, market data on quantities demanded at various prices can be generated. This method provides an initial estimate of the demand curve that can be used to equate marginal cost and marginal revenue.

Two common approaches to new product pricing, which reflect different marketing objectives and market conditions, are penetration pricing and skimming pricing. Penetration pricing refers to a new product price set close to what the planner feels the long-run price, after competitors enter the market, will be. As was pointed out in an earlier chapter, firms entering the market late may use price as the active variable in their marketing mix in order to gain market acceptance. This lower price is anticipated by the planner who uses it as the initial price for the new product. Sometimes called a "stay out" price, it discourages competitors from entering the market because of the low profit margin. This low price also may encourage product trial and speed penetration of the entire market for the product or service.

A skimming approach places a high initial price on the product or service and assumes some price inelasticity—that a substantial number of consumers will pay a high price, for example. This creates a very high profit per unit in the introductory stage of the product life cycle and helps recoup product development and early market development costs. The price is then lowered over time as the market expands and sales volume increases. This approach can attract competitors unless a unique product is involved or a strong patent is obtained on the product, which slows market entrance by competitors. One unique feature of the skimming approach is that it becomes possible to estimate points on the demand curve as price is lowered. This technique provides the data needed to estimate the marginal revenue curve and therefore a profit-maximizing price.

One increasingly popular management science tool for helping marketers set prices for new products is conjoint analysis. This technique is sometimes referred to as trade-off analysis because research respondents in a conjoint study indicate preference for different combinations of product attributes (e.g., for a car battery with a $60 price, lifetime warranty, and that is maintenance free versus one with a $55 price, five-year warranty, and that is maintenance free), which reveals where they are or are not willing to make trade-offs (e.g., Will they "trade-off" $5 more expense to get a lifetime rather than five-year warranty?).

Conjoint analysis has proven its value in thousands of studies as a means of helping marketers identify a price that target market consumers perceive as providing a good trade-off with the desired product features. It forces consumers to reveal how valued the product features really are to them by indicating when they will or will not pay more to get those features. This analytical tool overcomes the problems inherent in research methods, which merely ask participants to indicate independently the importance they attach to a product feature (e.g., most features are rated as important) and what they think the price should be (always low). Interested readers should refer to one of the more detailed descriptions of how conjoint analysis is conducted and the results used for setting prices and fixing product features.[2]

PRICING POLICY DECISIONS

Policies need to be developed for some aspects of pricing decisions. These are the reoccurring decision-making situations faced on a regular basis. The four policy areas to be discussed are: (1) price flexibility, (2) price discount, (3) geographic pricing, and (4) price lining.

Price Flexibility

These policies deal with the question of whether all customers who buy under the same conditions will pay the same price or pay a negotiated price policy. A one-price policy means charging all customers the same price. Retailers and wholesalers normally use this policy except for high-value items where individual price concessions are made. This does not mean that prices are not reduced for sales, out-of-season products, or damaged goods. It also does not mean that prices for goods or services bought under different conditions will be the same. No individual price negotiations are permitted when this policy is used. For low-value items (grocery items, for example), the time and effort involved in negotiating is not worth the trouble.

A flexible price policy results in a negotiated price, the actual price being determined by the negotiating skills of the buyer and seller and the range within which the seller will negotiate. This method is commonly used on high-value items. Situations in which the salesperson alters the price to beat a competitor's price are common for many types of products and services. Thus, different customers pay different prices for the same products.

Some manufacturers of consumer goods also use flexible price policies in their sales to different retailers based on geographical factors. Procter & Gamble uses this policy because of its desire to adjust prices by geographic area based on consumer demand and competitive pricing.[3]

Price Discount

Most firms offer three types of discounts to customers. Trade discounts are given to channel members to cover the costs of performing the marketing functions, quality discounts are given for purchases in large quantities, and a cash discount is given for quick payment of a bill.

Trade discounts are given to a retailer, for example, for performing the retail functions. This is a discount off the anticipated or list price of the product. Trade discounts are usually well established within a channel. Therefore, a manufacturer may have to accept the established discount.

Two types of quantity discounts that are often given to encourage larger purchases are cumulative and noncumulative. In cumulative quantity discounts, each order is added to previous orders to determine the total quantity purchased during a time period and therefore the price. This method encourages customers to concentrate their purchases with one source.

In noncumulative discounts, the discount on each individual order is calculated. Although this method encourages larger individual order, it does not encourage using a single source of supply. Planners must decide whether or not quantity discounts will be used, the type, and the quantities associated with various discount rates.

Cash discounts encourage quick payments of bills. A cash discount of 2/10 net 30, for example, means a 2 percent discount is given if the bill is paid within ten days of receipt and the full amount is due in 30 days. This increased turnover of accounts receivable reduces the firm's need for outside sources of cash. For the customer, taking advantage of a cash discount of 2 percent is equivalent to earning 36 percent a year on that money. In some channels, cash discounts are so established that a planner must use them.

Geographic Pricing

Geographic pricing policies are needed because transportation charges influence the price paid by the customer. The term FOB is used with a specific point, for example, "FOB Tulsa," to indicate that the seller, who is located in Tulsa, will load the products on a carrier. Title passes at that time to the buyer, who pays transportation charges and assumes the risks involved in shipping the product. If the seller agrees to pay the freight costs, then "FOB buyer's factory" is used.

Some firms develop a zone-delivered price to avoid the variations in price when an FOB shipping point is used. In zone-delivered pricing, the market areas in which a firm sells its products are divided into zones and all customers within a zone are charged a uniform price. Some buyers are actually paying more than the actual freight charges, whereas others are actually paying less, since an average freight cost is used in computing price. If the whole market area is considered one zone, there are uniform prices throughout.

The planner can use geographical pricing as a competitive tool because transportation costs paid by the seller result in the equivalent of a reduced price. That is, this factor can produce a lower price for the customer without a change in the list price.

Price Lining

A typical problem faced by retailers is establishing retail prices that reflect cost but are not too complicated for the consumer. A clothing retailer, for example, may sell men's suits that vary in cost from $165 to $200. If a 40 percent markup is used, retail prices would vary from $191, $193, $197, and so on. The retailer may decide to have just three price lines. All suits that cost between $165 and $175 might be priced at $205, all suits that cost between $176 and $185 might be priced at $215, and all suits that cost over $185 might be priced at $250. Thus, three price ranges are used rather than the thirty to forty that would result if each suit is priced individually.

This approach helps consumers because it is less confusing. Many consumers will establish their own price range for clothing items and then make the selection within that range based on style, quality, color, and so forth.

Retailers benefit because less work is involved in marking products and reduced levels of inventories are needed to carry a good selection at each price. It may also be easier to "trade up" a customer to a higher quality product. Finally, those who are best at making pricing decisions have come to realize certain "truths" about pricing, which combine the internal and external factors mentioned at the beginning of this chapter. Exhibit 13.5 shares some of these truths.

SUMMARY

Price, the last variable discussed in the marketing strategy, is extremely important in today's environment because of the consumer's heightened interest in it. Because of inflation, more consumers are aware of price changes and have become more sensitive to price as a variable. No brand loyalty or promotional or channel uniqueness may be present that a lower price by a competitor will not overcome.

Pricing influence on volume and profitability also reflects the importance of this variable in the strategy. The behavior of costs and

EXHIBIT 13.5. Ten timeless truths about pricing.

1. Pricing is just one part of an overall revenue-generating strategy. Marketers should think of it that way and try to become less price-dependent by diversifying revenue streams. There are many ways to boost revenue without raising price.

2. Pricing strategy is absolutely tied to market share strategy.

3. Pricing strategy always involves cost strategy, because if you're going to fight on price, eventually you're going to have to get down to costs.

4. Pricing strategy is derivative of the price-performance equation relative to one's competitor. Pricing is not an absolute science but rather a relative science. The customer obviously has multiple choices.

5. Pricing must always be considered relative to the segment or the group of customers being pursued; otherwise it's just average pricing and money is being left *on the table*.

6. Upward price leverage is clearly a function of brand equity. The more equity you have in the brand, usually the higher price premiums you can command. Obviously, it is important to contemporize brands, and doing so requires continuous investment in brand awareness and product improvement.

7. Astute pricing requires careful engineering of discount schedule design. Marketers have to consider the number and steepness of price breaks where minimum orders cut in and where maximum discounts cut out.

8. Pricing plans should not be too complex or too far out of sync with efficient shipping units. Complicated systems usually cause errors and compromise a total quality effort in marketing.

9. Marketers need to track price performance by centralizing bidding files, using graphs, studying win-lose bid ratios, and systematizing the measurement of price performance against list prices.

10. The results of a pricing plan ultimately depend on good one-on-one negotiating skills with customers. This calls for a search for win-win pricing scenarios and the maintenance of a very professional but friendly sales force. Price negotiating is just a small part of customer relationship building. The emphasis must be on gaining customers, not just orders.

Source: Magrath, Allan J. Ten Timeless Truths About Pricing. *Journal of Consumer Marketing,* winter 1991, pp. 5-13.

volume must be analyzed to set a price that reflects both the cost and the demand side of the pricing problem.

This chapter concludes the discussion of strategy and strategy variables. Chapter 14 examines the financial impact of marketing strategies.

Chapter 14

The Financial Impact
of Marketing Strategies

MARKETING PLANNING IN ACTION:
RAZOR WARS

The race continues in the men's wet-shaving razor market. The Gillette Company has unveiled a marketing deal with six of NASCAR's top drivers in an effort to stave off its rival Schick. Gillette is hoping to tap into the 75 million NASCAR fans with its new battery-operated M3Power razor, now the world's most expensive mass-market wet razor. At an average cost of $14.99, the battery-powered razor is Gillette's answer to Schick's Quattro, a four-bladed and much-marketed implement that has helped Schick's sales soar by 149 percent while Gillette's slipped 13 percent during the same period.

The users of the new battery-powered M3Power will press a button that will activate the motor and begin a slight pulsating action. The action is intended to stimulate hair upward and away from the skin for a closer shave. Although the target market may appreciate the performance of the new razor, the question is whether or not they will be willing to shell out the $14.99, both pricey and almost 67 percent more than Schick's Quattro. Gillette is banking on the current success of battery-powered toothbrushes as a sign that men will be willing to try the new shaving system. Even if only a small percentage of the market tries the M3Power, it could prove to be a real success for Gillette. Currently, the company holds 74 percent of the $7 billion wet-shaving market. Schick has only 12 percent. Even if only 10 percent of NASCAR fans were to try the M3Power, this would translate into sales for Gillette of roughly $112 million. Gillette's significant size of the market also gives it an advantage with promotional funding, evidenced by both the $20 million deal with NASCAR and its television commercials during the 2004 Super Bowl, the first for Gillette in a decade. Even though the M3Power is expensive, there appears that there is room for growth in the personal care market. William H. Steele, an analyst for Banc of America Securities suggests,

"Aging baby boomers want to look their best for as long as possible." That may mean they are willing to pay the price for a smooth shave.[1]

INTRODUCTION

Once the marketing strategy has been developed and decisions have been made about which market segments will be sought using what marketing mixes, the financial impact of these decisions should be evaluated. This step is directly in line with the societal marketing concept of satisfying consumers' needs *at a profit*. The same type of analysis should be undertaken by nonprofit organizations since break-even needs to be established.

Evaluating the financial impact of a specific strategy forces you to estimate sales, costs of sales, marketing costs, and administrative expenses associated with a strategy *before* the strategy is implemented. This step prevents overly optimistic or pessimistic biases from "muddying" the planning process. As was pointed out earlier, the strategy development process is interactive. A strategy must be specified before its financial impact can be evaluated. After the financial impact has been evaluated, changes in the strategy variables may be needed to meet sales and profit objectives, therefore altering the original objectives and/or strategy. This interactive approach makes the planning process more realistic and removes the "marketing wizard" connotations from planning, where the wizard's job is to dream up some unique strategy to accomplish whatever objectives have been set.

PRO FORMA INCOME STATEMENT

One of the most beneficial ways to approach the financial impact of the marketing plan is to rely on the pro forma income statement as the basic document to be generated in the evaluation process. This is a projected income statement for a specific future time period using estimates of sales and costs associated with that time period. It provides an estimate of cash flows to be produced by a given product. The cash flow can be discounted to determine the present value of a stream of income from the product. This estimate, in turn, is used to calculate the rate of return anticipated from offering a product, opening new facilities, and so forth.

A pro forma income statement for a proposed new product is shown in Exhibit 14.1. The approach used for this project was to develop three alternate income statements, each based on a different assumption about demand for the new product. This method permits identification of the most optimistic, most pessimistic, and most likely outcomes. This realistic approach to demand forecasting produces a range of sales revenue for new products. When products have been on the market for several years, a sales history is available to use in projecting sales.

Sales and costs change over the course of a product's life cycle. High investments in promotion to build a customer base produce losses in early years; reduced variable costs achieved by increasing efficiency may produce higher profit levels in later years. Since a suc-

EXHIBIT 14.1. Pro forma income statement (2006).

	Low (pessimistic)	Medium (most likely)	High (optimistic)
Sales	$3,500,000	$4,500,000	$5,500,000
Cost of sales	2,500,000	3,400,000	4,300,000
Gross margin	$1,000,000	$1,100,000	$1,200,000
Expenses			
Direct selling	$457,000	$480,000	$512,000
Advertising	157,000	168,000	180,000
Transportation and storage	28,000	38,000	48,000
Depreciation	15,000	15,000	15,000
Credit and collections	12,000	14,000	16,000
Financial and clerical	29,000	38,000	47,000
Administrative	55,000	55,000	55,000
Total expenses	$753,000	$808,000	$873,000
Profit before taxes	$247,000	$292,000	$327,000
Net profit after taxes	$128,440	$151,840	$170,040
Cash flow	$143,440	$166,840	$185,040

cessful marketing strategy may not be altered, the pro forma statement must be estimated each year for some assumed length of life for the product, or an "average" year three to five years into the future can be used. Then the discounted cash flow from this year is used as an average for the product's anticipated life to calculate the return on investment (ROI).

Developing a pro forma income statement requires a sales forecast and a forecast of operating expenses. The procedures for developing these estimates are discussed in the following section.

PRO FORMA FORECAST

The sales forecast for a product can be developed by using several techniques. The technique chosen depends on the sophistication of the planner, whether an existing or new product is involved, and the time and money available for forecasting. Sales forecasting techniques commonly used for existing products will be discussed first.

Forecasts for Existing Products

Jury of Executive Opinion

The jury of executive opinion involves asking several executives within a firm to estimate sales for a given product. The objective is to work out a consensus among the executives on a sales forecast. Although this method is easy to use, it may produce very poor results if the excessive reliance on past data does not reflect current market trends. This approach might work best after some other techniques have been used to forecast sales. Then the jury tries to reconcile differences in forecasted values produced by alternate techniques.

Mechanical Extrapolations

Mechanical extrapolations extend historical data into the future by using moving averages or least squares. The least-squares technique is a linear extrapolation of past sales; it may miss the turning points in a product's or service's revenue patterns unless both long- and short-run projections are used to simulate graphically a curvilinear sales curve.

Analytical Methods

Regression analysis is a commonly used analytical method for sales forecasting. In multiple regression analysis, several factors influencing sales are identified and their relationship to sales is analyzed. These factors are forecasted for future time periods, and their relationship to a firm's sales is used to forecast a product's future sales. When the sales pattern has been curvilinear, logarithms are normally used since they would be linear even when antilogs are not.

Forecasts for New Products

When new products are involved, no sales history is available and the techniques used to forecast revenues must reflect this fact. The jury of executive opinion could be used for new products, but by itself would involve only an educated guess. Three other techniques are commonly used in forecasting for new products.

Consumer Surveys

Surveys of potential consumers are often used for industrial products where the number of consumers is small and can be more readily identified. However, a survey can also be used for the ultimate consumer as well. This would involve drawing a sample of prospective customers and collecting data on the number of consumers who say they would buy a new product if it were offered to them.

Substitute Method

Most new products are substitutes for existing products on the market. If the size of these markets can be estimated, the sale of the new products, based on its replacement potential for existing products, can also be estimated. An acceptance rate would have to be estimated for the proportion of existing consumers who would switch to the new product when it is introduced. This rate could be estimated through consumer research.

Test Markets

The most reliable technique for estimating new product sales involves test marketing the product. Although test marketing is expensive and can alert competition to a potential new product, it provides actual market data on revenues for the product. The ideal test market would place the product in the market on a limited basis, with a marketing mix and market conditions similar to those anticipated with full-scale commercialization.

Although many variations in price, promotional expenditures, themes, and so forth can be evaluated through test markets, a key result is actual sales volume generated by the product. An example of the test market results for a new food product are shown in Exhibit 14.2. Based on these results, the rate of sales per 1,000 people was 3.2 cases (15,519/4,870), and the rate per 1 million dollars of retail sales was 8.6 (15,519/1,798). If total population of potential market areas was 65 million, the sales potential would be 65,000 (population in thousands) times 3.2 cases sold in the test market, or 208,000 cases. If retail sales in those market areas were 25 billion, sales potential would be estimated at 215,000. Since the test market was only for six months, these figures would have to be doubled to estimate annual sales, producing estimates of sales potential of 416,000 and 430,000 cases per year. If this quantity could be produced and distributed in all market areas within a three-year time period, case sales times price per case would produce an estimate of sales revenue for the pro forma forecast. This of course assumes a constant annual rate of sales (no

EXHIBIT 14.2. Test market results (case sales for six months).

Area	Case Sales	Retail food stores sales (millions)	Median household income	Population
Dallas	3,920	$407	$9,334	1,131,000
Memphis	2,010	239	7,875	785,000
Detroit	3,450	526	7,773	1,139,000
Columbus	2,929	311	9,563	883,000
Miami	3,210	315	8,681	932,000
Total	15,519	$1,798		4,870,000

seasonality) and minimal geographical consumption differences in test market cities and other markets.

PRO FORMA COST FORECAST

The second step in developing a pro forma income statement is to forecast cost associated with the new product. If the marketing plan is developed for an existing product, the cost can be estimated based on past and anticipated volume. For new products, a different approach must be used. Costs based on company experience for the test markets is one source of information. Another source is standard cost figures for the firm.

The estimates of marketing expenses depend upon whether the marketing plan is controlled by objectives or resources. In an objective-controlled plan the objectives determine the level of expenditures for marketing. In effect, this approach implies that the ends justify the means. The basic question to be answered is this: What level of marketing expenditures is needed to successfully sustain this product on the market? Since heavy marketing expenses will normally be experienced in the introductory period, and lower expenses will occur in later periods, an average level is used to project costs. After the product has been introduced and has reached early maturity, the level of expenditures for marketing should be about average for the whole life cycle unless some dramatic changes occur in the market.

If the marketing budget is resource-controlled, marketing expenditures would be computed as a percent of revenues or a set amount per case or per unit. When this approach is used, the marketing expenses can be computed from the sales forecast. Firms usually base the percentage or fixed sum per unit on considerable experience with similar products.

For services that involve a large-scale advertising campaign, expense estimates can be provided through ad agencies. Their experience with media costs and with other services provides a basis for estimation. If the product is already on the market but new to the company for which the plan is being developed, the current level of expenditures by competitors can be estimated by an ad agency and these figures can be used as a basis for estimating costs.

The administrative costs depend on the organizational changes brought about by the addition of a new product or change in existing strategy. If new personnel are not added, the new product would be allocated a share of the administrative expenses based on previous allocation procedures. When new personnel are hired, their compensation should be reflected in costs.

When cost analysis has been used on previous products, many of the cost-allocation decisions have already been made. All incremental costs must be estimated in all areas—personnel, marketing, and administration—to reflect the additions to costs associated with a new service. The pro forma income statement should reflect changes in sales and costs associated with a new product.

RETURN ON INVESTMENT

The third step in analyzing the financial impact of a strategy is to compute a return on investment (ROI), given the level of cash flow generated by the product or new strategy. ROI is a commonly used figure to determine the acceptance of a proposed plan. Many companies develop policies that specify a payback period or rate of return that any proposed project must attain in order to be introduced. The marketing plan must also be accountable for producing an acceptable level of profits from strategies used by the company. Since different strategies result in different levels of sales, costs, and returns, this step forces a consideration of the profit impact of various alternatives and brings profit accountability into the plan.

Although estimates of sales, costs, and returns had to be made in the feasibility study of the second stage of product development, the actual strategy costs could not be specified until after the strategy was developed. By the time full-scale commercialization is reached, much new data are available on personnel costs, marketing costs, and profit impact of the strategy.

Three commonly used methods for analyzing returns are payback, discounted rate of return, and excess present value.

Payback

The payback method evaluates a return in terms of the number of years it takes to recoup the initial investment. This method is simple to calculate and can provide answers similar to those provided by more sophisticated techniques.

If an investment of $2 million is expected to produce an average return of $500,000 annually, the payback is computed as:

$$\frac{\$2,000,000}{500,000} \text{ investment annual return} = \text{four-year period}$$

If two strategies are being compared, each requiring equal investment, the one with the shortest payback is accepted, if it meets minimum standards. This payback could alternatively be expressed as an unadjusted return of 25 percent by dividing the annual return by the amount invested.

Discounted Rate of Return

If returns from an investment in future years are to be compared with an investment made in present dollars, the returns must be converted to their present value. Future dollars are not as valuable as today's dollars because of the time difference. A dollar one year from now would presently be worth less because less than a dollar could be put in a savings account and earn enough interest to be equal to a dollar a year from now. The problem of time differences in returns can be resolved by converting future returns to present values. The discounted rate of return is computed by expressing future returns in terms of present values and dividing this amount by the amount invested in fixed and working capital to carry out a strategy.

The annual cash inflows from the strategy are converted to present values by using published tables of present values in annuity tables. In the previous example, if the returns were $500,000 annually for ten years, the rate that would equate the returns with the investment is about 22 percent. This is the discounted rate of return. The alternative with the highest rate is the one accepted. It was computed by:

1. finding the payback (four years);
2. finding a value in a table of annuities for $1 a year for ten years, which is close to four (3.923);
3. multiplying the annual inflow times the factor to see if that rate (22 percent) equates the present value of the inflows with the investment ($500,000 × 3.923 = $1,961,500 [about $2,000,000]). Thus, the discounted ROI is a little less than 22 percent.

Excess Present Value

Excess present values is computed by simply comparing the present value of the returns with the amount of the investment. A hurdle rate, the minimum acceptable rate of return, is used to enter the table of present values. The strategy with the highest excess present value is the one used. The hurdle rate is usually equal to or greater than what is currently being earned.

Given a hurdle rate of 18 percent, for example, the excess present value in the example previously used would be calculated by finding a value from a table of annuities for $1 a year for ten years at 18 percent. Then the calculations would proceed as follows:

> Present value of $1 a year for ten years at 18 percent = 4.494.
> Present value of $500,000 a year for ten years at 18 percent = $2,247,000
> Excess present value = present value–the investment:
>   Present value   = $2,247,000
>   Investment   = $2,000,000
> Excess present value = $247,000

If no other alternatives produce a higher excess present value, this one is accepted because the rate is higher than 18 percent.

When additional investments in facilities, equipment, and working capital are not required, a common approach is to compare the pro forma statement with and without the introduction of the new product or a change in strategy. (A planner would not normally propose a change in strategy unless financial benefits were expected.) This approach accomplishes the same objective since an evaluation of incremental revenues and costs must precede such an approach.

STRATEGY REVISIONS AND CONTINGENCY PLANS

If a proposed strategy would not produce the desired financial results, alternate strategies must be evaluated. These may require additional test marketing and other costs, but it is better to introduce a successful strategy than one that will not ultimately produce the desired financial results.

Several strategies should be developed and evaluated, each with a different set of assumptions about the nature of the market, competitive action, economic conditions, and so on. This approach gives you the possibility of developing contingency plans, should conditions warrant. Although it is not possible to develop a contingency plan for each of perhaps thousands of different combinations of events, at least the impact of various strategies will have been evaluated on a preliminary basis.

SUMMARY

This chapter concludes the development of strategy with the cold, hard facts of business life—profit accountability. Estimating the financial impact of decisions is extremely difficult work because of the many uncertainties of the future. However, the marketing area cannot make its full contribution to a firm's operations if this is not done. A firm's purpose cannot be carried out in the face of financial losses, nor can it exist over the long run under such conditions.

For many people, such emphasis on details and numbers is not a pleasant task. Great skill is needed in estimating revenues and costs, and the most reliable teacher is experience. Nowhere is a marketing planner's breadth and depth of knowledge more tested than in estimating the future financial impact of marketing strategies.

This chapter outlined a basic set of approaches that can be used to accomplish a difficult task. Chapter 15 discusses monitoring and controlling the plan.

PART V:
IMPLEMENTING AND CONTROLLING
THE MARKETING PLAN

Chapter 15

Marketing Plan Implementation

MARKETING PLANNING IN ACTION: THE FLUCTUATING POPULARITY OF THE HUMMER

When General Motors (GM) bought the rights to consumer product development for the Hummer vehicle back in 1999 from AM General Corporation, it had high hopes for translating the popular, but expensive, Humvee military vehicles into a multiline consumer product. With an average price of around $100,000, the Hummer was out of reach for the majority of American customers. With the addition of newer, lower-priced models, the demand for the Hummer brand was at an all-time high by the end of 2002.

What a difference a year makes, though. Once gleaning premium prices for its $50,000 H2s, GM found itself offering $2,000 dealer incentives on its remaining models in August 2003. One reason was that dealers had a ninety-one-day supply of vehicles on hand compared to the thirteen-day supply at the end of 2002. Touted as being part of the business plan, GM spokesman Pete Ternes said, "It is easier to sell a 2004 than a 2003 ... the incentive gives dealers the ability to clear the 2003 inventory."

Reasons cited for the slowing popularity of the Hummer vehicles included the low twelve-mile-per-gallon gas consumption and a somewhat tenuous economy. Despite these issues, GM is clearly moving forward with its plans for the brand. Attempting to tap the younger market segment, GM is unveiling its new H3, a slightly smaller version of its former Hummers. The new H3 will be a foot narrower than the H1 and will sell for less than the H2. In addition to the H3 SUV-type vehicle, GM is also planning the H3T, a concept vehicle that is a pickup truck version of the H3.

Other plans include the export of the H2 SUV to global markets, including Russia, where a very affluent market segment is reported. H2s will also be sold in Europe, the Middle East, and Japan. GM has also attempted to capitalize on brand equity by expanding into Hummer Footwear, a line of men's shoes and boots. The footwear is sold through higher-end retail establishments and differentiates itself from competitors by using unusual material components, such as Yak leather. Priced from an average $100 to $300, the footwear is aimed toward the younger market and those who may aspire to be Hummer vehicle owners, but cannot afford the price tag. "This is a lifestyle brand," said Jordan Saliman, president of Hummer Footwear. "We want to participate in consumers lives from the time they get up to the time they go to bed."[1]

INTRODUCTION

A 1986 *Harvard Business Review* article carried the title "Hustle As Strategy," the point being that more is gained from a good strategy with great implementation than from a great strategy with good implementation.[2] "Hustle," or implementation, can make or break a company in many marketing situations at the turn of the century. The firm that achieves excellence in the skills needed for implementing a marketing plan may achieve a competitive advantage that perhaps has eluded it in the strategy development stage of the planning process. However, excellent implementation of a poorly conceived strategy is akin to great advertising of a terrible product—the disaster occurs much sooner than if the excellence was not there! Thus, successful organizations have found ways to be good at both the development and implementation of marketing plans.

IMPLEMENTATION SKILLS

To this point of the book, our emphasis has been on developing marketing plans that focus on delivering customer value at a competitive advantage. Our societal marketing orientation adds to that goal the desire to consider the impact of our actions on the long-term, as well as short-term, welfare of our customers and of society at large. From an implementation perspective, the trick is to accomplish this feat by translating our strategy into a series of assigned activities in such a way that everyone can see their job as a set of value-added actions. These actions should be seen as contributive to the organization, by the people assigned those tasks, because they ultimately result in greater value being delivered to the customer. In *The Marketing Edge,* Bonoma suggests four types of skills that must be utilized in order for such a strategic goal to be successfully translated into implementation activities:

> *Allocating skills* are used by marketing managers to assign resources (e.g., money, effort, personnel) to the programs, functions, and policies needed to put the strategy into action. For example, allocating funds for special-event marketing programs or setting a policy of when to voluntarily recall a defective product are issues that require managers to exhibit allocating skills.
>
> *Monitoring skills* are used by marketing managers who must evaluate the results of marketing activities.
>
> *Organizing skills* are used by managers to develop the structures and coordination mechanisms needed to put marketing plans to work. Understanding informal dynamics as well as formal organization structure is needed here.
>
> *Interacting skills* are used by marketing managers to achieve goals by influencing the behavior of others. Motivation of people internal as well as external to the company—marketing research firms, advertising agencies, dealers, wholesalers, brokers, etc.—is a necessary prerequisite to fulfilling marketing objectives.[3]

Exhibit 15.1 continues the example begun in Exhibit 2.1 by showing how Eli Lilly might have used these four skills to implement the strategy and objectives formulated at the corporate, SBU, and product/market levels of planning. Note that in this example a consistency is found between every level and every action taken with respect to the various manifestations of strategy and tactics. Contemporary marketing managers, perhaps unlike their predecessors, would find it important to tell the sales force and external agents *why* these assignments were being made and not just what and how much to do.

INTEGRATING A SOCIETAL MARKETING ORIENTATION THROUGHOUT THE ORGANIZATION

A key indicator of whether a true societal marketing orientation exists within a company is the degree to which its philosophical tenets are held by people outside the marketing function. Inculcate ev-

EXHIBIT 15.1. Strategy hierarchy for Eli Lilly.

Corporate level

Objective: Maintain product leadership in each market we enter
Strategy: Product leadership, value, discipline

Strategic business unit level

Objective: Maintain a market share of the nonnarcotic analgesic market of 80 percent + for the next five years
Strategy: Introduce new products to take the place of high revenue-producing products when they lose patent protection

Product market level

Objective: Call on physicians to sell Darvocet as a more-advanced analgesic than Darvon with more efficacy and fewer side effects; call on pharmacists to leave order blanks for Darvon at sale prices.
Strategy: Product line extension and aggressive pricing.

Allocating— Assigning to sales force the targeted number and types of MDs and pharmacists to give a sales call during a specified period of time. Budgeting of funds to cover advertising, selling, direct mail, etc., expenses.

Monitoring—Annual plan controls will monitor sales to make sure total sales objectives are achieved as well as percent of sales to old versus new product, sales calls to MDs and pharmacists to ensure calls are made, pricing to ensure that the correct price for old and new products are printed and that "sale" announcements are received by pharmacists at specified time. Profitability controls will be used to monitor profitability by type of MDs, chain versus independent pharmacies, etc.

Organizing— Ensuring that existing market organization structure aids in the execution of the specified strategy and tactics.

Interacting—Motivating sales force to devote the effort necessary to make the number of calls needed to fulfill strategic plan. Providing sales force with information and material needed to change MDs' prescribing habits toward new product and obtain orders from pharmacies for both old and new product. Working with ad agency in preparation of promotional materials.

eryone within the organization as well as the external agencies with which the company works into having the customer orientation in the execution of their jobs. Institute training sessions to explain why such an orientation is needed in the globally competitive markets in which the organization competes, as well as set forth the management expectations for achieving the goal of generating satisfied, loyal customers. Several books have been devoted to the subject of building a customer focus within the organization.[4] In *Marketing Management Analysis, Planning, and Control, Fifth Edition,* Kotler illustrates the problems involved in integrating the efforts of key personnel when implementing a customer orientation with this example:

> The marketing vice president of a major airline wants to increase the airline's traffic share. Her strategy is to build up customer satisfaction through providing better, good, clean cabins, and better-trained cabin crews, yet she has no authority in these matters. The catering department chooses food that keeps down food costs; the maintenance department uses cleaning services that keep down cleaning costs; and the personnel department uses people without regard to whether they are friendly and inclined to serve other people. Since these departments generally take a cost or production point of view, she is stymied in creating a high level of customer satisfaction.[5]

Kotler goes on to point out that integrated marketing effort means two things. First, there must be a coordination of marketing effort among the various marketing functions (sales force, product management, advertising, marketing research, and so on). Too often, the sales force is angry at product management for setting an unrealistic sales goal; or the advertising agency and brand management cannot agree on an appropriate ad message. Second, marketing efforts must be well coordinated between marketing and the other departments within the organization. Marketing is the job of everyone in the company, even if the person is not part of the marketing department. IBM took the step of including in every one of its job descriptions an explanation of how that job impacts on the customer. IBM factory managers know that a clean and efficient production area can help sell a customer on a factory visit. IBM accountants understand that quick response to customer inquiries and accuracy in billing impact the image customers have of IBM.

TRANSITION FROM STRATEGY TO TACTICS

Implementation of a marketing plan includes turning the strategic elements of the marketing mix into tactics. These elements are discussed in the following text.

Product

Moving from a product positioning statement to a tangible product that delivers customer satisfaction in accordance with the positioning strategy and at a profit to the company is not easily accomplished. The design team must not lose sight of the product strategy as it applies a high degree of creative and technical skill to the tasks. The team must understand not only the strategic needs in the product's design before the sale, but also the entire product use/consumption experience to make the product as "user-friendly" as possible. The team must also consider the after-consumption disposal of the product and its packaging in the design of the product.

Product quality and service issues (see Chapter 10), market-entry timing, production scheduling, after-sale service, package handling, transportation, and many other issues must be decided. All of these decisions should be influenced by how they impact the delivery of customer value and correct tactical implementation of a predetermined strategy. We should never lose sight of the product strategy, which indicates where our competitive advantage lies when we engage in the myriad acts required in the exchange process with customers.

Place

Tactical issues for channels of distribution involve not only providing value by physical access to the production service, but also the performance of important marketing functions such as merchandising, personal selling, advertising, pricing, and after-sales service. All these functions play a role in implementing the positioning strategy and must be seen as parts of a whole strategy instead of autonomous tasks. Likewise, the type and number of outlets (intensive, selective, or exclusive distribution) play a major role in positioning the product in the minds of target market consumers.

Promotion

Many models exist for selecting promotional media to maximize reach and frequency objectives for a given audience at a given budget. However, models are never a perfect substitute for managerial judgment in this area. Promotional tactics involve the actual presentation of communication messages to target audience members. These messages must be formulated to be the most effective means possible of presenting the essence of the positioning strategy to potential customers. Many companies with a sound positioning strategy have "self-destructed" at the implementation stage by choosing an advertising approach totally unsuited to conveying the image they wished to project for their company or product. Sales promotions, special-event marketing, trade show displays, collateral material, and all other forms of promotion should also be carefully formulated to be the appropriate tactical implementation of the positioning strategy. Possible competitive reactions to promotional efforts should also be factored into tactical actions. Coherence with marketing strategy is as important with sales-force tactics as it is with the other promotional elements, sales training, sales support materials, and reward systems must be considered with overall strategy.

> If, for example, the core benefit proposition is to help customers solve a specific set of problems in using a particular plastic compound through better engineering and technical service, a consultative, problem-oriented selling process directed at establishing a partnership with the customer would probably be the best approach. If, however, the strategy is to be the lowest-cost producer and sell on the basis of price and availability, the sales presentation should emphasize price and delivery. In the latter instance, the selling would be "harder" than the "soft sell" of the partnership proposition.
>
> Recruiting criteria, training, and reward systems would also be different for the two strategies. In implementing the first strategy, a highly educated salesperson (e.g., a graduate engineer) who has completed a fairly elaborate training program (including on-the-job training under a seasoned, consultative salesperson) and is compensated with salary plus bonus would probably be the best choice. For the second low-price strategy, a less educated (e.g., a junior college graduate) and less elabo-

rately trained salesperson compensated largely by commission would probably be more appropriate. Both approaches could be successful in their respective strategy frameworks; the critical task is to match the correct sales management policies with the proper strategy.[6]

Price

Implementation of issues with respect to pricing were discussed, to some degree, in Chapter 13, under the headings of Price Flexibility, Price Discount, Geographic Pricing, and Price Lining. Policies established in these areas are in essence the implementation of a pricing plan that acknowledges as necessary adjustments to price to fit market conditions. Other price implementation issues include initiating price increases and responding to changes in competitors' prices.

As costs rise and productivity increases near the point of diminishing returns, companies feel the pressure to initiate price increases. The following types of price adjustments are commonly used:

- *Adoption of delayed quotation pricing*—A price for a product is not set until the product is produced or delivered. In this way, any price adjustments needed to maintain margins can be made once all costs have been determined.
- *Use of escalator clauses*—Customers pay a price at the time of order, plus any inflation increase that occurs before delivery is made. Such an escalator clause may be tied to a specific price index such as the cost-of-living index.
- *Unbundling of goods and services*—The product price is maintained, but previous services included are now priced separately, such as delivery or installation.
- *Reduction of discounts*—Policy changes might be initiated, which could prevent the sales force from offering normal discounts.[7]

Another pricing implementation issue concerns a company's reaction to a change in price by a competitor. Market leaders, in particular, must determine how they will react to a drop in price by major competitors. Several options are available:

- *Maintain price*—The market leader may decide to maintain its price without losing customers it wishes to retain. This strategy can be risky in some circumstances, but avoids giving the attacker confidence and avoids demoralizing the sales force.

- *Raise perceived quality*—Another option is to maintain price, but improved the perception of value of its products by strengthening the company's product, services, or communications.
- *Reduce price*—The leader might decide to drop its price in response to the competitor. This is commonly motivated by a belief that buyers primarily make choice decisions on the basis of price, and that a failure to lower its price will result in an unacceptable decline in market share. Quality should be maintained even if price is dropped, however.
- *Increase price and improve quality*—This approach is based on the belief that by establishing an elite image as the "best" on the market, a company can better capture the share of the market comprised of customers motivated by that status. Some firms pursuing this strategy simultaneously launch a less expensive "fighting brand," which is intended to compete against the lower-cost competitor.[8]

Any price implementation actions should be governed by the objectives a company sets for its price decisions (see Chapter 13).

SUMMARY

A great plan is only as good as the implementation activities that put it into action. Organizations must acquire the set of allocating, monitoring, organizing, and interacting skills required to successfully translate their strategies into tactics. Such tactics must be customer-oriented by whoever performs them, in or out of the organization. Consequently, marketers must assume the responsibility of integrating the societal marketing orientation into the process of people all along the value delivery chain, from suppliers to channel members. Finally, each element of the marketing mix must have a coherence between strategy and the tactical actions involved in the execution of the marketing plan.

Chapter 16

Monitoring and Controlling the Marketing Plan

MARKETING PLANNING IN ACTION: REINVIGORATING LEVI STRAUSS

One of the most well-known brands in the world is finding itself in the midst of a troubled sea. Levi Strauss & Co., the legendary jeans maker, was once the icon of American brands. Its classic denim jeans were born during the California gold rush and remained a symbol of work clothing until the 1960s, when they turned into the status of hip and alternative. During the past four decades they have remained the uniform of many baby boomers who began wearing them in their youth. However, Levis do not have the same cachet with today's younger market as they did with their older fans. Sales for the American company have declined from $7.1 million at their peak in the mid-1990s to about $4 billion in 2003. Several factors may have contributed to this decline including the corporate culture at Levi Strauss and its past marketing efforts. In a world of target segmentation and brand positioning, it is difficult to be "somewhere in the middle" in customer's minds. In many different types of markets those companies and brands who position themselves there find they cannot compete. Levis were not only positioned as neither hot nor cold in customers' minds, they were also distributed through the most middle-America of retail stores, JCPenney and Sears. Levi also lost out on those customers who were interested in discounted clothing, as they did not want to "devalue" the brand by distributing them through the likes of Wal-Mart or Target. At the other end of the spectrum, Levis did not have an image of being new, cool, or exciting. Younger buyers were turning to the newer brands such as Diesel, Lucky, and Juicy.

Levi Strauss reformulated its marketing plan, including hiring a former PepsiCo, Inc. executive, Phil Marineau, as its new CEO. Under his leadership, it has developed two new diverse jean lines and is trying several new marketing tactics. For the more expensive market, it has developed the Premium Red Tab jean which is sold through retailers such as Nordstrom and Neiman Marcus. It has also developed its new Signature label, targeted to teens and sold through the discount chains of Wal-Mart and Target, which thus far, is reported to be selling well. "Our plan is really to develop our grassroots brand building, and you can see the beginnings of that in what we've done already. Research shows us that brand awareness has currently doubled over what it was six months ago through these efforts" says Scott LaPorta, president of the Levi Strauss Signature division in the United States.[1]

INTRODUCTION

Many companies fail to understand the importance of establishing procedures to monitor and control the planning process, a failing that leads to less than optimal performance. This chapter reviews the need for control, what is to be controlled, and some control procedures. Control should be a natural follow-through in developing a plan. No plan should be considered complete until controls are identified and the procedures for recording and transmitting control information to managers are established.

The need for controls was clearly pointed out in a study of seventy-five companies of various sizes in several industries. The findings were as follows:

- Smaller companies had poorer control procedures than larger ones.
- Fewer than one-half of the companies knew the profitability of individual products, and one-third had no system set up to spot weak products.
- Almost half failed to analyze costs, evaluate advertising or sales force call reports, or compare their process to competitors.
- Many managers reported long delays—four to eight weeks—in getting control reports, and many of their reports were inaccurate.[2]

Such problems can be avoided when a sound control system is established. Failure to establish control is similar to looking once at a map before a long trip and then never looking at road signs, markers, or checkpoints as you travel. If you arrive at all, it is sheer luck.

INTEGRATION OF PLANNING AND CONTROL

Planning and control should be integrated processes. In fact, planning was defined as a process that included establishing a system for feedback of results. This feedback reflects the company's performance in reaching its objectives through implementation of the strategic marketing plan. The relationship between planning and control is depicted in Exhibit 16.1.

The planning process results in a specific plan being developed for a product or service. This plan is implemented (marketing activities are performed in the manner described in the plan) and results are produced. These results are sales revenues, costs, profits, and accompanying consumer attitudes, preferences, and behaviors. Information on these results is given to managers who compare the results with objectives to evaluate performance. This performance evaluation identifies the areas where decisions must be made. The actual decision making controls the plan by altering it to accomplish stated objectives, and a new cycle begins. The information flows are the key to a good control system. Deciding what information is provided to which managers in what time periods is the essence of a control system.

EXHIBIT 16.1. Planning and control model.

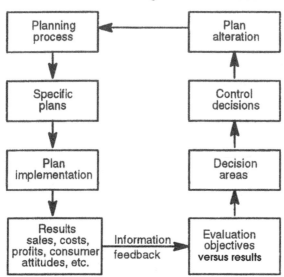

TIMING OF INFORMATION FLOWS

The strategic plan in the firm is composed of many annual operating plans. An economist once noted that "we plan in the long run but live in the short run." If each of our annual operating plans is controlled properly, the long-run plans are more likely to be controlled. The planner cannot afford to wait for the time period of a plan to pass before control information is available. The information must be available within a time frame that is long enough to allow results to accrue but short enough to allow actions to align results with objectives. Although some types of businesses may find weekly or bimonthly results necessary, most companies can adequately control operations with monthly or quarterly reports. Cumulative monthly or quarterly reports become annual reports, which in turn become the feedback needed to control the plan.

Auditing the planning process is necessary not only for control but also for improvement in the planning process. This will be discussed in detail in Chapter 17.

PERFORMANCE EVALUATION AND CONTROL

Performance should be evaluated in many areas to provide a complete analysis of what the results are and what caused them. The four key control areas are sales, costs, profits, and consumers. Objectives have been established in three of these areas for the operating and strategic plan. The fourth, costs, is a measure of marketing effort and is directly tied to profitability analysis.

Sales

Sales control data are provided from an analysis of sales by individual segments (products, territories, etc.), market share data, and data on sales inputs (sales force, advertising, and sales promotion).

Sales by Segment

Sales performance can be evaluated by segment by developing a sales performance report as shown in Exhibit 16.2.

EXHIBIT 16.2. Sales performance report—Quarter 1 (by products).

Product	Sales objective	Actual sales	$ variation	Percent variation	Index
A	$100,000	$90,000	−10,000	−10.0	.90
B	95,000	102,000	+7,000	+7.4	1.07
C	120,000	92,000	−28,000	−23.0	.77
D	200,000	203,000	+3,000	+1.5	1.02

When such a format is used, the sales objectives stated in the annual operating plan are broken down on a quarterly basis and become the standard against which actual sales results are compared. Dollar and percentage variations are calculated because in some instances a small percentage can result in a large dollar variation.

A performance index can be calculated by dividing actual sales by the sales objective. Index numbers of about 1.00 indicate that expected and actual performance are about equal. Numbers larger than 1.00 indicate above-expected performance, and numbers below 1.00 reveal below-expected performance. Index numbers are especially useful when a large number of products is involved because they enable managers to identify those products that need immediate attention.

The same procedures can be followed to analyze sales performance by customers or territories. They could also be combined to check performance of products in various territories or sales to various customer types.

Market Share Data

Another important type of sales control data is provided through market share analysis. A firm's performance should be compared to the competitors', and a common method is to calculate a firm's share of a market. External forces do not affect all firms in the same way, and their impact can be analyzed through market share analysis.

To calculate market share, the relevant market must be identified. It is possible to calculate market share on at least two bases:

1. *Share of total market.* The firm's sales divided by the total sales in the markets in which the firm is exerting marketing effort.
2. *Relative market share.* One firm's share of the market held by the top two, three, or four firms. It reflects the firm's share of the market captured by the major competitors.

Unless some effort is made to understand why a firm's market share has changed or failed to change, this analysis is more of a score-keeping task. If the components of market share are analyzed—such as number of customers reached, product loyalty, repeat purchases—meaningful control decisions can be made.

Sales Input Data

A great deal of analysis of performance can be done on sales inputs. For the sales force, these inputs can be divided into qualitative and quantitative inputs.

Qualitative inputs:
- Time management
- Planning effort
- Quality of sales presentation
- Product knowledge
- Personal appearance and health
- Personality and attitudes

Quantitative inputs:
- Days worked
- Calls per day
- Proportion of time spent selling
- Selling expenses
- Nonselling activities
  — Calls to prospects
  — Display setups
  — Service calls
- Miles traveled per call

Analysis of these factors will help a sales manager evaluate the efficiency of the sales effort. For many of these input factors, a sales force average can be computed to serve as a standard for analyzing individual salespersons. If the number of sales calls per day for one salesperson is three and the company average is six, this case warrants attention. The low number of calls per day could be caused by a large, sparsely populated territory, or it could be that the salesperson is spending too much time with each customer. Whatever the problem, management must be alerted to its existence.

Advertising inputs are difficult to evaluate but must be dealt with nonetheless. Several factors can be evaluated that help determine the efficiency of this input:

- Competitive level of advertising
- Readership statistics
- Cost per thousand
- Number of sales inquiries stimulated by an ad
- Number of conversions of inquiries to sales
- Changes in store traffic generated by an ad campaign

These measures help evaluate the results of advertising decisions. Tracking these data over several years can help identify successful appeals, ads, or media.

Many sales promotional tools can be directly evaluated if objectives are set before their use. For example, if a firm is going to enclose a cents-off coupon in a packaged product, the number of coupons redeemed is one measure of the results. The number of people who visit a trade show, the number of customers who try a product through in-store demonstrations, and so forth are all examples of how data on these activities can be used to evaluate their effectiveness.

The key to evaluating sales input performance is the setting of objectives, which become the standards by which actual performance can be evaluated.

Cost

Several tools are available for establishing cost control procedures, including budgets, expense ratios, and segment and functional costs analysis. Budgets are a common tool used by most organizations for anticipating expense levels on a yearly basis. The budget is often established by using historical percentages of various expenses as a percent of sales. Thus, once the sales forecast is established, expense items can be budgeted as a percent of total sales. If zero-based budgeting is used, the objectives to be accomplished must be specified

and the expenditures necessary to accomplish these objectives estimated. The estimates are the budgeted expenses for the time period.

Once the budget is established, expense variance analysis by line
item or expenditure category is used to control costs. Although standard costs cannot be established for marketing expenditures, the budget amounts are the standards used to perform variance analysis. A
typical procedure is to prepare monthly or quarterly budget reports
showing the amount budgeted for the time period and the dollar and
percentage variation from the budgeted amount, if any exists. Expenditure patterns that vary from the budgeted amounts are then analyzed
to determine why the variations occurred.

Expense ratio analysis is another tool used to control costs. An important goal of every plan is to maintain the desired relationship between expenditures and revenues. Calculations of expense ratios provide information on what this relationship is at any time. Monthly,
quarterly, and yearly ratio calculations should satisfy most managers'
needs for this type of data. Common expense ratios are as follows:

- Profit margins
- Selling expense ratio
- Cost per sales call
- Advertising expense ratio

Many other financial ratios, such as asset turnover, inventory turnover, and account receivable turnover, also provide measures that can
be used to reduce or maintain costs levels.

Segment and functional costs analyses were described in detail in
Chapter 4. These types of analysis permit evaluation of cost by individual products, territories, customers, and marketing activity. Analysis of these costs in relation to sales volume produced by segment is
a key type of analysis for identifying profitable and unprofitable
products, territories, and customers.

Profit

Profit control begins with profitability analysis by products, territories, and customers. As outlined in Chapter 4, this method involves
a breakdown of sales and costs by various market segments to determine either a profit contribution or a contribution to cover indirect
costs and earn a profit. Profitability analysis is the only way to iden-

tify the strong and weak products, territories, or customers. Until specific products can be identified as unsuccessful, no action can be taken to correct the situation. A manager needs specific information about a product or customer on both sales revenues generated and the costs associated with a given level of revenue.

Profit control is achieved through the action taken once the specific information is available. Exhibit 16.3 presents data on order size for a grocery wholesaler. Many of the customers were placing small orders, which actually resulted in losses.

When the costs of goods sold and other direct expenses of sales commission, order picking, and delivery were calculated, a negative contribution margin for orders under $200 was left. Sales revenues did not cover direct expenses. A naive decision would be simply to stop selling to these customers. This would reduce sales revenue, but the decrease in direct expenses would more than offset the decrease in revenues.

A more analytic approach would be to determine why the orders were small and what could be done to increase their size. It could be that these are all small retailers, and little could be done to increase order size; or it could be that these retailers are splitting orders with several wholesalers. Some of the corrective actions that could be taken are as follows:

1. Get several small retailers to pool their orders.
2. Have the salespeople call on them less frequently, thus increasing the size of individual orders.
3. Start a cash-and-carry operation to deal with these retailers.
4. Have these retailers order by phone or from product portfolio listings.

EXHIBIT 16.3. Number of customers by order size.

Number of customers	Order size
31	over $1,000
50	$800-$999
80	$600-$799
90	$400-$559
75	$200-$399
65	less than $200

5. Encourage them to concentrate their purchases with one source of supply.

Several possible corrective actions could improve their order size and permit the wholesaler to continue to deal with them. If none of the corrective actions evaluated were feasible, a minimum-size order could be established. This may eliminate some customers, but it can not be avoided if profitability is to be improved.

Consumers

The final area of performance evaluation is customers and involves analysis of customer awareness, knowledge, attitudes, and behaviors. Chapter 12 pointed out that communications efforts are goal-oriented. The goals are to have consumers become aware of products, services, or stores; possess certain knowledge; and exhibit certain attitudes and behaviors. These should be specified in the operating and strategic objective statements and then become the standards to which current consumer data are compared.

Data on consumers must be collected either by the company or a research firm. Many research firms specialize in providing commercial data to companies, either as a one-time research project or on a regular basis. Store audits, awareness studies, and attitudinal surveys are available by subscription for most consumer goods. Several research firms specialize in industrial consumer research and provide appropriate data on these consumers.

Consumer data are especially valuable if collected over a long period of time because awareness levels, attitudes, and purchase behavior can be analyzed to reveal trends and areas for further investigation. Also changes in the consumer's attributes can be related to marketing activities, such as coupons or the introduction of a new advertising theme. One area of customer feedback that has received considerable attention is customer satisfaction measures. Much has been written about how to define and measure customer satisfaction, and the importance of obtaining this type of feedback on a regular basis so that corrective action can be taken when areas of dissatisfaction appear. It has also been argued that customer satisfaction measures are too narrowly focused and that "customer value delivery" is a more important gauge of how well a company is doing with its customer.[3] Here, the organization is seeking to determine the level of customer loyalty by determining the customers' sense of value delivered to him or her via the organization's value package: price, product quality, innovation, service quality, and company image relative to the competition. All of these areas should be monitored to determine the degree to which customers are loyal to the organization versus which are at risk to be lost to competitors.

ESTABLISHING PROCEDURES

None of the performance evaluation data previously described are going to be available unless they are requested and funds are made available to finance them. Thus, data-collecting and reporting procedures must be set up by the planner in consultation with the managers who are going to use the control data in decision making.

The procedures will usually change over time as some types of analysis or reporting times are found to be better than others. The most important requirement is that the data meet the needs of managers in taking corrective actions to control marketing activities.

SUMMARY

No planning process should be considered complete until monitoring and control procedures have been established. Without such information, managing marketing activities with any sense of clarity about what is actually happening in the marketplace is impossible.

Performance evaluation of sales, costs, profits, and consumer data is vital for control decisions. Information from these areas tells a manager what has happened and serves as the basis for any actions needed to control the activities of the organization toward predetermined objectives.

PART VI:
PLANNING ANALYSIS

Chapter 17

The Marketing Planning Audit

Although 2003 was a tough year for many drug companies, Johnson & Johnson's stock performance trailed behind most of its competitors. The company, which makes numerous product lines, from baby shampoo to artificial knees, did see a rise in sales and profit, yet it must analyze and redirect its efforts in order to sustain its historical levels of 10 percent annual growth in revenue. In the past, Johnson & Johnson has relied on several different strategies to sustain its market growth, including new product development and diversification through acquisition. However, with new pharmaceutical products taking sometimes years to develop and approve through the Food and Drug Administration, the company needs to find additional means to obtain market growth. Today, Johnson & Johnson spends 50 percent of its drug-development budget on new compounds, compared to only 20 percent just five years ago. The remainder of the budget is used to find new uses for existing drugs.

An audit of the company's position reveals that for now, Johnson & Johnson has no new major products in the developmental stages, which means it is time to redevelop its strategy. Johnson & Johnson has come up with an action plan for the next few years that it hopes will hold off its competition. The plan consists of four major strategic areas: acquisitions, new drug uses, cost cutting, and teamwork. In the next few years it plans to continue shopping for new acquisitions, but its focus will be on smaller companies who can produce blockbuster drugs. Johnson & Johnson also plans to focus more of its efforts on finding new uses for its existing drug portfolio. The downside to this strategy is that the new uses will still require FDA approval, but the payoff is that the "line extensions" will be likely to sell well, helping boost revenue. Johnson and Johnson also plans to cut costs by merging operations and increasing its centralized purchasing division so it can apply the funds toward new pharmaceutical development. Finally, the company plans to encourage more teamwork across divisional lines in order to develop both products and drug-delivery systems. Johnson & Johnson does not dispute the challenges it faces. Its CFO, Robert J. Darretta, says "We've been going through a period well above historic averages. The next couple of years look tougher." He believes however, that their action plan will enable it to sustain the 10 percent growth in revenue and 13 percent growth in earnings it has experienced in the past.[1]

INTRODUCTION

In Chapter 1, planning was described as a managerial activity that involves analyzing the environment, setting objectives, and deciding on specific actions needed to reach objectives and provide control of results. Planning is a process that can be studied and improved. Improvements are centered on decisions concerning who will participate in the planning process and how the process will actually be executed.

This chapter focuses on how the marketing planning process can be improved within a company. The marketing planning audit is described as a basic framework for analyzing the planning process and identifying specific actions to improve it. Improvements in the process result in better analysis, more realistic objectives, better strategies, and more appropriate control mechanisms.

THE PLANNING AUDIT

The concept of a marketing planning audit was derived from accounting, where audits have traditionally been used as a procedure for internal financial control. The term has been defined in a number of ways: from simply "a marketing audit is a systematic and thorough examination of a company's marketing position,"[2] to "a marketing audit is a *comprehensive, systematic, independent,* and *periodic* examination of a company's—or business unit's—marketing environment, objectives, strategies, and activities with a view to determining problem areas and opportunities and recommending a plan of action to improve the company's marketing performance."[3] But, in essence, a *planning audit* is a critical, unbiased review of the philosophies, personnel, organization, purpose, objectives, procedures, and results associated with some activity. Everything associated with the marketing planning process within a company is reviewed.

Audits are appropriate for virtually any type of organization—new to old, small to large, healthy or ailing, engaged in service or physical products. The need for a marketing planning audit may stem from changes in: target markets, competitors, internal capabilities, the economic environment, and so forth. Consequently, an audit may have many purposes:[4]

- Appraise the total marketing operation.
- Evaluate objectives and policies and the assumptions that underlie them.
- Aim for prognosis as well as diagnosis.
- Search for opportunities and means for exploiting them as well as for weaknesses and means for their elimination.
- Practice preventive as well as curative marketing practices.

The marketing audit process can be lengthy and complex. A great deal of prior planning and preparation are necessary. Ultimately, it involves (1) deciding who will do the audit; (2) agreeing on its objectives, scope, and breadth; (3) identifying sources of data; and (4) deciding on the format used to present its results.

AUDIT PERSONNEL

Kotler offers six ways in which a marketing audit may be conducted:

1. Self-audit
2. Audit from across
3. Audit from above
4. Company auditing officer
5. Company task force audit
6. Outsider audit.

Generally speaking, the best audits are likely to come from experienced outside consultants who have the necessary objectivity and independence, broad experience in a number of industries, some familiarity with this industry, and the undivided time and attention to give to the audit.[5]

Basically, the choice is between internal and external auditors. Internal auditors have the advantage of working relationships and familiarity with the company's operating environment. If the audit is not a self-audit but is done by high-level executives or an auditing staff, this approach can be less time-consuming and perhaps less costly. However, one basic assumption must be made for the full benefits of the audit to be realized when company personnel are used: internal auditors are not myopic in their knowledge of planning procedures; that is, they must have a good understanding of how planning should take place in any organization and not just in their particular company. Unless the analysts possess the depth and breadth of knowledge needed in marketing, many of their judgments will be naive. An understanding of marketing planning is needed in addition to an understanding of planning.

External auditors can provide some of the breadth of knowledge needed if their experience is broad-based. Consulting firms specializing in marketing may bring a perspective to the firm's planning process, which could not otherwise be obtained, especially for firms with inbred executives. The major disadvantage of using external auditors is the time needed for them to gain an understanding of the company's approach to planning and the qualifications and training of the people involved in the planning process. A long-term relationship with the same consulting group would help alleviate this shortcoming.

OBJECTIVE, SCOPE, AND BREADTH OF AUDIT

Audits should begin with a meeting between the company officer(s) and the marketing auditor(s) to work out an agreement on the objectives, coverage, depth, data sources, report format, and the time period for the audit. A detailed plan as to who is to be interviewed, the questions to be asked, the time and place of contact, and so on, is carefully prepared so that auditing time and cost are kept to a minimum. The cardinal rule in marketing auditing is to avoid reliance solely on the company executives for data and opinion. Customers, dealers, and other outside groups must be interviewed. Many companies do not really know how their customers and dealers see them, nor do they fully understand customer needs.[6]

The audit can be most effective when its philosophy is built on three attributes: comprehensive, systematic, and periodic. An audit should not be considered comprehensive unless all aspects of planning are analyzed. A fee audit or promotional audit by itself provides depth but is not comprehensive enough to evaluate relationships among personnel, organization, and procedures. The audit must be comprehensive to be effective. It should contain an examination of six major components of the company's marketing situation:

- *Marketing environment.* Analyze the major macroenvironmental forces and trends that are the key components of the company's task environment. These include markets, customers, competition, distributors, and dealers, suppliers, and facilitators.
- *Marketing strategy.* Review the company's marketing objectives and marketing strategy to appraise how well these are adapted to the current and forecasted marketing environment.
- *Marketing organization.* Evaluate the capability of the marketing organization, implementing the necessary strategy for the forecasted environment.
- *Marketing system.* Examine the quality of the company's system for analysis, planning, and control.
- *Marketing productivity.* Examine the profitability of different marketing entities and the cost-effectiveness of different marketing expenditures.
- *Marketing function.* Conduct in-depth evaluations of major marketing-mix components, namely products, price, distribution, sales force, advertising, promotion, and publicity.[7]

A systematic audit is one that follows logical, predetermined steps. An outline to such an approach is shown in Exhibit 17.1. The areas covered (based upon the major components of the marketing situation) and the types of questions asked provide the basis for systematically analyzing a company's procedures.

This systematic approach should uncover a great deal of data about the planning process within a company. The continual questioning of "why" about procedures, decisions, and controls is the key to uncovering who did what with what efficiency and provides input for answering, "Are we doing the right things?"

EXHIBIT 17.1. The marketing planning audit format.

Part I: The company marketing environment
  A. Purpose
    1. Has a meaningful statement of company purpose been developed?
    2. Has it been effectively communicated to all marketing personnel?
  B. Organization
    1. Has the responsibility for developing the marketing plan been assigned within the organization?
    2. Are the right people involved in preparation, review, and approval of completed planning documents?
  C. Product/market analysis
    1. Has a general environmental analysis been completed to identify salient factors in the company's operating environment?
    2. Has an environment analysis been completed to identify the product/market's boundaries (i.e., set of customer needs for particular customer segments served by alternative technologies)?
    3. Have the movements along these product/market dimensions been tracked over time to identify evolving trends?
    4. Have the major market growth factors been identified and their relation to revenue studied?
    5. Have these market growth factors been properly forecasted for the planning Period?
    6. Have the key success factors for the product/market been identified?
    7. Has an analysis of sales and costs been conducted by market segment served?
  D. Customer analysis
    1. Have customers' needs been carefully studied by market segments?
    2. Are sufficient data on customers available for planning? What are the nature and time periods covered by these data?
    3. Have customers' motivations been analyzed? What approaches were used to accomplish this?
    4. Has purchase behavior been studied in detail over time? What patterns were identified?
    5. What conclusions were reached about customers' needs, motivations, and behavior?
    6. Have the product/markets been segmented? Have the segment profiles been determined? Have segments been targeted?
  E. Competitive analysis
    1. Has the firm's competitive advantage for each market segment been identified? Does it conform to the four criteria for competitive advantage?
    2. Have the sources of competitive advantage been evaluated for strength and sustainability?

3. Have competitors been identified at all the levels of competition (e.g., desire, generic, etc.)? Do we know the level at which consumers are making their choice among competitors?
4. Have the strategies used by competitors been analyzed and evaluated?

F. Opportunity analysis
1. Were the opportunities identified and described in detail?
2. Were sufficient data used to evaluate these opportunities?
3. Was the compatibility of these opportunities studied in relation to the resources of the firm?
4. Were economic, legal, technological, and cultural factors analyzed for each opportunity? What decisions were made?

Part II: Objectives
A. Nature of objectives
1. Were specific objectives developed?
2. Did these objectives meet the requirements of good objectives? How was this tested?

B. Types of objectives
1. What types of objectives were established?
2. Was a sufficient database used to establish realistic objectives?

Part III: Strategy
A. Have all five elements of the strategy been addressed at the three planning levels?
B. Were alternative strategies evaluated? How?
C. Were product positioning, quality, and service strategies set?
D. What approach was used in establishing prices? Place? Promotional mixes?
E. Were sufficient resources available to implement the strategy?
F. Was the financial impact of the strategy evaluated? How did this influence strategy decisions?

Part IV: Monitoring and control feedback
A. Was a control system established in the planning process?
B. What types of data were collected and how periodically was this done?
C. Where these data and time periods appropriate?
D. What results were achieved? Were these compared to objectives?
E. Was performance evaluation completed on all products by market segment? What types of performance were evaluated?
F. Was corrective action taken as a result of this feedback? What specific actions were taken?

The audit should be undertaken periodically to avoid crisis circumstances. Many firms do not audit their managerial activities until a crisis has arisen, but in many cases a crisis can be avoided by an audit. Few marketing planning processes are so successful that yearly or second- or third-year audits should not be used.

AUDIT DATA AND REPORTING FORMAT

The data for the audit must be provided through source documents (sales reports, sales training procedures, advertising budgets, media schedules, etc.) and interviews with personnel involved in marketing planning. Top management must ensure that auditors have complete cooperation from these personnel and access to any information needed to complete the audit, especially when external auditors are used. Failure to provide access to the same data available to the planners is sure to lead to a superficial audit. Again, auditors must have access to customers, dealers, and other outside groups relevant to the marketing situation. Failure to do so can result in an incomplete and misleading audit report.

Most companies assign one high-level executive as the key person for the external auditor to work through. Information requests routed through that executive carry authority "by virtue of office."

A variety of reporting formats are possible, but one of the most appropriate is a finding, which is a written report of recommendations. In such a report, the auditors' findings are written out for each area of study in the audit and a specific recommendation for improvement is stated for each finding. Thus, the reporting format is action-oriented, and specific actions can be evaluated for improving the planning process.

INCREASING THE LEVEL
OF SOPHISTICATION IN PLANNING

As the marketing planning process is used, audited, and restructured, it becomes possible to raise its level of sophistication. For example, once a database for market analysis or revenue forecasting is established, other factors can be added or simulation models or input-output models can be developed. Online data retrieval for control, as well as other improvements, can be made available for managers in companies with data processing equipment.

Some companies have established internal positions called *marketing controllers* to monitor marketing expenses and activities. These people work in the controller's office and have specialized in the marketing side of the business. Previously, controller offices have concentrated on watching manufacturing, inventory, and financial expenses and did not include staff that understood marketing very well. The new marketing controllers are trained in finance and marketing and can perform a sophisticated financial analysis of past and planned marketing expenditures.[8]

The level of sophistication of the managers and planners should determine the level of sophistication used in planning. More training for current managers or hiring new managers with higher levels of skills permits moving the planning process to more complex approaches.

SUMMARY

This chapter discussed the final aspect of marketing planning, the planning audit. The audit is designed to improve the planning process within a company and can increase level-of-planning sophistication. Thus, the marketing planning process can be studied and improved through the analysis undertaken in the planning audit.

Appendix A

Worksheets

CHAPTER 1: GETTING STARTED

1. Using Exhibit 1.1 as a guide, determine the orientation that guides your business.

   _____

   _____

   _____

2. What changes, if any, are needed to move the orientation of key decision makers to a societal marketing orientation?

   _____

   _____

   _____

3. At what level(s) is planning conducted in your organization (see Exhibit 1.2):

   Corporate?   SBU?   Product/Market?

   _____   _____   _____

   _____   _____   _____

   _____   _____   _____

4. Provide tentative answers to the questions at each planning level. (You will develop more comprehensive answers as you complete the worksheets for each chapter, but this exercise is intended to start you thinking about these critical questions.)

   What is our business? What should it be?

   _____

   _____

   _____

Where should we be going?

_____

_____

_____

How do we get there?

_____

_____

_____

CHAPTER 2: ORGANIZATIONAL CONSIDERATION

1. Define your organization's purpose and mission:

   _____

   _____

   _____

2. Which value discipline does your organization most closely pursue in fulfilling this purpose and mission:

Operational excellence?	Product leadership?	Customer intimacy?
_____	_____	_____
_____	_____	_____
_____	_____	_____

3. Ensure a consistency of objectives and strategy as you move through the planning levels (see Exhibit 2.1 for an example):

   Product line or service _____

   Corporate level _____

   Objective _____

   Strategy _____

   Strategic business unit level _____

   Objective _____

   Strategy _____

   Product/market level _____

   Objective _____

   Strategy _____

CHAPTER 3: INFORMATIONAL NEEDS

Answer These Questions First

1. What kinds of information do you need to make a decision about which course of action to take? Stated another way, if you knew this, would it enable you to make a decision? If yes, the "this" you specified is the information you need.

   _____

   _____

   _____

2. Who is going to be responsible for getting this information? Someone within the organization? An external person or group?

   _____

   _____

   _____

3. If someone within the organization is to collect the data, are there any resource people who could be used to give guidance or input? Who are these people?

   _____

   _____

   _____

4. Has a budget been set aside for this research project? If not, where will the funds come from?

   _____

   _____

   _____

Now Identify Your Information Needs

1. What data is needed as an input to the marketing plan?
   A. _____
   B. _____
   C. _____

2. How would you recommend getting the data to accomplish the objectives?
   A. What information is needed? _____

   _____

   _____

B. From whom should you collect data? _____

_____

_____

C. From how many people should you collect data? _____

_____

_____

D. What kinds of questions do you need to ask? _____

_____

_____

E. How will you collect the data? In person? By telephone? Do you need a formal questionnaire? Is a market database available internally or externally? _____

_____

_____

F. How will you combine the data gathered from different individuals so you can summarize their answers? _____

_____

_____

CHAPTER 4: PRODUCT/MARKET ANALYSIS

1. Describe the conditions or events in each of these segments, which could make a significant impact on the marketing plan for your product or service.

   Economic _____

   Technological _____

   Cultural _____

   Social _____

   Legal _____

   Political _____

2. For each product/market you are analyzing for the marketing plan, indicate the current status and evolving trends for each of the following dimensions (see Exhibit 4.2):

   Customer needs _____

   Customer segments _____

   Alternative technologies _____

3. What are the market growth factors in the product/market and what trends are these factors experiencing?

   _____

   _____

   _____

4. What key success factors are present in the product/market? Which ones are basic to all competitors and which ones do competitors meet with differing degrees of success?

   _____

   _____

   _____

5. What is your performance for these factors?

   Key success factor   Our performance

   _____   _____

   _____   _____

   _____   _____

6. Sales analysis by product/region:

Product total sales	Regional sales			
	A	B	C	D
a. _____	_____	_____	_____	_____
b. _____	_____	_____	_____	_____
c. _____	_____	_____	_____	_____
Totals	_____	_____	_____	_____

7. Cost analysis by product/region:

Cost type	Product A	Product B	Product C
Direct	_____	_____	_____
Indirect	_____	_____	_____
Total	_____	_____	_____
Net Profit	_____	_____	_____

CHAPTER 5: CONSUMER ANALYSIS

1. Describe your target market consumers and characteristics that influence their need for, choice of, or consumption of product or service:

   _____

   _____

   _____

2. For business-to-business products or services, describe those characteristics of organizational buyers that influence their behavior (e.g., who are the decision makers, what are their motives, how is the purchase decision made, etc.).

   _____

   _____

   _____

3. If you are able to define different groups with different characteristics, what can you do to meet the needs of each group differently?

   _____

   _____

   _____

4. Can your product/market be segmented? If so, what basis should be used to segment the market?

   _____

   _____

   _____

5. Identify the market segments:

   _____

   _____

   _____

   Segment name characteristics (demographics, lifestyles, usage patterns, motives, etc.)

   A. _____

   B. _____

   C. _____

6. For each segment identified, estimate the size of each segment in terms of units purchased.

Segment name   Size in units

A. _____   _____

B. _____   _____

C. _____   _____

D. _____   _____

7. Which segments will you choose as target markets?

_____

_____

_____

CHAPTER 6: COMPETITIVE ANALYSIS

Answer These Questions First

1. Do you have a competitive advantage? For each segment chosen as a target market (from #7 of the Chapter 5 worksheet), determine the existence of a competitive advantage.

Target segment   Is the advantage

A. _____   Real? _____

B. _____   Important to the customer? _____

C. _____   Specific? _____

                               Promotable? _____

2. What is the source of your advantage?

Target segment

A. _____   The way you compete _____

B. _____   Basis of competition _____

C. _____   Where you compete _____

                               Whom you compete against _____

3. At what level do you compete in each product/market?

Target segment

A. _____   1. Desire _____

B. _____   2. Generic _____

C. _____   3. Form _____

                               4. Type _____

                               5. Brand _____

Competitive Analysis by Segment

4. Segment name   Specific competitors

A. _____   1. _____

                               2. _____

                               3. _____

B. _____   1. _____

                               2. _____

                               3. _____

C. _____   1. _____

                                       2. _____

                                       3. _____

5. Marketing mix audit by segment

    Segment name _____

	Competitor A	Competitor B	Competitor C
A. Products offered			
1. Number	_____	_____	_____
2. Quality	_____	_____	_____
3. Reputation	_____	_____	_____
B. Place			
1. Location	_____	_____	_____
2. Channels used	_____	_____	_____
3. Distribution services	_____	_____	_____
C. Prices			
1. Price level	_____	_____	_____
2. Dealer/trade discounts	_____	_____	_____
3. Quantity discounts	_____	_____	_____
D. Promotion			
1. Quality	_____	_____	_____
2. Quantity	_____	_____	_____
3. Budget	_____	_____	_____

CHAPTER 7: SUMMARY OF SITUATION ANALYSIS

Basic questions answered	Segment identification			Segment rank
	Segment 1	Segment 2	Segment 3	

Factors analyzed:

Environmental
Are the general factors in the environment favorable to this market segment?

Market
What are the specific market growth factors and key success factors for this segment?

Market potential
How many consumers are in this segment and what are potential sales?

Competition
Do you have a competitive advantage with this segment?

Consumer analysis
What are the characteristics that describe this segment?

Alignment with purpose
Would going after this segment be in line with overall purpose?

Alignment with resources
Marketing
Production
Finance
Management
Do we have or can we acquire the marketing, financial, production, and management resources required by this segment?

Other factors
Economic
Technology
Political and legal
Cultural and social
Are each of these factors favorable or unfavorable in relation to each segment?

Total score

CHAPTER 8: MARKETING OBJECTIVES

Answer These Questions First

1. What do your objectives need to relate to—sales, profits, customers, or all three?

_____

_____

_____

2. What needs to happen for your program to be successful? In other words, what level of profits or how much sales volume do you need?

_____

_____

_____

3. When do you want this to happen? By what specific date?

_____

_____

_____

Now Write Your Objectives

Use the information in your answers to these three questions to write statements of your objectives.

Objective 1: _____

_____

_____

Objective 2: _____

_____

_____

Objective 3: _____

_____

_____

Now test each statement using the criteria given in this chapter. Is each statement relevant to the basic purpose of your organization? Is each statement practical? Does each statement provide a challenge? Is each statement stated in objectively measurable terms? Do you have a specific date for completion? Does each statement contribute to a balance of activities in line with your firm's strengths and weaknesses?

CHAPTER 9: MARKETING STRATEGY DEVELOPMENT

Answer These Questions First

1. What are the distinctive competencies of your firm? What do you do well?

   _____

   _____

   _____

2. What market segment(s) should you select to match your firm's skills and resources with customers' needs in those segments?

   _____

   _____

   _____

3. Do you have the skills/resources to pursue several segments or should you concentrate on one segment? Is that segment large enough to sustain your firm and allow for growth?

   _____

   _____

   _____

Now Develop Your Positioning Statement

1. Distinctive competencies _____

   _____

2. Segments sought _____

   _____

3. Products offered _____

   _____

4. Promotion orientation _____

   _____

5. Price levels _____

   _____

   _____

6. Growth orientation _____

_____

_____

Using the five strategic components described in Chapter 9 and Exhibit 9.1 as guides, fill in the following table. Your strategies should be informed by the situation analysis you conducted in the worksheets for Chapters 3 through 7 and the objectives detailed in Chapter 8's worksheet. The basic concept is that good strategies are "good" because they "fit" the market segment's conditions (i.e., leverage a real competitive advantage with a market segment whose consumers are well understood by management).

Strategy components	Corporate strategy	SBU strategy	Product/market strategy
Scope	_____	_____	_____
	_____	_____	_____
	_____	_____	_____
Goals and objectives	_____	_____	_____
	_____	_____	_____
	_____	_____	_____
Allocation of resources	_____	_____	_____
	_____	_____	_____
	_____	_____	_____
Sources of competitive advantage	_____	_____	_____
	_____	_____	_____
	_____	_____	_____
Sources of synergy	_____	_____	_____
	_____	_____	_____
	_____	_____	_____

CHAPTER 10: PRODUCT DECISIONS

Answer These Questions First

1. Is there any evidence that your existing products need to be changed (low sales volume, complaints, etc.)? What evidence do you have?

   _____

   _____

   _____

2. Is this product vital to your firm? In other words, do you need to continue this product? Why?

   _____

   _____

   _____

3. Are there additional products that you need to add in order to better meet the needs of your customers? What specifically?

   _____

   _____

   _____

4. Determine the appropriate positioning strategy for your product(s).

   A. What product features/benefits are used by target-market (segment) members to evaluate products?

   _____

   _____

   _____

   B. What positions do existing competitors occupy along these dimensions?

Segment	Competitor	Positioning
A._____	A._____	A._____
B._____	B._____	B._____
C._____	C._____	C._____

   C. What niches are largely unoccupied by competitors with particular market segments?

Segment	Unoccupied niche (Features/benefits positioning)
A._____	A._____
B._____	B._____
C._____	C._____

D. Write a positioning strategy for each selected segment.

Segment	Positioning base	Positioning strategy
A. _____	Attribute _____	_____
B. _____	Price/quality _____	_____
C. _____	Use or application _____	_____
D. _____	Product user _____	_____
E. _____	Product Class _____	_____
F. _____	Competitor _____	_____

5. Have you considered the long-term impact to targeted customers and to society from marketing this product?

_____

_____

_____

6. Establish a product quality strategy.

Support of top management? _____

Understands customer needs? _____

Closes gaps in meeting needs? _____

Avoids untimely delays? _____

Empowers people? _____

Rewards appropriate actions? _____

Seen as continuous concern? _____

7. Establish a customer service strategy.

_____

_____

_____

Does it include the following dimensions:

Tangibles? _____

Reliability? _____

Responsiveness? _____

Assurance? _____

Empathy? _____

8. Have the following gaps been "closed"?

Gap between customer expectations and management perceptions?

_____

Gap between management perceptions and service quality specifications? _____

Gap between service quality specifications and service delivery?_____

Gap between service delivery and external communications?_____

CHAPTER 11: PLACE DECISIONS

1. What kinds of services have to be provided to end users by marketing channels in order to assure target end user satisfaction, regardless of the specific channels employed?

_____

_____

_____

2. What kinds of marketing and/or logistical activities or functions have to be performed to generate those services?

_____

_____

_____

3. Which types of institutions or agencies are in the best position to perform these activities, taking into account their effectiveness and efficiency at doing so?

_____

_____

_____

4. What specific middlemen are needed to implement your positioning strategy?

_____

_____

_____

5. What degree of market exposure is needed for each of your firm's products?

_____

_____

_____

Products   Market exposure desire
A._____   _____
B._____   _____
C._____   _____

6a. How many additional locations or middlemen are needed? Where should they be located?

Facility A _____

_____

Facility B _____

_____

6b. How will these be selected?

_____

_____

_____

7. What changes are needed to improve the distribution of your product?

Better middlemen _____

More locations _____

Better physical distribution _____

8. For each area previously listed, describe your plan for making these changes happen.

Area	Your plan
A. _____	_____
B. _____	_____
C. _____	_____

9. For each product, specify how transportation and storage are to be handled.

Product	Storage facilities	Transportation mode
A. _____	_____	_____
B. _____	_____	_____
C. _____	_____	_____

CHAPTER 12: PROMOTION DECISIONS

Advertising

Answer These Questions First

1. What positioning strategy will you execute through your promotional efforts?

   _____

   _____

   _____

2. What is the targeted group for this positioning strategy? What are the characteristics of this group that would influence how the members perceive messages or where they might receive messages?

   _____

   _____

   _____

3. What do you want to say to this group? What message(s) do you want to communicate? Are you going to send repeated messages to this group about this topic? If so, would a theme help tie messages together?

   _____

   _____

   _____

4. What media will you use to deliver this message? Are there other media you could use? Have you evaluated these in terms of costs, frequency, reach?

   _____

   _____

   _____

5. How much do you plan to spend for this specific promotion? What percent of your total budget is required by this specific promotion project? Do you have accurate estimates on production costs, number to be printed, aired, etc?

   _____

   _____

   _____

Now Plan Your Advertising Strategy

First, write a general statement of how promotion is to be used to inform, persuade, or remind prospects about your organization's products. This is your overall strategy statement. Now use the information from the answers to the previous questions to write several statements concerning what is to be communicated to whom, through what media, and at what costs. These statements now specify your promotions strategy statement.

Overall strategy statement: _____

_____

_____

Target of promotion: _____

_____

_____

Messages to be communicated: _____

_____

_____

Media to be used: _____

_____

_____

Budget: By media
                       1. _____
                       2. _____
                       3. _____
                       Total _____

Personal Selling

Answer These Questions First

1. What is the targeted group for personal selling? What are the characteristics of this group, which would influence what messages they need?

_____

_____

_____

2. What needs to be presented to the individuals in this group? What information do you need to convey to them?

_____

_____

_____

3. How much time should the salesperson plan to spend with each prospect contacted? How many calls will be made each day?

_____

_____

_____

4. How much follow-up is needed to effectively serve customers?

_____

_____

_____

Now Plan Your Personal Selling Strategy

After answering the previous questions, develop your statement of the personal contact strategy for your plan.

Quality level of representatives needed: _____

_____

_____

Quantity of representatives needed: _____

_____

_____

Motivation/training plan to be used: _____

_____

_____

Reporting policies and procedures: _____

_____

_____

Publicity

Answer These Questions First

1. Who is to be responsible for publicity in your firm?

   _____

   _____

   _____

2. What types of publicity would best fit your firm?

   _____

   _____

   _____

3. What event/story would most likely be of interest to the public you want to reach?

   _____

   _____

   _____

Now Plan Your Publicity Strategy

After answering the previous questions, develop a specific publicity plan for an event.

1. Event(s) to be publicized:

   _____

   _____

   _____

2. Specific media to be contacted:

   _____

   _____

   _____

3. Details of the event:

   _____

   A. Who _____

   B. What _____

   C. When _____

   D. Where _____

   E. Why _____

   F. Budget _____

Sales Promotion

Answer These Questions First

1. Who is to be responsible for your firm's sales promotion activities?

   _____

   _____

   _____

2. What types of sales promotion activities would be best to help coordinate your advertising/personal selling efforts?

   _____

   _____

   _____

3. Do you have the policies, procedures, and staff set up to handle the promotions? Do you need an outside organization's help in putting the promotions together?

   _____

   _____

   _____

Now Plan Your Sales Promotions

After answering the previous questions, develop a specific plan for each promotional activity used.

1. Exact nature of the promotion:

   _____

   _____

   _____

2. Specific needs of the promotion:
   A. Outside organization(s) needed:

   _____

   _____

   _____

   B. Special staff:

   _____

   _____

   _____

C. Duration of the promotion:

_____

_____

_____

D. Budget for the promotion:

_____

_____

_____

CHAPTER 13: PRICE DECISIONS

Answer These Questions First

1. Does your existing price strategy fit what you want to accomplish in terms of profitability? Positioning?

_____

_____

_____

2. Does the nature of the internal and external factors identified in the chapter indicate the need for a change in your price strategy?

_____

_____

_____

3. Do you have enough cost information available to determine your average cost per unit?

_____

_____

_____

Develop a Price Strategy

1. Identify your price strategy by product, i.e., below, with, or above the market.

Product	Strategy
A._____	_____
B._____	_____
C._____	_____

2. What is your current list price for each product? What discounts apply to each product?

Product	List price/unit	Discount used	Actual price
A._____	$ _____	_____	$ _____
B._____	$ _____	_____	$ _____
C._____	$ _____	_____	$ _____

Perform a Cost Analysis

1. Fill out a cost worksheet similar to the following for each of your products.

Cost Category	Amount
A. Production cost in total	$_____
B. Marketing costs in total	_____
C. Inventory carrying costs	_____
D. Administrative overhead assigned	_____
Total cost	$_____

2. Now estimate unit cost by dividing the total cost by the number of units you sold last year.

   Total costs from above = Average cost per unit $___Number of units sold

3. Now compare this cost with the price you identified under the previous level section. Do your prices reflect these costs? Do you need to raise/lower your price based on consumer preference, offerings of others, etc.?

Product	Price
A. _____	$_____
B. _____	_____
C. _____	_____

CHAPTER 14: FINANCIAL IMPACT

Answer These Questions First

1. Do you have the data necessary to complete the pro forma statement? If not, how will this data be generated?

   _____

   _____

   _____

2. What techniques will be used to
   A. forecast sales? _____

   _____

   _____

   B. forecast costs? _____

   _____

   _____

3. What techniques will be used to analyze the return on investment?

   _____

   _____

   _____

4. Will additional investment be needed to offer this service? Plant? Equipment? Distribution facilities?

   _____

   _____

   _____

Now Fill Out the Following Pro Forma Statement

	Low	Medium	High
1. Sales			
Cost of sales	_____	_____	_____
Gross margin	_____	_____	_____
Expenses	_____	_____	_____
Direct selling	_____	_____	_____
Advertising	_____	_____	_____
Transportation and storage	_____	_____	_____
Depreciation	_____	_____	_____
Credit and collections	_____	_____	_____
Financial and clerical	_____	_____	_____
Administrative	_____	_____	_____

Total Expenses
Profit before taxes
Net profit after taxes
Cash Flow
2. New investments:
Fixed capital
Working capital
Total new investment
3. Return on investment:

CHAPTER 15: PLAN IMPLEMENTATION

1. Indicate how you will use the following skills to tactically implement the strategic elements of your marketing plan:

A. Product

Allocating	Monitoring	Organizing	Interacting
_____	_____	_____	_____
_____	_____	_____	_____
_____	_____	_____	_____

B. Place

Allocating	Monitoring	Organizing	Interacting
_____	_____	_____	_____
_____	_____	_____	_____
_____	_____	_____	_____

C. Promotion

Allocating	Monitoring	Organizing	Interacting
_____	_____	_____	_____
_____	_____	_____	_____
_____	_____	_____	_____

D. Price

Allocating	Monitoring	Organizing	Interacting
_____	_____	_____	_____
_____	_____	_____	_____
_____	_____	_____	_____

2. Ensure that these tactics are consistent with the objectives and strategies at the corporate, SBU, and product/market levels.

	Corporate		SBU		Product/Market	
	Strategy	**Objective**	**Strategy**	**Objective**	**Strategy**	**Objective**
Consistent tactics	_____	_____	_____	_____	_____	_____

3. Have the implementation activities been coordinated among the various marketing functions?

	Product management	**Sales force**	**Advertising**	**PR**	**Trade promotion**	**Other**
Product management	_____	_____	_____	_____	_____	_____
Sales force	_____	_____	_____	_____	_____	_____
Advertising	_____	_____	_____	_____	_____	_____
PR	_____	_____	_____	_____	_____	_____
Trade promotion	_____	_____	_____	_____	_____	_____
Other	_____	_____	_____	_____	_____	_____

4. Have the implementation activities been coordinated between marketing and other business functions?

	Marketing	**Production**	**Service**	**Accounting**	**Suppliers**	**Other**
Marketing	_____	_____	_____	_____	_____	_____
Production	_____	_____	_____	_____	_____	_____
Service	_____	_____	_____	_____	_____	_____
Accounting	_____	_____	_____	_____	_____	_____
Suppliers	_____	_____	_____	_____	_____	_____
Other	_____	_____	_____	_____	_____	_____

Action Plan Worksheet

Key result area: _____

Objective: _____

Benefit statement: _____

Strategies:

    A. _____

    B. _____

    C. _____

    D. _____

    E. _____

Action plan person responsible: _____

Resources required: _____

Date started: _____

Date completed: _____

Budget: _____

CHAPTER 16: MARKETING CONTROL

Answer the Following Questions

1. What kinds of information do you need to evaluate your firm's or a specific product's success?

_____

_____

_____

2. Who should receive and review this information?

_____

_____

_____

3. What time periods do you want to use to analyze the data? Weekly? Monthly? Quarterly?

_____

_____

_____

4. What record-keeping system do you need to devise to make sure the information you want is recorded for the time periods you specified in question 3?

_____

_____

_____

Now Set Up Your Control Procedures

1. Specify the areas to be controlled:
   A. _____
   B. _____
   C. _____
2. Specify the format of the data for each area. (Is it to be sales by month by product? Do you want dollar and percentage variations?)
   A. _____
   B. _____
   C. _____

3. Specify how the data are to be collected, who is to collect and analyze the data, and who is to receive the results of the analysis:

A. How data are to be collected? _____

_____

_____

B. Who has responsibility to collect and analyze the data? _____

_____

_____

C. Who is to receive what type of analysis?

Manager's name	Types of analysis
1. _____	1. _____
2. _____	2. _____
3. _____	3. _____

CHAPTER 17: MARKETING PLANNING AUDIT

Part I: The Company Marketing Environment

A. Purpose
   1. Has a meaningful statement of company purpose been developed?

_____

_____

_____

   2. Has it been effectively communicated to all marketing personnel?

_____

_____

_____

B. Organization
   1. Has the responsibility for developing the marketing plan been assigned within the organization? _____

_____

_____

   2. Are the right people involved in preparation, review, and approval of completed planning documents? _____

_____

_____

C. Product/market analysis
   1. Has a general environmental analysis been completed to identify salient factors in the company's operating environment? _____

_____

_____

   2. Has an environmental analysis been completed to identify the product/market's boundaries (i.e., set of customer needs for particular customer segments served by alternative technologies)? _____

_____

_____

   3. Have the movements along these product/market dimensions been tracked over time to identify evolving trends? _____

_____

_____

4. Have the major market growth factors been identified and their relation to revenue studied? _____

_____

5. Have these market growth factors been properly forecasted for the planning period? _____

_____

6. Have the key success factors for the product/market been identified?

_____

_____

7. Has an analysis of sales and costs been conducted by market segment served? _____

_____

D. Customer analysis
  1. Have customers' needs been carefully studied by market segments?

_____

_____

  2. Are sufficient data on customers available for planning? What are the nature and time periods covered by these data? _____

_____

  3. Have customers' modifications been analyzed? What approaches were used to accomplish this? _____

_____

  4. Has purchase behavior been studied in detail over time? What patterns were identified? _____

_____

  5. What conclusions were reached about customers' needs, motivations, and behavior? _____

_____

  6. Have the product/markets been segmented? Have the segment profiles been determined? Have segments been targeted? _____

_____

E. Competitive analysis
   1. Has the firm's competitive advantage for each market segment been identified? Does it conform to the four criteria for competitive advantage? _____

   _____

   _____

   2. Have the sources of competitive advantage been evaluated for strength and sustainability? _____

   _____

   _____

   3. Have competitors been identified at all the levels of competition (i.e., desire, generic, etc.)? Do we know the level at which consumers are making their choice among competitors? _____

   _____

   _____

   4. Have the strategies used by competitors been analyzed and evaluated?

   _____

   _____

   _____

F. Opportunity analysis
   1. Were the opportunities identified and described in detail?

   _____

   _____

   _____

   2. Were sufficient data used to evaluate these opportunities?

   _____

   _____

   _____

   3. Was the compatibility of these opportunities studied in relation to the resources of the firm?

   _____

   _____

   _____

   4. Were economic, legal, technological, and cultural factors analyzed for each opportunity? What decisions were made?

   _____

   _____

   _____

Part II: Objectives

A. Nature of objectives
   1. Were specific objectives developed? _____
   _____
   _____

   2. Did these objectives meet the requirements of good objectives? How was this tested? _____
   _____
   _____

B. Types of objectives
   1. What types of objectives were established? _____
   _____
   _____

   2. Was a sufficient database used to establish realistic objectives? _____
   _____
   _____

Part III: Strategy

A. Have all five elements of the strategy been addressed at the three planning levels? _____
_____
_____

B. Were alternative strategies evaluated? How? _____
_____
_____

C. Were product positioning, quality, and service strategies set? _____
_____
_____

D. What approach was used in establishing prices? Place? Promotional mixes? _____
_____
_____

E. Were sufficient resources available to implement the strategy? _____
_____
_____

F. Was the financial impact of the strategy evaluated? How did this influence strategy decisions? _____

_____

_____

Part IV: Monitoring and Control Feedback

A. Was a control system established in the planning process? _____

_____

B. What types of data were collected and how periodically? _____

_____

C. Were these data and time periods appropriate? _____

_____

D. What results were achieved? Were these compared to objectives? _____

_____

E. Was performance evaluation completed on all products by market segment? What types of performance were evaluated? _____

_____

F. Was corrective action taken as a result of this feedback? What specific actions were taken? _____

_____

_____

Appendix B

Sample Marketing Plan:
Water-Oriented Recreation Park

Prepared by
Triad Consulting and Research
2900 Cameron
Monroe, LA 71201

SITUATION ANALYSIS

Environmental Trends

Although the concept of a water-oriented park was not new, there were no close competitors in the market area. The following trends and forecasts for recreation were taken from industry literature:

1. Americans have a growing preoccupation with outdoor recreation.
2. Based on past trends, a doubling of recreational expenditures can be expected in the next eight to ten years.
3. Expenditures for leisure activities are increasing faster than consumer spending as a whole.
4. More and more people are moving to the Sunbelt; the South and Southwest are expected to be major growth areas, and people tend to be more recreationally active there.
5. Leisure spending does not appear to be as heavily influenced by adverse economic conditions as other expenditures.
6. Total leisure spending is expected to grow to $400 billion within six years.
7. Tops on the list of popular sports in the United States is swimming—some 103 million people regularly swim.

Note: Names and dates in this plan have been altered for anonymity.

8. Admissions revenue for sporting events grew from $15 billion to $35 billion over the last ten years.
9. Water-related activities accounted for five of the top twenty-five outdoor recreational activities.
10. Experts state that participation in summertime outdoor recreational activities is four times greater than it was forty years ago.
11. Many theme parks are currently in trouble financially because of saturation, competition, and inflation.
12. Experienced theme-park operators have learned how to keep guests for several hours and offer many alternative ways to spend money.
13. A major cost problem for theme parks is the attempt to add a newer, more thrilling ride every two years—at continuing inflated costs.
14. A nearby water-oriented recreation project is successful, appealing mainly to a younger market, ages eight to twenty-three; but very few families participate.

Although large theme parks recently had trouble, the overall climate for outdoor recreation ventures is favorable, and water-related activities in the Sunbelt appear to have a high probability of success.

Product/Market Analysis

1. *Customer needs:* The core need that we will be serving is water-related recreation with other supplemental entertainment and recreation activities available.
2. *Customer segments:* The segments of greatest interest are local youth, ages eight to eighteen, who will travel with their peers to enjoy group recreational activities.
3. *Alternative technologies:* The core technology will be waterslides, waterflume, wave pond, and swimming pool; but video/electronic technologies will also be available in the arcade, and go-cart, miniature golf, and other technologies will be offered.
4. *Success factors:* Research has shown the following key success factors are present in this product/market:
   Location—People will not travel long distances to use such a facility. Less than fifteen miles from the Anytown center is ideal.
   Hierarchy of "dangerous fun"—Youth in the targeted segment want to have available activities that offer different degrees of "danger." Amusement parks provide roller coasters requiring different degrees of courage to ride, and our park should do the same with the water-based activities. The names of the activities should communicate the differing degrees of "danger" (e.g., The Slip-n-Slide versus Terminal Velocity).

Ancillary activities—If you are to attract the targeted segment to spend the day at the facility you must provide non-water-based activities as well (e.g., video arcade, go-cart racing, batting cage, miniature golf, etc.). Once attracted to the water activities it will be possible to get more of the target market's recreational dollars with other activities that will keep them at the park.

Promotion—A variety of promotional methods must be used, supported by a substantial budget, over the entire summer season.

5. *Hours of operation:* Recreational attractions must be open at night and during the day to maximize usage by target audience (youth ages eight to eighteen).

Consumer Analysis

The market segments for the park are shown in the market grid in Exhibit B.1. Two major characteristics of the market influence marketing activities outlined in the plan. One is the size of the party involved. Research evidence collected from this project confirms that the primary market is youth and single adults, and also many consumers indicated they would probably go with a group to this type of attraction. Although families will certainly not be ignored, the size of this market compared to the other two warrants less marketing effort.

Another consumer category is area resident versus tourist. Again, the tourists will not be ignored, but primary emphasis will be placed on the resident segments because of their size and accessibility.

EXHIBIT B.1. Market segments.

Type of party	Size of party		
	Individuals/couples	Families	Groups
Area residents	Youth eight to eighteen Single adults, nineteen and over Young couples	Young, no children Older, young children Older, older children	Churches Colleges Organizations
Tourist	Single adults Young couples	Young, no children Older, young children Older, older children	Churches Schools

Research reveals that the major motives for going to this type of park are as follows:

1. *Fun:* This is a key word used by many consumers.
2. *Peers:* People like to be with people their own age.
3. *Physical attraction of combination of sun and water:* People like to be near water in hot weather.
4. *Boredom:* People want activities other than staying home, watching television, and so on.

Consumers appear willing to spend $5 to $8 for this type of event per person, and most youths report spending $15 to $20 a month on outdoor recreational activities during the summer. A high degree of consumer acceptance of water-related activities such as a waterslide are also evident; most youths have been to a waterslide and most adults with children are aware and approve of them. This means a favorable consumer mind-set for the park.

The demographics of the market are favorable in terms of the major segments to be sought as customers. Statistics on Anytown reveal the sizes of the market segments, as shown in Exhibit B.2. Population projections show a near doubling of the county population in the next twenty years. Thus a strong population base is apparently to continue in the market area for the next two decades.

Income statistics for Anytown also reveal a very strong market. Exhibit B.3 shows the *Sales Management* magazine's recent estimate of household effective-buying income.

Income in Anytown is not much different from the state; at least 48.8 percent of the households had an income of $30,000 or more. The median income for Anytown was $29,622. Overall, Anytown provides a stable economic base with future population growth and income levels that will support additional recreational facilities.

EXHIBIT B.2. Population distribution by age groups.

Age group*	Total number
6-17	70,758
18-34	150,134
35-64	92,700

Source: Statistical Abstract, Planning Department, City of Anytown, USA. Statistics are based on most recent census. Includes most of the 40,000 to 60,000 students enrolled at the area colleges.

*in years

EXHIBIT B.3. Household effective-buying income for Anytown, USA (percentage of households).

Income (dollars)	Anytown (%)	State (%)	U.S. (%)
0-7,999	26.4	27.3	25.4
8,000-9,999	7.3	6.9	6.6
10,000-14,999	17.5	17.6	18.0
15,000-24,999	26.9	28.7	30.8
25,000 and over	21.9	19.5	19.2

Source: Sales and Marketing Management, Survey of Buying Power.

Competitive Analysis

An analysis of competitive daytime recreational facilities revealed the data shown in Exhibits B.4 and B.5. Although many competing recreational activities can be found in Anytown, no competitor offers facilities comparable to the proposed park. In fact, at current prices for waterslides in the area, the park will draw most of those consumers because of the cumulative attraction of other activities and the positive park value. Each alternate recreational facility is a competitor of the park; but given the nature of the project, no major daytime or nighttime competitor is available.

Marketing Opportunities

Given the overall positive environment for outdoor recreational activities and the "ripeness" of the Anytown market, a definite marketing opportunity for the project was found. The opportunities can be characterized as follows:

1. Opportunity for major water-oriented park appealing mainly to youths and young adults.
2. Opportunities for many nonadmission revenues from locker rentals; swimsuits, sunglasses, suntan lotion, and T-shirt sales; concession sales; and arcade sales.
3. Major opportunities for group sales.
4. Opportunity for other revenue-producing activities such as religious group concerts, craft festival days, and so on.

EXHIBIT B.4. Indoor recreational daytime competitors.

Type	Number	Average price
Theaters	23	$6.50/twelve years and over
Skating rinks	4	3.50/person
Bowling alleys	5	3.70/person
Racquetball courts (public)	2	9.50/person
Arcades	10	.75/game
Pistol ranges	3	4.00/person

EXHIBIT B.5. Outdoor recreational daytime competitors.

Type	Number	Average price
Waterslide	2	1/2 hours—$4.00 1 hour—$6.00 All day—$9.00
Race cars	1	$2.50/lap usually spend $15/person
Skateboard park	1	Not open
Swimming pools (public)	6	$2.00/person
Miniature golf	3	$3.00/person
Tennis courts (public)	6	$2.50/person
Amusement park	2	$.25/ticket 3-4 tickets per ride

OBJECTIVES

Short-Term Objectives—One Year

1. *Sales:* To generate a minimum of 190,000 paid attendance.
2. *Profits:* To break even on the profit and loss statement and show a positive cash flow from operations.
3. *Consumers:* To create at least 75 percent awareness of the existence and nature of the park to market segments and a 50 percent penetration of market by the end of the first year of operation. Also have each customer attend at least three times during the first season.

Long-Term Objectives—Five Years

1. *Sales:* To grow at a minimum rate of 15 percent in attendance and an additional minimum of 10 percent per year in ticket price. This results in a 25 percent increase in revenues at the end of five years.
2. *Profits:* To provide a minimum of 20 percent return (cash flow on cash investment) by the end of five years.
3. *Consumer:* To create a 95 percent level of awareness of the existence and nature of the park among continuous residents (excluding immigration) and an 85 percent level of penetration of the market by the end of the fifth year of operation. Also maintain repeat business of three times a year by the end of five years.

STRATEGY

Scope

1. *Target market:* The primary market is youth ages eight to eighteen in the local area; the secondary market is families, and visitors from outside the area.
2. *Product/market development plan:* Offer a new, water-oriented, outdoor recreational facility that is well designed, well laid out, and has several participation-oriented activities. Offer several related products and services for additional entertainment and enjoyment, concessions, T-shirts, arcade, go-carts, miniature golf, etc.
3. *Goals and objectives:* See Objectives section.
4. *Allocation of resources.*

Product/Service Strategy

1. Offer major activities of waterslide, waterflume, wave pool, and swimming pool and select a name that is suggestive of water.
2. Build ancillary areas for jogging and volleyball, as well as a covered picnic area with tables and chairs for large groups.
3. Offer a kiddie pool for children with a slide and other play equipment close to the pool and play area but some distance from major activities; install a small fence around the children's area.
4. Build an air-conditioned recreational building with an arcade of electronic games and a concession area with seating and outside window service. A large covered area for spectators should be provided either in the building or adjacent to it.

5. Offer shopping facilities for swimsuits, sunglasses, suntan lotion, bathing towels, T-shirts, and souvenirs.
6. Provide a large bathhouse for changing clothes, complete with restroom facilities, showers, built-in hair dryers, and rental locker baskets for clothes.
7. Provide rental umbrellas and sunbathing mats.

Place Strategy

1. The park would be located within a fifteen-mile radius of Anytown. Research evidence indicates that this is the maximum distance parents would drive their children for an activity. Location within a five-mile radius of center of town is most desirable.
2. A consistent image of water and water-related activity should be projected by park facilities; for example, men's restroom signs could say "buoys" and women's could say "gulls"; the recreational building could be designed to look like a boat; and so on. These are all image-building features.
3. The entire facility should be completely fenced, well-lighted, and well-manned. Sufficient rules should be established and a sufficient number of lifeguards should be on duty at all times.
4. Physical facilities, rules, lifeguards, and so on should create an image of safety and sanitary conditions for water-oriented activities.
5. The facility should be laid out to facilitate the traffic flow within the park—for instance, the long lines of people waiting for the flume ride should not be standing in front of the concession stand.
6. Landscaping should provide privacy for sunbathers and participants who are in the park and minimize onlookers around the fences. It also encourages more people to come into the park.
7. The facility should be laid out in anticipation of other uses—for example, there should be a large area for people to sit on the ground for a concert and an area that could be used for a craft display. Expansion of retail facilities should be anticipated.

Promotional Strategy

1. Plan a major impact on the market to introduce concept and raise level of awareness and interest. Saturate media two weeks before opening date to four weeks after opening.
2. Work with an ad agency to develop a theme and a consistent set of messages to focus on basic consumer motivations. Messages on T-shirts, posters, billboards, and so on should all support and/or expand basic theme.

3. Two separate promotional plans should be developed—one for individuals, couples, or families and the other for group sales.
4. Promotional expenditures should approximate $100,000 in the first year and $50,000 thereafter at current price levels. After impact on market is made, promotional emphasis should shift to reminder-type advertising, thereby reducing expenditure.
5. The promotional effort should be related to the season of activities, with at least 50 percent of the yearly budget spent in a six-week period surrounding the grand opening, two weeks before and four weeks after the opening. The rest of the budget should be allocated evenly over the rest of the season and should continue to be a mix of informative and reminder-type messages.
6. The largest proportion of the media budget should be spent on radio since this is the primary medium for reaching teenagers.
7. The most popular radio station for this market segment should cooperate in opening ticket giveaways, broadcasts on location for opening, and so forth.
8. Billboards (road signs) should be used for information and location promotion. This is a technique for reaching the tourist market.

Price Strategy

1. A package price policy should be used—admission price covers use of basic services. A price of $9.95 per day and $5.95 for evenings (5 p.m. to 10 p.m.) is a good value for the services offered.
2. Additional charges should be made for use of all other facilities and equipment—sunbathing mats, lockers for clothes, and so on.
3. Prices of food, beverages, T-shirts, souvenirs, and so on should not be excessive—no $1 soft drinks. Reasonable prices encourage greater use of facilities and minimize problems of people bringing their own food and drinks.
4. Discounts should be used for return visits to encourage repeats; careful control must be exercised to avoid giving discounts to new users.
5. Group rates should be discounted and prorated on the number in the group, which encourages larger groups to cut down individual costs. The minimum-size group for discounts should be established at around twenty.
6. After-hour rental of the facility for approved activities should be encouraged to expand sales.
7. The price should be emphasized in promotion—one price for up to ten hours is a good value.

Sources of competitive advantage: Comprehensive set of attractions centered around the water-based facilities. No other competitive recreational attraction can meet this success requirement. Also, being open at night as well as during the day capitalizes on another success requirement at an advantage over competitors.

Sources of synergy: Offering accessories related to the water recreational activities such as locker rentals, swimsuits, sunglasses, suntan lotion, slide mats, etc.

Pro Forma Analysis

The results of the analysis of attendance, revenues, and costs are presented in Exhibits B.6 and B.7. The admission charge was anticipated to be about $10 per person, giving the following alternative sales forecasts.

A sales range of about $2,134,375 to $2,570,500 was estimated. To derive a figure for the pro forma income statement, the following probabilities were assigned to each forecast: low = .25, most likely = .50, and high = .25.

This final value ($2,134,375) was used as the estimated sales revenue to be generated from attendance sales in the pro forma income statement. Other revenues from mat rentals, concessions, and miscellaneous sales were estimated but not included in this analysis. Costs were estimated by management for each of the expenses shown in Exhibit B.7. The figures were derived from cost figures of other company operations with similar labor, material, and overhead structures. The ROI for twenty years was 26 percent, which represents an above-average ROI for company projects. Therefore the strategy is feasible as planned.

CONTROL PROCEDURES

The following control procedures are to be used for each annual plan:

1. A profit-center accounting system for each of the following profit centers:
   a. Attendance
   b. Rentals
   c. Food and beverage operations
   d. Retail shop operations
   e. Miscellaneous
2. An awareness-penetration consumer study at the end of each operating season to be conducted by an outside research organization
3. An ROI and ratio analysis at the end of each operating season

EXHIBIT B.6. Attendance projections.

Alternative forecasts for year 1	Attendance		
Facts/assumptions	Low	Most likely	High
Attendance/penetration			
Local market—target population	xxx	xxx	xxx
Target market (ages ten to twenty-five)	112,000	112,000	112,000
Penetration	.65	.70	.85
Attendance	72,800	78,400	95,200
Local market—general population			
Population	103,087	103,087	103,087
Penetration	.03	.05	.07
Attendance	3,100	5,100	7,200
Regional market			
Population	90,000	90,000	90,000
Penetration	.10	.15	.20
Attendance	9,000	13,500	18,000
Tourist market			
Population	225,000	225,000	225,000
Penetration	.03	.05	.07
Attendance	6,750	11,250	15,750
Group sales market			
Attendance	18,275	20,350	25,700
Repeat business			
Attendance	72,800	78,400	95,200
Total attendance (sum of above)	182,725	207,000	257,050

Low forecast—$1,827,250 (182,725 × $10)
Most likely—$2,070,000 (207,000 × $10)
High forecast—$2,570,500 (257,050 × $10)

EXHIBIT B.7. Pro forma income statement (end of year 1).

Sales		$2,134,375
Expenses		
Salaries and wages	$105,000	
Supplies	123,000	
Utilities	48,000	
Deprection	133,000	
Advertising	50,000	
Taxes and insurance	73,638	
Other administrative expenses	<u>38,000</u>	
	$570,638	
Total operating expenses		<u>570,638</u>
Net income before taxes		$1,563,737
Taxes (state and federal)		<u>781,869</u>
Net income after taxes		$781,868
Total investment	$3,000,000	
Payback period	3.8 years	
Discounted rate of return	26%	

Low forecast .25
Most likely   .50
High forecast .25

The expected sales revenue was then computed as follows: E_{SR} = ($1,827,500) (.25) + ($2,070,000) (.50) + (2,570,000) (.25) E_{SR} = $2,134,375.

The manager of each profit center is to prepare a yearly pro forma statement at the beginning of each operating season. An evaluation of variances and recommendation for performance improvement are to be submitted by each manager within a week of the close of each month during the operating season—six reports in total. In addition, a summary report is to be submitted within two weeks of the close of the operating season.

CONSUMER STUDY

This section of the report develops the methods for collecting consumer information and presents the results of the Anytown consumer study.

Assessment of consumer attitudes on this new concept began with a technique called focus group interviews. These interviews were conducted with twelve teenagers between the ages of twelve and eighteen. Males and females were evenly mixed, and most of the participants would be considered opinion leaders to some extent. The interviews proceeded from a general discussion of recreation, to outdoor activities, to water-related activities. The concept was described, and many questions were asked about participation, price, repeat trips, and so on.

The findings of the group interviews were confirmed in the consumer survey. A consistent pattern of responses emerged from both data collection techniques. The methodology and findings of the survey follow.

Introduction

Purpose

The purpose of this study was to provide data for market analysis and planning for the project. The study provided data and a wide range of topics related to outdoor recreational activities and market participation. These data were the basis for the marketing plan developed for the park.

Research Objectives

This study sought to accomplish several research objectives:

1. Identify the type of recreational activities Anytown residents participate in and the extent of participation by family unit.
2. Determine the price levels anticipated by consumers for an outdoor recreational activity such as the proposed park.
3. Determine exactly which consumer segment was most likely to be appealed to by the project.
4. Identify reasons for anticipated participation or lack of participation in the proposed project.
5. Identify socioeconomic characteristics of the anticipated target markets.

Methodology

Sampling

Respondents for this study were selected through the use of a cluster sampling procedure of Anytown area residents listed in the current telephone book. The original clusters consisted of 1,500 residential listings.

This rather large number was necessary to produce a sample of 300 respondents—225 adults and 75 young people. Many disconnected numbers, respondents who would not cooperate, and potential respondents who could not be reached were anticipated, and therefore a larger number of residents was selected initially to assure the desired sample size.

Survey Instrument and Data Collection

A telephone questionnaire was prepared for this study and pretested for validity. The following topics were covered:

1. Participation in outdoor recreational activities
2. Types of outdoor activities participated in
3. Vacationing recreational activities
4. Total family expenditures anticipated for an outdoor activity
5. Familiarity with and reaction to waterslides
6. Motivation for participation in water-related recreational activities
7. Socioeconomic classification data

A separate questionnaire was designed to be administered to young people to assure collection of data from consumers most likely to use a recreational facility such as the proposed. The data were collected during the second week of February by interviewers selected and trained by the consultants. Although little difficulty was encountered in obtaining cooperation or in administering the questionnaires, many interviews were aborted completely by respondents who were not participants in outdoor activities or who were unfamiliar with water-related activities. Approximately ten minutes was required for completion of the adult interview and approximately five minutes for the youth questionnaire.

Data Tabulation and Analysis

The data were hand tabulated and organized by topical area. All tabulations were then put in percentages to provide patterns of responses. Descriptive statistics were then calculated to represent the basic response modes of consumers and permit further analysis of the data.

Findings

Outdoor Recreational Participation

Most of the respondents interviewed in the study (71 percent) do participate in outdoor recreational activities. The most popular activities were swimming, jogging, and tennis. For those respondents who have children living at home, 65 percent participate with their children in outdoor activities. Swimming, tennis, and camping appear to be the most popular activities for these families.

When on vacation, they were not as likely to participate in outdoor recreational activities; only 52 percent reported such participation. However, most families participated together in the activity when traveling. Swimming was the major activity again, and this was probably associated with a motel stay.

Most respondents reported traveling less than five miles to participate in an outdoor activity. Most parents would only be willing to travel up to ten miles to take their children to an outdoor recreational activity.

Reactions to Water-Related Recreational Activities

The majority of respondents (79 percent) had heard of a waterslide, but only 39 percent had actually been to one. Of those respondents who had been to a waterslide, the majority (69 percent) participated in and enjoyed the activity.

Although a waterslide does not really compare directly with the park concept, the type of activity does, and respondents' image of that type of activity was analyzed. A very consistent pattern of responses emerged. The majority of respondents felt that that type of activity was for children. Fifty-nine percent stated that it was for children, 8 percent for families, 3 percent for adults, and 16 percent for everyone. These responses were consistent with earlier findings from the focus group interview. This type of activity was clearly seen as an activity for youths by both adults and young people interviewed.

The majority of adults with children indicated a preference for staying and watching their children participate in an activity if a comfortable place was provided. Adults also seemed extremely concerned with safety for their children in this type of activity. Eighty-five percent of the respondents identified safety as their major concern.

Expenditure Data

Respondents were asked how much they would spend per person to participate in an outdoor recreational activity if they could stay for up to ten hours as a family. The median response was $8.00 per person. When asked how much they would be willing for one of their children to spend for that type of activity, the median or average response was $10.50.

When youths were asked the same question, their average response was $10.00. Since the current price for all day at a waterslide in Anytown is

$6.00, a price of $9.95 or more for the park complex would be a good value. Youths reported spending an average of $26.00 a month for recreational activities during the summer.

Socioeconomic Characteristics of Respondents

A typical adult respondent in this study can be profiled as follows: median income of a little over $25,000, about thirty years old, male, caucasian, worked in a professional or technical occupation, and median level of education was some college completed. The majority of youths interviewed were between the ages of twelve and seventeen.

Summary and Conclusions

Based on the findings outlined in this study, the following conclusions and summary statements have been made:

1. Findings of this study parallel entirely the earlier focus group interview—a consistent pattern of responses in viewing outdoor recreational activities.
2. Many families are involved in outdoor recreational activities when at home and while on vacation. However, the variety of activities is much more limited when on vacation.
3. The majority of adults and youths view water-related activities such as a waterslide as being for young people—not for families or older adults.
4. A price of $10 to $12 or more for the park complex is entirely in line with what adults and youths would expect to pay.
5. The major reason for participation in water activity is summed up in one word—fun. Also, hot weather and water activities appear to be part of the consumer mind-set.
6. The major concern of adults for this type of activity will be safety in use.
7. Most youths appear to be interested in participating in this type of activity with a group of friends.

Notes

Chapter 1

1. Adapted from Daniels, Cora. Mr. Coffee. *Fortune,* April 2003, pp. 139-140.
2. Mayros, Van and Dennis J. Dolan. How to Design the MKIS That Works for You. *Business Marketing,* January 27, 1980, p. 47.

Chapter 2

1. Adapted from Vajta, Peter G. When It Comes to Organization, Think Simple. *Business Month,* May 1989, p. 85.
2. Drucker, Peter F. *Management: Tasks, Responsibilities, Practices.* New York: Harper and Row Publishers, 1974, p. 75.
3. Ibid.
4. Adapted from Ben & Jerry's Homemade, Inc., corporate Web site. Available online at <www.benjerry.com>.
5. Terry, George R. *Principles of Management,* Sixth Edition. Homewood, IL: Richard D. Irwin, Inc., 1972, pp. 40-41.
6. Treacy, Michael and Fred Wiersema. *The Discipline of Market Leaders.* New York: Addison-Wesley, 1997.
7. Stanton, William J., Rosann L. Spiro, Greg A. Rich, and William E. Prentice. *Management of the Sales Force,* Eleventh Edition. Homewood, IL: Richard D. Irwin, Inc., 2002, p. 72.
8. Dale, Ernest. *Organization.* New York: American Management Association, 1967, p. 9.
9. Stanton et al., *Management of the Sales Force,* pp. 78-83.
10. For a more detailed discussion of line and staff functions and responsibilities, see Griffin, Ricky W., *Management.* Boston: Houghton-Mifflin Company, 1984, Chapter 10.
11. The Search for the Organization of Tomorrow. *Fortune,* May 18, 1992, p. 93ff.
12. Eisenhart, Tom. Playing Together: Marketing and Communications Catch the Team Spirit. *Business Marketing,* July 1989, pp. 40-46.
13. Jain, Subhash C. *Marketing Planning and Strategy,* Sixth Edition. Cincinnati: South-Western Publishing Co., 1999, pp. 301-304.

Chapter 3

1. Adapted from Merrick, Amy. The 2000 Count: Counting on the Census. *Wall Street Journal,* February 14, 2001, p. B1.

2. Bernstel, Janet B. Smart Move: Creating an "Intelligent" Database. *ABA Bank Marketing,* 34(9), 2002, p. 14.

3. Database Marketing, *Business Week,* September 5, 1994, pp. 56-62.

4. Morgan, Michael S. Research Boosts Database's Power. *Marketing News,* 35(October 8), 2001, p. 16.

5. Mason, Robert L. and John C. Young. Another Data Mining Tool. *Quality Progress,* 36, 2003, p. 76. For additional information on data mining, see Berry, Michael and Gordon Linoff, *Mastering Data Mining: The Art and Science of Customer Relationship Management.* New York: Wiley Computer Publications, 2000.

6. Weiss, Shari. More Customers, More Visits, More Profits. *Nation's Restaurant News,* 36(October 28), 2002, p. 12.

7. Jackson, Rob and Paul Wang. *Strategic Database Marketing.* Chicago, IL: NTC Business Books, 1994.

8. Space limitations prevent us from covering marketing research at length. Interested readers are referred to Wrenn, Bruce, Robert Stevens, and David Loudon, *Marketing Research: Text and Cases.* Binghamton, NY: The Haworth Press, 2002.

9. Sablosky, Tanja L. The Value of Research: More Navigating, Less Drifting. *ABA Bank Marketing,* 35, 2003, p. 25.

10. Amato-McCoy, Deena. Blockbuster Aims to Improve its Customer Communications. *Stores,* 85(April), 2003, p. 36; Mason, Tania. Bacardi-Martini's Leisure Arm Boss to Handle Events. *Marketing,* March 22, 2001, p. 4.

11. Sales Staff Also Does Some Research. *Marketing News,* 19(September 13), 1985, p. 1.

12. Ray, Nina M. and Sharon Tabor. Cybersurveys Come of Age. *Marketing Research,* 15(1), 2003, p. 32.

13. Long, Ju, Kerem Tomak, and Andrew Whinston. Calling All Customers. *Marketing News,* 37(January 20), 2003, p. 18.

Chapter 4

1. Adapted from Parloff, Roger. From Betamax to Kazaa: The Real War over Piracy. *Fortune,* October 27, 2003, p. 150; Recording Industry Association of America, Research and Data, November 11, 2003. Available online at <www.riaa.com/news>; Anonymous. Business: In a Spin; The Music Industry. *The Economist,* 366(8313), 2003, p. 67; and Elkin, Tobi. Record Labels Turning to Web to Boost Sales. *Advertising Age,* June 9, 2003, p. 16.

2. Robinson, William T. and Claes Fornell. Sources of Market Pioneering Advantages in Consumer Goods Industries. *Journal of Marketing Research,* August 1985, pp. 305-317.

3. Moore, Michael J., William Boulding, and Ronald C. Goodstein. Pioneering and Market Share: Is Entry Time Indigenous and Does it Matter? *Journal of Marketing Research,* February 1991, p. 97.

4. Drucker, Peter F. *Management: Tasks, Responsibilities, Practices.* New York: Harper and Row Publishers, 1973, p. 45.

5. Abell, D. F. *Defining the Business: The Starting Point of Strategic Planning.* Englewood Cliffs, NJ: Prentice-Hall, 1980.

6. See David A. Aaker, *Strategic Market Management*, Sixth Edition. New York: John Wiley, 2002.

7. Ibid., pp. 88-89.

8. De Vasconcellos, Jorge Alberto Souse and Donald C. Hambrick. Key Success Factors: Test of a General Theory in the Mature Industrial-Product Sector. *Strategic Management Journal,* July/August 1989, pp. 376-382.

9. Stanton, William J. and Richard H. Buskirk. *Management of the Sales Force.* Homewood, IL: Richard D. Irwin, Inc., 1987, p. 413.

Chapter 5

1. Adapted from Beatty, Sally. New Wrinkle—Hot at the Mall: Skin-Care Products from Physicians; "Cosmeceutical" Creams Tap Antiaging Market. *Wall Street Journal,* November 14, 2003, p. A1; and Samuelson, Robert J. Adventures in Agelessness. *The Washington Post,* October 29, 2003, p. A5.

2. See Frank, R.E., W.F. Massy, and Y. Wind. *Market Segmentation.* Englewood Cliffs, NJ: Prentice–Hall, 1972, for a discussion of how to conduct market segmentation research. See Weinstein, Art, *Market Segmentation.* Chicago, IL: Probus, 1994, for a discussion of contemporary segmentation approaches.

3. Hayes, Jack. No Kidding: Casual Chains Make Play for Youth Market. *Nation's Restaurant News,* September 2, 2002, p. 1.

4. For a more detailed discussion of consumer-behavior issues involved in the use of geodemography as a base for segmenting markets, see Schiffman, Leon and Leslie Kanuk. *Consumer Behavior,* Eighth Edition. Englewood Cliffs, NJ: Prentice-Hall, 2003.

5. Adapted from Simon, Ruth. Sweat Chic. *Forbes,* September 5, 1988, pp. 96-101.

6. Segmenting Markets by Corporate Culture. *Business Marketing,* July 1988, p. 50.

7. Reinhartz, Werner and V. Kumar. The Mismanagement of Customer Loyalty. *Harvard Business Review,* July 2002, pp. 86-94.

8. Bland, Vikki. Customer Relationship Management: Keeping Customers Loyal. *New Zealand Management,* September 2003, p. 53.

Chapter 6

1. Adapted from Lukas, Paul and Maggie Overfelt. UPS: United Parcel Service. *FSB: Fortune Small Business,* 13(April), 2003, p. 24; and Brooks, Rick. Leading the News: UPS Cuts Ground-Delivery Time; One-Day Reduction Aims to Repeat FedEx Assault on Company's Dominance. *Wall Street Journal,* October 6, 2003, p. A3.

2. Schnaars, Steven P. *Marketing Strategy.* New York: Free Press, 1991, p. 161.

3. Cohen, William A. *The Marketing Plan,* Third Edition. New York: John Wiley & Sons, 2001.

4. Reed, Keith. America West Cuts Spark Fare War. *Boston Globe,* August 21, 2003, p. C1.

5. Mateja, Jim and Rick Popely. Car Notes. *Chicago Tribune,* November 13, 2003, p. 7.

6. Intarakomalyasut, Nondhanada. Asahi Brewer to Tap Market for Japanese Beer Fanatics, *Knight Ridder Tribune Business News,* November 29, 2004, p. 1.

Chapter 7

1. Adapted from Grossman, Adam. New Kids Challenge Barbie's Dominance. *Marketing Week,* July 24, 2003, p. 20; Bannon, Lisa. Fashion Coup? New Doll Grabs Some of Barbie's Limelight. *Wall Street Journal,* November 29, 2002, p. A11; Seger, Ira, and Brian Hindo. Ho, Ho, Ho, Here's What's Selling. *Business Week,* December 22, 2003, p. 16; Palmeri, Christopher. To Really Be a Player, Mattel Needs Hotter Toys. *Business Week,* July 28, 2003, pp. 64-65; Tkecik, Maureen. Dolled Up: To Lure Older Girls, Mattel Brings in Hip-Hop Crowd; It Sees Stalwart Barbie Lose Market Share, So "Flavas" Will Take on the "Bratz"; Battle of the Big Heads. *Wall Street Journal,* July 18, 2003, p. A1; Rao, Akshay and Humaira Maji. The Price of Launching a New Product: Empirical Evidence on Factors Affecting the Relative Magnitude of Slotting Allowances. *Marketing Science,* spring 2003, pp. 246-252.

2. Balto, David. Recent Legal and Regulatory Developments in Slotting Allowances and Category Management. *Journal of Public Policy and Marketing,* fall 2002, pp. 289-295.

3. Paying for Shelf Space. *Business Week,* August 7, 1989, pp. 60-61.

Chapter 8

1. Adapted from Bandler, James. Ending Era, Kodak Will Stop Selling Most Film Cameras. *Wall Street Journal,* January 14, 2004, p. B; Chandiramani, Ravi. Can Kodak Thrive Amid the Digital Revolution? *Marketing,* July 3, 2003, p. 13; Bandler, James. Kodak to Cut Staff up to 21 percent Amid Film Business Shrinks, Company Retools for the Future; New Blow to Rochester, NY, *Wall Street Journal,* January 22, 2004, p. A1; and Bandler, James. Kodak Shifts Focus from Film, Betting Future on Digital Lines. *Wall Street Journal,* September 25, 2003, p. A1.

2. This section was adapted from Thompson, Arthur A. Jr. and A. J. Strickland *Strategy Formulation and Implementation,* Third Edition. Plano, TX: Business Publications, Inc., 1986, p. 52.

Chapter 9

1. Adapted from Taylor, Alex III. Mercedes Hits a Pothole. *Fortune,* October 27, 2003, pp. 140-145.

2. Adapted from Boyd, Harper W., Orville C. Walker, John Mullins, and Jean-Claude Larreche. *Marketing Management,* Fourth Edition. Chicago, IL: McGraw-Hill Irwin, 2002, p. 41.

3. Troy, Stewart. This Isn't the Legend Acura Dealers Had in Mind. *Business Week,* November 28, 1986, pp. 71-76.

4. Edmondson, Gail. Will Yankee Drivers Buy VW Luxury? Its Upscale Move Is Meeting Resistance in Europe, so the U.S. Push Is Critical. *Business Week,* November 3, 2003, p. 51.

5. Geld, Betsy and Gabriel Geb. New Coke's Fizzle—Lessons for the Rest of Us. *Sloan Management Review,* fall 1986, pp. 71-76.

6. Troy, This Isn't the Legend, p. 74.

Chapter 10

1. Adapted from Gunther, Mark. Tree Huggers, Soy Lovers, and Profits. *Fortune,* June 23, 2003, pp. 98-104.

2. Rust, Roland T., Zeithaml, Valarie, and Lemon, Katherine. Customer-Centered Brand Management, *Harvard Business Review,* September 2004, pp. 110-118.

3. Aaker, David A. and J. Gary Shansby. Positioning Your Product. *Business Horizons,* May/June 1982, pp. 56-62.

4 The following section is adapted from Jain, Subhash C., *Marketing Planning and Strategy,* Sixth Edition. Cincinnati: South-Western Publishing Co., 1999, pp. 417-424.

5. Gale, Bradley T. and Robert D. Buzzell. Market Perceived Quality: Key Strategic Concept. *Planning Review,* (March/April 1989), p. 11.

6. Boyd, Harper W. Jr., Orville C. Walker Jr., John Mullins, and Jean-Claude Larreche. *Marketing Management,* Fourth Edition. Chicago: McGraw-Hill Irwin, 2002, pp. 472-473.

7. McBride, Sarah. Actor to Hollywood: Think Direct-to-Home Movies, *Wall Street Journal,* January 18, 2005. p. B4.

Chapter 11

1. Adapted from Zellner, Wendy. Call It Mall-Mart: As Anchor Department Stores Fail, Big Discounters Move In. *Business Week,* July 14, 2003, pp. 40-44; and Coughlan, Anne, Erin Anderson, and Louis W. Stern. *Marketing Channels,* Sixth Edition. Upper Saddle River, NJ: Prentice-Hall, 2001, p. 197.

2. Stern, Louis W., Adel I. El-Ansary, and Anne Coughlan. *Marketing Channels.* Upper Saddle River, NJ: Prentice-Hall, 2001, p. 188.

3. For an extended discussion of why the balance of power has shifted to retailers, see Coughlan et al., *Marketing Channels,* pp. 71-76.

4. Weiner, Edith and Arnold Brown. The New Marketplace. *The Futurist,* May/June 1995, pp. 12-16.

5. McIntosh, Jay. Internet Sales: A Bright Spot in Retailing. *Chain Store Age,* 79(9), 2003, p. S1.

6. Arthur Andersen and Co. *Facing the Forces of Change 2000.* Washington, DC: Distribution Research and Education Foundation, 1992, pp. 163-173.

7. Verdon, Joan. Toys "R" Us Hopes Birthday Club Entices Shoppers Year-Round, *Knight Ridder Tribute Business News,* May 20, 2004, p. 1.

Chapter 12

1. Adapted from *CBS Sunday Morning,* television program transcript. CBS News Productions, September 15, 2002; Linnett, Richard and Wayne Friedman. "Green Hornet" Shops for a Car. *Advertising Age,* May 26, 2003, p. 1; Stilson, Janet. Placements Push to Front. *Advertising Age,* June 9, 2003, p. S8.

2. Irwin, Tanya and Karl Greenberg. Chrysler, Mercedes Take Show on the Road. *Adweek,* April 28, 2003, p. 8.

3. Media Faxing. *Marketing and Media Decisions,* October 1988, p. 138.

4. Whitaker, Leslie. Ads Unplugged. *American Demographics,* June 2001, pp. 30-34.

Chapter 13

1. Adapted from Binkley, Christina. Hotel Rebound is a No-Show—Has Demand Fallen Permanently in Sept. 11 Aftermath? *Wall Street Journal,* February 24, 2003, p. B6; and Rich, Motoko. Hotels Offer Price Guarantees—Sort Of. *Wall Street Journal,* March 12, 2003, p. D1.

2. A good discussion on conjoint analysis can be found in many marketing research texts. See, for example, Tull, Donald S. and Dell I. Hawkins. *Marketing Research.* New York: Macmillan, 1993, pp. 405-419.

3. Swasy, Alecia and Greg Stucharchuk. Grocery Chains Pressure Suppliers for Uniform Prices. *Wall Street Journal,* October 21, 1988, p. B1.

Chapter 14

1. Adapted from Anonymous. Business Brief—Gillette Company: NASCAR Marketing Deal Is Part of Push to Outdo Rival Schick. *Wall Street Journal,* November 17, 2003, p.1; and Symonds, William. Can Gillette Regain Its Edge? *Business Week,* January 26, 2004, p. 46.

Chapter 15

1. Adapted from Hawkins, Lee Jr. GM to Offer Dealer Incentives on Hummer H2s. *Wall Street Journal,* August 26, 2003, p. D8; Carty, Sharon Silke. GM May Sell a Smaller Hummer Model. *Wall Street Journal,* December 11, 2003, p. D2; Anonymous. GM Preps H2 for Russia. *Ward's Auto World,* August 2003, 39(8), p. 11; and Sanders, Lisa. Hummer Markets Shoes for Offroad Set. *Advertising Age,* 75(2), 2004, p. 3.

2. Bhide, Amar. Hustle As Strategy. *Harvard Business Review,* September/October 1986, pp. 59-65.

3. Bonoma, Thomas V. *The Marketing Edge: Making Strategies Work.* New York: Free Press, 1985.

4. See Naumann, Earl and Kathleen Giel. *Customer Satisfaction Measurement and Management.* Cincinnati: Thomson Executive Press, 1995; and Naumann, Earl. *Creating Customer Value.* Cincinnati: Thomson Executive Press, 1995.

5. Kotler, Philip. *Marketing Management,* Eleventh Edition. Upper Saddle River, NJ: Prentice-Hall, 2002, pp. 21-22.

6. Urban, Glen L. and Steven H. Star. *Advanced Marketing Strategy.* Englewood Cliffs, NJ: Prentice-Hall, 1991, p. 462.

7. Kotler, *Marketing Management,* p. 518.

8. Ibid., pp. 521-522.

Chapter 16

1. Adapted from Zellner, Wendy. Lessons from a Faded Levi Strauss; It Has One of the World's Best-Known Brands, But It's Not Hip. *Business Week,* December 15, 2003, pp. 44-45; Sheth, Jagdish and Rajendra Sisodia. *The Rule of Three: Surviving and Thriving in Competitive Markets.* New York: The Free Press, 2002, pp. 2-6; LaPorta, Scott. Levi Strauss Signature Rolls Out at Target. *DSN Retailing Today,* February 9, 2004, p. 13; and Cuneo, Alice. Levis Struggles to Peddle Signature to Men. *Advertising Age,* December 1, 2003, p. 12.

2. Kotler, Philip. *Marketing Management Analysis, Planning, and Control,* Fifth Edition. Englewood Cliffs, NJ: Prentice-Hall, Inc., 1984, p. 765.

3. Fredericks, Joan O. and James M. Salter. Beyond Customer Satisfying. *Management Review,* May 1995, pp. 29-32.

Chapter 17

1. Adapted from Arner, Faith. J&J: Toughing Out the Drought. *Business Week,* January 26, 2004, pp. 84-85.

2. Bell, M.L. *Marketing: Concepts and Strategies,* Second Edition. Boston, MA: Houghton Mifflin Co., 1972, p. 428.

3. Kotler, Philip. *Marketing Management Analysis, Planning, and Control,* Fifth Edition. Englewood Cliffs, NJ: Prentice-Hall, 1984, p. 765.

4. Shuchman, A. The Marketing Audit: Its Nature, Purposes, and Problems. In *Analyzing and Improving Marketing Performance,* Report Number 32. New York: American Management Association, 1959, p. 15.

5. Kotler, *Marketing Management Analysis,* p. 765.

6. Ibid., pp. 765-766.

7. Ibid., p. 766.

8. Ibid., p. 771.

Index

Page numbers followed by the letter "f" indicate figures and exhibits; those followed by the letter "t" indicate tables.

For Product Safety Concerns and Information please contact our EU
representative GPSR@taylorandfrancis.com Taylor & Francis Verlag GmbH,
Kaufingerstraße 24, 80331 München, Germany

Printed and bound by CPI Group (UK) Ltd, Croydon, CR0 4YY

08/05/2025

01864489-0001